Constitutional Violence

Constitutional Violence

Legitimacy, Democracy and Human Rights

Antoni Abat i Ninet

EDINBURGH
University Press

To my wife Marisol, the light of my life

First published in hardback in 2013
This paperback edition 2014

Edinburgh University Press Ltd
The Tun – Holyrood Road
12 (2f) Jackson's Entry
Edinburgh EH8 8PJ
www.euppublishing.com

Typeset in Sabon by
3btype.com, and
printed and bound in Great Britain by
CPI Group (UK) Ltd, Croydon CR0 4YY

A CIP record for this book is available from the British Library

ISBN 978 0 7486 6954 7 (hardback)
ISBN 978 0 7486 7538 8 (paperback)
ISBN 978 0 7486 6955 4 (webready PDF)
ISBN 978 0 7486 7537 1 (epub)

Contents

Preface

Sociologist and legal theorist Max Weber argued that states claimed a monopoly on the legitimate use of violence. The monopoly is most successful, of course, when the overt use of state violence is minimised, acting as a sword of Damocles affecting the behaviour of everyone over which it hangs. Robert Cover sought to bring into view the violence implicit in the routine deployment of law – not merely in the use of police forces to arrest people for what all concede to be arguable violations of existing and uncontroversial law, but in the normative claims that ordinary and constitutional law make, which induce people to believe that whatever contrary views they might hold are somehow illegitimate.

Constitutions often *originate* in violence, as revolutionaries displace by force regimes they regard as oppressive. Even relatively peaceful revolutions can occur against a background of violence, as dissidents withdraw their assent to the legitimacy of the state's monopoly of violence, and thereby enable the possibility that some other entities might now claim – and use – violence as a legitimate weapon available to them no less than to the state. Overt violence can *sustain* constitutions as well, suppressing secession and its predecessor, mere dissent. More interesting, perhaps, are the matters Cover addressed, where violence lies behind state actions, but never appears openly, even as normative communities other than the state find themselves squeezed out of existence.

Antoni Abat i Ninet offers us a wide-ranging re-theorisation of the role of violence in maintaining the constitutional order. He begins from the common observation that constitutionalism and democracy are inevitably in tension. Democracy seems to require that the current policy judgements of today's majority be implemented, while constitutionalism seems to require that some such judgements be thwarted. Rather than accepting the equally common observation that constitutionalism's limits on democracy enable greater democratic choice in the long run, an observation captured by the implications of the cynical phrase about elections in new democracies, 'One person, one vote, one time', Abat i Ninet argues that constitutionalism prevails over democracy through the regular, albeit sometimes concealed, exercise of violence.

Some readers will be provoked by his wide-ranging overview of constitutionalism's foundations in religious and political theory. Others will find his case studies of the violence of constitutionalism in modern societies ranging from the United States to France and Spain valuable, in light of the usual judgement that these nations are 'stable' democracies not pervaded by the open deployment of state violence. I suspect that every reader will find something with which to disagree in the argument. I know that I have such disagreements. And yet surely there is something here worth thinking about. Scholars of constitutional law should bring Weber out of the shadows into open view. Abat i Ninet's project provides one source of illumination.

Prof. Mark Tushnet
William Nelson Cromwell Professor of Law
Harvard Law School

1

Introduction

This book is the result of an extended process of thinking that began with the draft of my paper 'Playing at being Gods'.[1]

After this work I started to focus my interest on the main issues addressed in this book: constitutional legitimacy and the relationship between democracy and constitutions. The topics analysed in this book emerged progressively as a consequence of thinking about the preceding issues. The first question to be developed, constituting the opening premise, was that of the origins and influences of the religious discourse in the configuration of the modern constitutional system. Particularly important were the sacred conception of the US Constitution and the expansion of this phenomenon to the rest of the world's modern constitutions.

The drafters of the US Constitution consciously played the role of a civil God; the US Supreme Court developed the role of secular prophets; the Constitution was the sacred tablets; and the people of the United States became the chosen people. As the law was received by Moses on the tablets, so too did the Constitution adopt a legal, moral and religious character. This sort of metaphysical phenomenon and full authority was sought deliberately by the Founding Fathers and the drafters of the US Constitution, to obtain the kind of sovereignty and power that they needed.[2] The new fundamental norm of the state came outfitted with a sort of undisputed legitimacy, an almost divine authority.

The first issue analysed in this book considers the fundamentally religious character of the secular constitutions that eventually became what we understand as the modern American Constitution, and the undemocratic nature of constitutions in general. The founding of this constitutional doctrine, supported by this type of sacred speech, was not fortuitous. This consecrated supra-legitimacy sought, and still seeks, somehow to coerce the freedom of the people, requesting compliance instead of citizen participation. The first section of Chapter 2 deals with this new sort of theology and the influences of the religious discourse on the modern constitutional discourse, and also how jus-positivism contributed to the consolidation of this sacred-civil language. Various manifestations and theological concepts (that is, Messianism, eschatology and idolatry) have been applied to achieve undisputed legitimacy. Political and legal theologies are also analysed in Chapter 5, when constitutional violence proceeds against human rights. The conflict between human rights and constitutional dispositions unmasks the mundane reality of constitutions and constitutionalism.

The first premise (the application of the religious discourse by the new sovereign) raises the topic developed in the following section, 'Sovereignty and Subject', which consists of a synthesis of the concept of sovereignty and its relationship with modern constitutionalism. The starting point of the section is a definition of sovereignty, with particular attention to its multi-disciplinary nature, types of sovereignty, the complexity of this notion and its current significance. To develop a comprehensive theory of the concept of sovereignty, I analyse classic and modern theories, different realities and fields of study, but always keeping contact with the main framework of this book, constitutional violence.

The main goal of this section is to provide a comprehensive notion of sovereignty, highlighting some of the fundamental characteristics of this notion that appear in the work of Hobbes, Kelsen, Schmitt and Derrida, for example. The selection of authors and features is based on the relationship between the role developed by the sovereign and violence. Once the definitions and features are set forth, the role of sovereignty and its relationship with violence is discussed by way of a conclusion. Then, by introducing a definition of sovereignty and the concept's need for genuine democratic legitimacy, I deduce why we can state that a given sovereignty is so and where its legitimacy comes from.

Chapter 2 goes on to analyse the Athenian experience of the fifth century BC, in which there was a change from popular sovereignty to the sovereignty of law. I attempt to obtain compelling premises and conclusions applicable to contemporary notions of sovereignty. The main conclusions drawn are that: (a) there is a real possibility of the sovereign switching from aristocracy to democracy, from the constitution to the people, and vice versa; (b) this alteration occurred gradually over time and not necessarily traumatically; (c) popular sovereignty functioned fully in Athens; and (d) the Athenian experience can be studied as an example of democratic establishment and in order to learn about the events that led to regression through the sovereignty of law.

The next topic studied, 'constitutional sovereignty', is also a consequence of the preceding section. This issue begins with a jus-positive study of constitutional texts. Who or what is legitimated as a sovereign in a constitutional text? Who or what bestows this attribution? Having described, in the first section of this chapter, the origins and influences of religious discourse on the configuration of the modern constitutional system, and how this fact predetermined the expansion of this phenomenon to the rest of the world's modern constitutions, I go on to point out that real sovereign is not actually defined in the constitution but is the constitution itself.

This third section locates the real sovereign, highlighting the difference between the *de jure* sovereign and the *de facto* sovereign. It explores the difference between the constitutional text and its real enforcement in relation to the factual possessor of the sovereignty. The section ends with some reflections about the catharsis that affects the citizenry and what provokes the illusion. Chapter 2 performs a critical introductory function by establishing an analytic baseline, a fundamental premise of the book's argument: that current constitutional legitimacy is ultimately based on violence.

Chapter 3, is entitled 'Democracy', where, after clarifying who the real sovereign is in our modern constitutional states, it is necessary to analyse the relationship between the *demos* and the *politeia*. As Derrida says: 'there is a sort of "semantic indeterminacy" at the core of democracy', and because of this indeterminacy the relationship between democracy and sovereignty remains problematic.[3] Chapter 3 asks whether this disjunction might have its roots in the vagueness of the concept of democracy. Democracy is a concept that has had various meanings throughout history. Even knowing this difficulty, it is essential to redefine the meaning of democracy because of its relationship with the main object of this book. If democracy is the only way to give legitimacy to constitutionalism, we need to know what democracy means. The chapter starts by dealing with an etymological and historical definition of democracy, trying to concrete the semantic indeterminacy (Derrida) that affects the notion.

The second section of Chapter 3 deals with an important issue related to the foundation of popular sovereignty: who are 'the people'? And who determines who the people are? Then, I address the matter of who the *optimum* are. These questions will be answered for each legal system from a positive-law perspective, but this issue affects many other disciplines of thought, giving rise to a wide variety of answers depending on each discipline's particular casuistry. The section also faces two more questions related to the US Constitution and, therefore, to other constitutional documents. Once the people and the optimum are defined, I deal with the legitimisation of the role of the judiciary, which has been the subject of ongoing analysis by Anglo-American jurisprudents. I develop this section analysing the work of Michelman, Ackerman and Tushnet, but also Raztrying to define the role of the judiciary from different perspectives.

Then, Chapter 3 addresses a central question: the considerable tensions between constitutionalism and democracy. This section focuses on different methods for enhancing constitutional legitimacy: contractualism (or contract-based legitimacy); consensualism (acceptance-oriented legitimacy);

procedural-dialogical legitimacy; constitutional authorship; and, finally, the rule of recognition. In the exposition of these theoretical categories I direct my attention to the way legitimacy is attributed and the role of the *demos*. In this chapter my point is to analyse the lack of democratic legitimacy in the 'founding moment', the approval of the basic norm using Kelsen's terminology, the first constitution. I contend that the undemocratic and violent founding (US independence and eighteenth-century France) has consequences for the development of the potentialities of democratic legitimacy in modern constitutional systems. Once the constitution is approved without real democratic legitimacy, I wonder where the undemocratic constitutional legitimacy comes from.

Chapter 4 is related to the link between violence and constitutional legitimacy. This chapter is a legal theoretical analysis of violent interactions in legal systems and specifically in constitutions. The main conclusion of this chapter is that without democratic legitimacy the only factor that ensures compliance with a constitutional system and constitutional enforcement is violence.

A definition of legal violence, its characteristics and categories, is given in the first section of the chapter. I illustrate the concept and effects of legal violence, analysing and complementing the works of Walter Benjamin, Derrida, Foucault, Cover and Sarat, but always restricting this definition to the constitutional sphere. The section includes a definition of coercion and the threat of violence, and how the constitutional system exploits these elements.

In Chapter 4, I expound various notions, the starting point being the relationship between law's legitimacy and its dependence on violence. Why do people obey the law? To answer this question I analyse different theories (habit of obedience, risk of punishment, and the role of legitimacy and authority). The next section of Chapter 4 deals with a definition of legal violence that is suitable to apply to the main objective of this book, namely, to define constitutional violence. The description of this relationship begins with a historical analysis, from Hebrew law to the role that violence played in the understanding and conceptualisation of law in Athens and Rome. I stress the importance of concepts such as *vis*, unlawfulness, self-help and *vindicatio* in our understanding of law, conditioned by the concept of violence. Then, we focus our attention on the eighteenth and nineteenth centuries and the birth of modern constitutionalism, conditioned by bloody revolutions and violence. The main point of this section is to emphasise the violent origins of law and how violence has always been closely related to law. Chapter 4 goes on to supplement this historical account with a contemporary critique of law's violence. Then the chapter considers how legal violence is used by constitutions and constitutionalism, why a constitution without legitimacy involves violent implementation, and how this violent implementation is viewed as 'legitimate' by the enforcers. Violence affects law in different manners, in different spheres, internally as a feature of law, and externally through codification or the determination, interpretation and enforcement of legal meaning. This chapter analyses these different connotations. The key point of this structure is to highlight the need to differentiate violence depending on how this phenomenon acts and affects law.

Some may argue that in the end violence is simply violence, but this differentiation will be helpful to analyse how violence interacts in the *nomos* of constitutionalism. The last paragraph is a sort of conclusion summarising the ideas that appear in the section; the final argument being that violence is ultimately the factor that 'legitimises' law. The main issue of this book is constitutional violence, which is a subtype of legal violence.

Chapter 5 is an exercise in comparative constitutional violence. It is a switch from the world of theory to the world of praxis. It begins with US constitutional violence, based on the application of the death penalty in Puerto Rico against the requirements of the Puerto Rican Constitution, the will of the people of Puerto Rico, the position of the Puerto Rican public institutions (governor, senate and municipalities) and, finally, against human rights and international conventions.

The next case analysed is French constitutional violence, which is set forth in two interrelated cases. The first deals with the constitutional accommodation of the debate between 'national sovereignty' and 'popular sovereignty', and its consequences in the whole French legal system. The case reveals how French constitutional violence produces violent homogenisation through constitutional legitimacy. The second example is strict case law, and reveals how the state apparatus has interpreted and enforced national identity in everyday aspects. The next examples in the book, Turkey and Chile, are clearly affected by the French understanding of constitutionalism and ethno-nationalism.

The example of Turkish constitutional violence is based on the military tutelage of political institutions, constitutions and a sort of pseudo-democracy of the state. The next case is Chilean constitutional violence. The analysis of this case is based primarily on the role that Chilean constitutionalism has developed in relation to the indigenous peoples. The Constitution as a founding act replaced the sovereign, created a new state, a new people and forced the assimilation of the different minorities into the new nation. The only alternative to assimilation was extermination. The role of constitutionalism was at least the juridification of this new political order. In other words, constitutionalism in Chile gave legal coverage to genocide. The last example is Spanish constitutional violence as a new way of determining democracy. After a period of transition from a military fascist dictatorship to democracy, the Constitution appeared to juridify the new Spanish democracy and 'transition'. As we will see, the Spanish Constitution of 1978 has some 'shadows' and 'reminiscences' of a military, undemocratic past.

After the American constitutional experience, constitutionalism and a religious conception of modern constitutions has almost completely triumphed. Almost every state in the world has a written constitution. The great majority of these declare the constitution to be the law controlling the organs of the state. We tend to label our liberal political systems as 'constitutional democracies', dividing the system into two different domains: a domain of politics, where the people rule; and a domain of law, which is set aside for a trained elite.

The relationship between these two domains has evolved since 1776, and we have tried to express the existence of an entente cordiale, a status in which the two 'sovereigns' do not interfere in the other's field. The American system, designed by *The Federalist Papers*, *Democracy in America* and the founding documents, has been consolidated over time by an elite of judges and lawyers.

Doctrinal texts have repeatedly shown that constitutionalism is the best guarantee for safeguarding fundamental rights. In this respect, Article 16 of the Declaration of the Rights of Man and of the Citizen is an excellent example. However, the two-headed system (constitution and people) is a fiction that remains in effect because of undemocratic factors that ultimately depend on various types of violence. The people has never been the true sovereign in our system. 'Constitutional democracy' is simply a euphemism, since there is only one sovereign, and there is no 'we the people'. The main conclusion of this work is to confirm that Hobbes' famous statement, *Autoritas, non veritas facit legem*, stills stands in force; and that violence is the only way to achieve legitimacy in constitutional law.

Since the work of Robert Cover in the late twentieth century, the violence of the law has not been a common topic in American legal jurisprudence. Cover's theorisation was a reflection on the contemporary situation of the law and the work of thinkers such as Walter Benjamin, Jacques Derrida and Emmanuel Levinas. This book is a continuation of the work of these and other authors – but referring strictly to the constitutional domain.

Constitutional Violence is a multidisciplinary work of legal scholarship that examines the legitimacy of constitutional violence. The book analyses sovereignty, democracy and constitutionalism, and concludes that constitutions are legitimised by legal force and violence. The book seeks to challenge constitutional legitimacy, submitting the concept to a type of *elegkhein*, and discussing this process with theoretical and practical examples.

Legal, political and constitutional practices demonstrate that constitutionalism and democracy seems to be irreconcilable. This book tries to mediate constructively in the dichotomy that Hamilton considered in 1776, namely, that good government is feasible and the constitutional system can be the best device to rule the country, but to achieve this objective it is necessary to reconcile 'we the people' and the constitution. The first step in this reconciliation is to recognise that constitutional democracy as such is impossible and that constitutional legitimacy is based on violence. This book concludes that human rights and democracy are the only solutions for deactivating the violence of a state when applied and legitimised through a constitution.

Portions of this work have been taken, greatly revised, from articles that appeared in *Ratio Juris*, *Philosophia Quarterly of Israel*, *American Journal of Comparative Law*, *Vienna Online Journal of International Constitutional Law* and *Springer Publications Hot Topics 6237*.

This project and parts of the book were presented and discussed in a book presentation at the State University of New York (SUNY) and in the workshop 'New Agents in International Law' at Stanford University. Here I especially want to thank James A. Gardner, Makau Mutua, Guyora Binder, John Schlegel and Kenneth Ehrenberg, participants in the book presentation at the SUNY at Buffalo. Others that I wish to recognise for their help, comments and guidance are Mark Tushnet, Larry Kramer and Bruce Ackerman.

I also benefited greatly from research assistance and facilities provided by the staff of the Stanford Law School Library. I owe thanks to Michael Halliday and Tobby Willet for linguistic corrections and comments, without whose help this book would not exist at all. I want also to express my deep gratitude to John Watson and Edinburgh University Press for its willingness to support this book.

Finally, with this book I want to pay tribute to the Critical Legal Studies and honour the memory of my friend Luay, who died in Benghazi, Libya fighting for democracy.

Notes

1. A. Abat i Ninet, 'Playing at being gods', *Philosophia Quarterly of Israel*, 38(1), 2008, 41–55.
2. *Ibid.*, p. 2.
3. J. Derrida, *Rogues: Two Essays on Reason*, Stanford, CA: Stanford University Press, 2005, p. 64.

2

Sovereignty and Constitution

This chapter provides a critical introduction by establishing an analytical baseline. A fundamental premise of the book's argument is that current constitutional legitimacy is ultimately based on violence. The first issue of this chapter considers the fundamentally religious character of the secular constitution – which eventually became what we understand as the modern American Constitution – and the undemocratic character of constitutions in general. I contend that the founding of a constitutional doctrine supported by religious language was not fortuitous. This consecrated supra-legitimacy seeks to coerce the freedom of the people by requesting compliance instead of participation. Chapter 2 deals with this new sort of theology and the influences of religious discourse on modern constitutional discourse, as well as the contributions of jus-positivism in the consolidation of this religious-civil language. This chapter also reviews the concept of sovereignty. The main goal is to provide a comprehensive notion of sovereignty, highlighting some of the fundamental aspects of the work of Hobbes, Rawls, Kelsen, Schmitt and Derrida. The selection of authors and features is based on the relationship that they have with the role of violence. Once the definitions and features are highlighted, the role of sovereignty and its relationship with violence is discussed as a conclusion. Then, by introducing a definition of sovereignty and the conceptual need for genuine democratic legitimacy, I show what type of sovereignty is applied and where its legitimacy originates.

CONSTITUTIONAL THEOLOGY

> Then render to Caesar what belongs to Caesar, and to God the things that are God's.[1]

My goal in this chapter is to consider both the fundamentally religious character of what we understand as modern constitutions and the undemocratic character of constitutions in general. Political theology is an old but also a very modern issue.[2]

Hamilton argued that: 'the fabric of American empire ought to rest on the solid basis of the consent of the people. The streams of national power ought to flow immediately from the pure, original fountain of all legitimate authority.'[3] But did the people understand the role of the constitution as a new sort of Torah restricting their power, or the Founding Fathers and drafters of the US Constitution as shepherds authorised to decide in the name of the people? Yet the drafters of the US Constitution needed this sort of sacred discourse to establish constitutional legitimacy undemocratically.

As Ferejohn emphasises, Madison was really concerned with the problem of legitimating the Constitution; the Founding Father desired to protect the basic norm from the vicissitudes and troubles of ordinary politics.[4] Madison anticipated the necessarily different treatment and special qualification that a constituting act deserves.

A juridical text like the Bible is a prescriptive text. The US Constitution continues the transposition of theological to juridical thought. As Jefferson warned, the '"veneration" of the Constitution has become a central, even if sometimes challenged, aspect of the American political tradition', and according to Kristol, 'The flag, the Declaration and the Constitution constitutes the holy trinity of what Tocqueville called American civil religion.'[5]

The use of a sacred discourse solved the lack of democratic legitimacy of the basic norm. In this sense, Madison's fears of the disruptive action of normal politics to the constitutional text were protected by a discursive shield, a sacred understanding of the Constitution. This sort of discourse warrants a non-discursive admission of the constitutional text by the people, and builds up, in Levinson's terms, a constitutional faith. Religious discourse and methodologies tend to affect citizens' understanding of the Constitution to facilitate a sort of blind veneration, to treat it as a holy text. The reference to the constitutional draft as the 'Miracle of Philadelphia' and statements like that of the former Arizona Governor Evan Mecham that the Constitution was inspired by God contribute to the progressive emergence of a sacred understanding of the Constitution. The Constitution was considered a holy document. But the use of political theology did not conclude once the draft had been deemed legitimate – it has continued until the present. The political use of constitutional faith has been constant, and there are many examples throughout US constitutional history of this phenomenon. For example, Levinson points out the use of oaths, a ritual of allegiance that requires officers to affirm their primary loyalty to civil religion, which established a substitute for the religious test with which the colonists were familiar under the established Anglican Church.[6]

Another important consequence of the application of the means and logic of the religious discourse to the constitutional system can be seen in the debate between originalism and non-originalism. Originalism focuses on finding the 'original meaning' of constitutional provisions. For originalism, fidelity to the constitution requires fidelity to the original meaning of the constitutional text and to its underlying principles.[7] Non-originalism is more related to the concept of a living constitution.[8] The latter doctrine considers that the constitution is adaptable, is and re-interpreted every day according to the principles of each generation. As if it were a sacred text, the constitution has its 'sects'. The discussion between Christian Catholics and Protestants, between Jewish Pharisees and Sadducees, and between Muslim Sunnis and Shias has a parallel application in the constitutional system because of the understanding of the constitution as a sort of holy text.

The drafters of the US Constitution consciously played the role of a civil God; the US Supreme Court developed the role of secular prophets; the Constitution was the sacred tablets; and the people of the United States became the chosen people. As the law was received by Moses on the tablets, so too did the constitution adopt a legal, moral and religious character. The new scripture established the authority, the new sovereign and the state, and not the opposite. The main result of this metaphysical authority was the understanding of the constitution as a sort of sacred civil code. With the triumph of Christianity in the Roman Empire every rule of the Jewish Scriptures that was legal passed over into the later Roman Law. The United States, with the draft of the Constitution, became another link in the chain. The step was made in 1776,[9] when the Americans used their constitution to establish a new kind of religion, based on this document.

As Grey states, the maxim *Vox populi, vox Dei* hints at the connection between the Bible and the Constitution: 'Just as Christians and Jews take the word of God as sovereign and the Bible as the world of God, so Americans take the will of the people as a sovereign, at least in secular matters, and the Constitution as the most authoritative legal expression of the popular will.'[10] The Constitution is not the expression of the popular will; the drafters were creating a new sovereign and a new supreme authority in the Constitution itself. Grey omits one of the main aspects of US constitutional theology, its main function: to enhance a vehicular discourse to legitimise the undemocratic republic. I am aware that this argument directly contradicts Kramer's opinion of the democratic character of the drafters,[11] but a literal interpretation of Madison's words in *The Federalist Papers* 10, will be enough argument to show the doubts of the Founding Father about democracy.

Madison argued:

> Hence it is that such democracies have ever been spectacles of turbulence and contention; have ever been found incompatible with personal security or the rights of property; and have been as short in their lives as they have been violent in their deaths. Theoretic politicians, who have patronized this species of government, have erroneously supposed that by reducing mankind to a perfect equality in their political rights, they would at the same time be

perfectly equalized and assimilated in their possessions, their opinions, and their passions.

A republic, by which I mean a government in which the scheme of representation takes place, opens different prospects and promises the cure for which we are seeking ...

The two great points of difference between a democracy and a republic are: first, the delegation of the government, in the latter, to a small number of citizens elected by the rest; secondly, the greater number of citizens and greater sphere of country over which the latter may be extended.

The effect of the first difference is, on the one hand, to refine and enlarge public views by passing them through the medium of a chosen body of citizens, whose wisdom may best discern the true interest of their country and whose patriotism and love of justice will be least likely to sacrifice it to temporary or partial considerations. Under such a regulation it may well happen that the public voice, pronounced by representatives of the people, will be more consonant to the public good than if pronounced by the people themselves, convened for the purpose.[12]

Frequent constitutional appeals to the people would have a pernicious effect, as Madison warned in *The Federalist Papers* 49, for they would 'deprive government of that veneration which time bestows on every thing, and without which perhaps the wisest and freest governments would not possess the requisite stability'.[13]

I concur with Rakove when he includes *The Federalist Papers* in his rather loose concept of 'pure theory' to capture the somewhat abstract way in which many modern commentators, especially legal scholars and political scientists, have described the original intentions and understandings of 1787–1788. This pure theory placed a notable emphasis on the ideas of James Madison, especially as they were encapsulated in his best-known writings, the essays of *The Federalist Papers*. It assumes that these views represent an authoritative, accurate and relatively unproblematic account of the underlying concerns that gave meaning and purpose to the spare prose of the constitutional text.[14]

Therefore, republican politics is based on the rule of law and not on democracy, regardless of the size of any constituency within the society; so, as Arendt stated, resolutions and deliberations should have been taken back (to the people).[15] The drafters of the Constitution needed to establish a basic norm to consolidate a new nation, an instrument to provide stability to politics, not only in the relationship between the states but also between economic classes.

The drafters needed the theological discourse to bring consistency to the constitutional fiction. The Constitution as a truth is undisputed. In this respect, this civil version of the religious discourse has incorporated the fundamental contribution of legal normativity and legal positivism.[16] Both theories have collaborated in the establishment and maintenance of this internal juridical logic that wants to remain in a parallel and self-sufficient world. The Kelsenian theory and the US form of constitution making are a sort of symbiosis. Kelsen finds the perfect empirical sample to elaborate his basic norm theory, and the US constitutional system finds a theoretical legitimation of the non-democratic constituent act.[17] In this sense the well-known work of Kelsen establishes as one of the central aspects of pure theory that legal norms are objectively valid if they are derived from the basic norm, which is itself valid.[18] The same is true of moral or ethical norms.[19] This means a complete independence of the legal norm, which, being the supreme reason of validity of the whole legal order, constitutes its unity. Therefore, the first constitution (the first basic norm) is the norm of norms. Kelsen contends:

> the basic norm of a religious norm system says that one ought to behave as God and the authorities instituted by Him command. Similarly, the basic norm of a legal order prescribes that one ought to behave as the 'fathers' of the constitution and the individuals – directly or indirectly – authorized (delegated) by the constitution command.[20]

He continues, arguing that certainly one may ask why one has to respect the first constitution as a binding norm.

The characteristic of so-called legal positivism is, however, that it dispenses with such religious justification of the legal order. This theory demonstrates the need for sacred and non-discursive language to provide legitimacy to the first constitution. So this new juridical universe requires a new sort of faith. I understand that this need is a clear *contradictio in terminis*, because the whole system is founded on a presupposition of validity of the basic norm. The basic norm is presupposed to be valid, because without this presupposition no human act could be interpreted as legal, especially as a norm creating act.[21] In Kelsen's terms, the basic norm is something that we will find out, not something that we create, as the Holy Scriptures were found by the people of Israel. This presupposition is the sort of analogous application of religious discourse to the civil sphere that the drafters of the US Constitution founded. We presume that the Bible is valid, and, consequently, all the norms must respect this basic norm. In this same sense Kelsen affirms: 'if there is a constitutional form, then constitutional laws must be distinguished from ordinary laws. There exists a special procedure, a special form for the creation of constitutional laws, and a different procedure for the creation of ordinary laws.'[22]

Consequently, the main difference between constitutional law and ordinary law resides in the procedure of creation of each kind of norm. But when the process of creation affects the basic rule it becomes the main gap in the pure theory that only a secular sacred faith, such as the one used in the US constitutional case, can fill. I agree with Bulygin when he states that the normative validity of legal norms cannot be based on a mere hypothesis and still less on fiction.[23] Rabbi Joel Roth stated: 'Since in the halakhic system, as in all others, presupposing the existence of a grundnorm requires a "leap of faith", the truth or falsity of the historical claims of the grundnorm is legally irrelevant.'[24] Following this logic, Hannah Arendt and Kelsen considered the method of constitution creation as irrelevant.[25] I do not agree with this statement if the constitutional fiction signifies the enablement of a non-democratic system, and because the constitution is a secular document and not the word of God, and therefore needs a different sort of legitimation.

The US constitutional system has been exported/imported to the rest of the world as an example of a democracy based on the constitution. After the American constitutional experience, the triumph of constitutionalism appears almost complete. Just about every state in the world has a written constitution. The great majority of these declare the constitution to be the law controlling the organs of the state. This development is generally thought to be a tribute to an especially American idea.[26] Although there is considerable variation in the substantive contents and structural machinery of constitutionalism in various countries, the central idea, forged in the American founding, of public power controlled by enforcement of a superior law is present everywhere constitutional government is proclaimed.[27]

I agree with this statement, but would contend that it requires more specificity. The different constitution-making processes must be included within the considerable variations. These modifications in the constituent process will determine the relationship between democracy and constitution.

The US constitutional system is a mixed model, even though historically one doctrinal sector has denied that such a thing is possible.[28] Ancient mixed constitutional influences on the framers of the US Constitution came from the work of Plato, Aristotle, Cicero and Polybius.[29] The main justification for mixed constitutions is to be found in a qualitative analysis. In regarding the basis of government as qualitative rather than quantitative, we assume certain simple forms of constitution to be dependent on certain principles, for example, democracy to be based on the idea of numerical equality, oligarchy or timocracy on the idea of what Aristotle calls proportional equality regulated by wealth.[30]

The framers needed to establish a basic norm to consolidate a new nation, with a mixed constitution and a republic in Madison's terms, where the equilibrium between the poor people (*demos*) and the rich people (aristocracy) is warranted, within a lower risk of revolution (Aristotle). Madison, in *The Federalist Papers* 10, argued:

From this view of the subject it may be concluded that a pure democracy, by which I mean a society consisting of a small number of citizens, who assemble and administer the government in person, can admit of no cure for the mischiefs of faction. A common passion or interest will, in almost every case, be felt by a majority of the whole; a communication and concert result from the form of government itself; and there is nothing to check the induce-ments to sacrifice the weaker party or an obnoxious individual.[31]

I contend that the decision made by the framers, to establish a mixed constitution instead of a constitution through a popular executive power, has been crucially important for the rest of the constitutional systems around the world. The framers opted for such a mixed system after studying the texts of Plato, Aristotle, Plutarch, Cicero and Polybius, among others, and analysing the traumatic experiences of pure democratic constitutions. Probably the main needs of the new state were stability and equilibrium, as Madison affirms in *The Federalist Papers* 10 and 49, and not democracy in a wide sense.[32] Like von Fritz, I consider that the influences of the mixed consti-tution theory, the system of checks and balances, and the separation of powers decisively influenced the shaping of constitutions adopted in Western Europe in the nineteenth and twentieth centuries.[33] But unlike von Fritz, I believe that the US Constitution was the main source of mixed constitu-tionalism in Europe, or at least the modern adaptation of the theory. The legitimacy and validity of the constitution requires not only popular ratification, but also real (or true) democratic involvement. A constitution made though ordinary parliaments and representatives is unacceptable.

But the role that the constitution develops in our systems is also rein-forced by another theological idea: the Messianic theory. Messianism is a mystical theory that has been applied analogously in political and constitu-tional theories in order to achieve undisputed legitimacy. But Messianism is not simply mysticism, but is also an important tool to analyse human experience. In this respect, political (Schmitt) and legal constitutional (Kelsen) thought have adapted the Messianic trend in order to achieve legitimacy, recognition and obedience to the sovereign (Schmitt) and the constitution (Kelsen). The role that the constitution plays in Hans Kelsen, and therefore the Continental constitutional conceptualization, can be compared and analysed with the position and features that the Messiah develops in Jewish mysticism.[34]

To apply the Messianic idea to constitutional theory is a difficult challenge that requires starting from a comprehensible definition of the Messianic idea in Jewish spirituality. To achieve this purpose the work of Scholem is the baseline, in conjunction with a historical approach to Messianism in the Old Testament, the Middle Ages and modern Jewish philosophy.[35]

The indeterminacy of the term has led to antagonistic theories, huge doctrinal differences and doctrinal inconsistencies that must be pointed out in order to obtain a feasible theory of Messianism. Part of the difficulty lies in applying a mystical theory to the secular (constitutional) world. In this regard, Messianism reproduces part of the inherent problems of other theological theories applied to the political or legal spheres. Another element that complicates a suitable definition is the evolution of the term over time, and the allocation of specific trends in each age, for example, medieval Judaism (Maimonides) introduced rational tendencies as basic features of Messianism, contradicting other rabbinic sources. But these difficulties are in fact issues that enrich the theory, allowing a possible application to constitutional thought.

The term Messianism has different meanings ranging from the belief in the arrival of a Messiah as the saviour of humankind to religious devotion to an ideal or cause.[36] Taubes stated that Messianism is nonsense, and dangerous nonsense at that, but the historical study of Messianism is a scientific pursuit. Messianism and the 'Messianic idea' are meaningful inasmuch as they disclose a significant facet of human experience.[37] Messianism can be a useful theory in order to analyse and understand constitutional theoretical constructions. The constitutional use of the Messianic idea consists in the replacement of the deity by the constitution.

The application of the Messianic idea is controversial because it mixes two spheres, the religious and secular.[38] However, to deny this relationship is a way of limiting the effects and potentialities of the Messianic trend in the secular (constitutional) world. Thus, the application of Messianism to and by Rosenzweig, Cohen, Levinas, Benjamin, Schmitt or Kelsen will never secularise the religious nature of the theory.

The work of Maimonides is an excellent instrument with which to link law, legal theology and Messianism. Maimonides has perhaps been Judaism's most trustworthy advocate of the Messianic character of future and utopia (Bouretz), but also a reference in the law. *The Guide of the Perplexed*, for instance, is devoted to 'the difficulties of the Law' and the 'secrets of the Law'.[39] Strauss argues that Maimonides seems compelled by the intention to transgress the law, for the first intention of the law as a whole is to destroy every vestige of idolatry; and yet Maimonides, as he openly admits and even emphasises, has studied all the available idolatrous books of this kind with the utmost thoroughness. Nor is this all. The law also forbids one to speculate about the date of the coming of the Messiah, yet Maimonides presents such a speculation, or at least its equivalent, in order to comfort his contemporaries.[40] Like others before him, Maimonides perceived catastrophe, wars and upheavals as presentiments of the footsteps of the Messiah. He saw these events as Messianic travails, 'the pangs of the Messiah', hardships of the restoration of prophecy, and a Messianic advent in the near future.[41]

The Messiah for Maimonides is both prophet and ideal king. He will free Israel from its enemies, rebuild the Temple, gather the dispersed Jews and usher in a period of world peace in which all nations acknowledge and worship the one God.[42] In this regard, the 2011 peaceful Arab revolutions in Tunisia, Egypt and Yemen, but also the war in Libya for 'democracy and constitution', can be equated with the role of the Messiah. The arrival of the Messiah is substituted by the arrival of constitutional democracies.

Maimonides argued that:

> The Messiah will arise and restore the kingdom of David to its former might. He will rebuild the sanctuary and gather the dispersed of Israel. All the laws will be reinstituted in his days as of old ... Rather it is the case in these matters that the statutes of our Torah are valid forever and eternally. Nothing can be added to them or taken away from them.[43]

It is important to highlight the link between the restorative Messiahs and the Torah.

Scholem argues that there was a rational limitation to the Messiah's restorative components. This limitation occurs only in the medieval varieties of Messianism, and there is a great difference here between medieval and modern rationalism, which must be maintained against obvious tendencies to efface it. To the extent that the rationalism of the Jewish and European Enlightenment subjected the Messianic idea to ever advancing secularisation, it freed itself of the restorative element, stressing instead the utopian element. Messianism became tied up with the idea of eternal progress and the infinitive task of humanity perfecting itself.[44] In other words, there is no restoration and recognition of the Messiah without full compliance with the Torah. The binding force of law does not cease and the lawful order of nature does not give way to any miracles. For Maimonides, the intervention of heaven on earth constitutes no criterion for the legitimacy of the Messiah and of his mission.[45] Legitimacy appears clearly as an element of Messianism. Even the Messiah needs legitimacy to be recognised, as his legitimacy is not presupposed but earned and recognised.

For Maimonides this legitimacy comes from respect for the Torah. In the secular analogies of the theory the Messiah is self-attributed; there is no higher or independent source. The new Messiah is the only source of legitimacy. In our constitutional democracies, constitutions have the same features. Our constitutions are the only source of legal legitimacy. The sovereign is a self-attributed condition that uses the constitution to juridify and consolidate its power.

SOVEREIGNTY AND SUBJECT: 'SUPERIOREM NON RECOGNOSCENS'

Sovereignty becomes a central issue of constitutional violence. Derrida relates the two concepts thus: *'la souveraineté de l'État comme monopole de la violence'*.[46]

This part of the book does not attempt to answer the question of what is sovereignty, but to define the cyclical or symbiotic relationship between violence and the sovereign, to illustrate how violence legitimates the sovereign and vice versa.

The section begins with different definitions of sovereignty. The main goal is to provide a comprehensive notion of sovereignty, highlighting some of the fundamental characteristics that appear in the work of Hobbes, Kelsen, Schmitt and Derrida. Once the definitions and characteristics of sovereignty are expounded, the next step is to link the comprehensive definition with violence. This theoretical exercise concludes with a proposal to change – or at least share – the holder of sovereignty, from the aristocracy and its constitution to – or with – the people.

Sovereignty is a term discussed in multidisciplinary discourses, in law and the political and social sciences, as well as in economics and the ongoing discussion of 'philosophical' terms. The first difficulty, which is at the same time part of the richness of the phenomenon of sovereignty, lies in the concept's differing character, definition and implications depending on the discipline concerned. The fact that sovereignty is a topic of investigation in different branches of knowledge determines its analysis and predetermines some of the conclusions. In fact, it is noted that the concept of sovereignty is mainly discussed because of its descriptive nature with respect to a particular characteristic of an active political entity, which is not necessarily clearly identified with specific political realities. The notion of sovereignty performs different roles.

Whereas it would seem relatively simple to describe as 'sovereign' a particular set of actors in international political relations, how these actors are 'sovereign', who attributed 'sovereignty' to them (e.g., the people, the nation, the monarchy) and what this attribution implies (e.g., full powers, legitimate representation, legal authority) are characteristics that can vary significantly from case to case. The complexity surrounding the definition of sovereignty gives rise to a lack of unanimous consensus on its historical origins.

Doctrine has reinterpreted the concept of sovereignty, but there are also some schools of doctrine that require the restriction or total cancellation of sovereignty, especially when dealing with conflicts involving international law, human rights and state sovereignty.

One common definition is that sovereignty has been, and continues to be, the concept applied to support old forms of legitimacy and responsibility,

as well as the basis upon which power becomes authority.[47] Its first characteristic is that it is an abstraction, a legal fiction that continues to evolve.[48]
The concept of sovereignty is permanently evolving and adapting itself to
each particular historical moment. Its continuous evolution is determined by
the need to legitimise authority: the sovereign must justify its power at any
given time, regardless of whether the source that legitimates its authority
becomes invalid in the future.

Another complication, as Bartelson states, is that a history of basic
political concepts such as sovereignty necessitates a change in methodological orientation from what is established practice within the study of political
(but also juridical and economic) ideas.[49] If there is a danger of misinter-
preting and misunderstanding the ideas to which they could not or did not
give expression, with political ideas like sovereignty this possibility is real.

One of the most complicated task has been to narrow the definition of
the concept of sovereignty to the subject of this work, constitutional
violence. The lack of consensus in determining the origins of sovereignty is
a demonstration of the intrinsic problem of the notion.

Kahn examines the evolution of the relationship between power and the
state to introduce the current conception of sovereignty and its mystical and
sacred character for states.[50] This sacred character has its origins in the fact
that the sovereign will, for centuries, was quite literally embodied in a subject:
the monarch was the mystical corpus of the state. That incorporation
borrowed explicitly from Christology. From this standpoint, the idea of
sovereignty is critical, while the representation of the sovereign in the monarch
is not. The monarch claimed to be the 'mystical corpus of the state', but
was vulnerable to competing symbolic representations of national will. The
sovereign as mystical corpus survives long after the monarch disappears.[51]
Revolution kills the king, but also announces the presence of a new sovereign:
'we the people'. The revelatory act – the moment of grace – is now that of
self-revelation by the popular sovereign. In the politics of the nation-state,
man – understood as the popular sovereign – has become divine. The source
of the state's creation is the will of the popular sovereign. Kahn examines
the evolution of the relationship of power within the state to introduce the
current conception of sovereignty and the mystical and sacred character of
states themselves: faculty and object have become identical.[52]

In this respect, Derrida views the sovereign as Aristotle did, as the *prima
causa*, the unmoved mover. Nothing and nobody can escape a sovereignty
thus understood, not even deconstruction.[53]

This same logic is utilised by the drafters of the Constitution of the
República Bolivariana de Venezuela, where they state that since the pre-
existing people to the arrival of the first Europeans were also pre-existing to
the formation of national states and that is why they are named 'Indians'.[54]

This constitutional statement is contradictory with one of the major essences of the notion of sovereignty: its evolution and openness to progress. Therefore, the use of the notions sovereignty and sovereign has been tendentious.

Sovereignty can be identified as the power to enforce a predominant '*nomos*' or 'logion' in a society. This logion is imposed on all other discourses. Therefore, when analysing constitutional violence we are forced to consider who the sovereign is, who applies this violence and where his legitimacy comes from. I agree with the mutation that Derrida contends, from *la bête et le souverain* to *la bête est le souverain*; in law the reason of the strongest is not the best, should not, will not be the best.[55] The last chapter in this book is an example of the imposition of the sovereign logion and *nomos*.

Hobbes held that a sovereign can come by conquest or by 'acquisition'; the sovereign has the same power in either case, whether brought about conquest or by authorisation, or institution via social contract.[56] The sovereign is our agent and acts with authority.[57]

Rawls adds important qualifications to this sort of fictitious authorisation; he states that authorisation is not simply the renunciation of a right on my part. Rather, authorisation enables someone else to use my right to act in a certain way. Thus, we do not renounce or abandon our rights in authorising the sovereign; rather we authorise the sovereign to use our rights in certain ways. The person who has the use of my right and who is my agent now has a right which that person did not have before; authorisation can be for a longer or shorter period of time and that, of course, depends on the grant of authority and its purpose and the like.[58]

These gradations are directly applicable to the final object of this work. When the sovereign acts against the will of he who authorises, contradicting or exceeding the authorisation, the contract is broken. Then the enforcement of this sort of action is based exclusively on violence. Acting against the authoriser invalidates the main role of the sovereign of stabilising and thereby maintaining the social state for everyone.[59]

Rawls expounds an evolution of Hobbes' theory about 'authorisation'; in his previous work, *De Cive*, the sovereign is not authorised, but rather everyone renounces certain rights that would enable them in some conditions to resist the sovereign. In *Leviathan* everyone confers the use of their right on the sovereign by means of a contract with each other, so the sovereign becomes their agent.[60] This transformation is important in order to configure the relationship between the sovereign and the people (authoriser), but both works are based on the premise of separating the people from the sovereign entity. This separation contradicts the reality preached by modern constitutions. The separation between authoriser (people) and authorised (aristocracy, constitution or fictitious person) describes the *de facto* truth. Authorisation can be understood in this context as a synonym of consent.

The first of the major features of the notion of sovereignty related to the subject of this section is abstraction, a legal fiction that continues to evolve.[61] There are different definitions and conceptions to characterise sovereignty as an abstraction: a metaphysical entity (Derrida); a legislative hypothesis (Kelsen); or an ideality (Hegel). But even in this feature there is not a unanimous doctrine. Kelsen considered that sovereignty was a legislative hypothesis, identical to positive law (the constitution) and different from facticity; Schmitt believed that sovereignty was a *de facto* situation (who decided in the state of exception); Hobbes considered the sovereign as an artificial person (the Leviathan), because the sovereign is someone whom members of society have authorised to act on their behalf. Among these different conceptions and features Hegel's ideality, related to unity, must be stressed. In this respect, Hegel contends:

> The fundamental characteristic of the state as a political entity is the substantial unity, i.e. the ideality, of its moments.
>
> (a) In this unity the particular powers and their activities are dissolved and yet retained. They are retained, however, only in the sense that the authority is no independent one but only one of the order and breath determined by the Idea of the Whole; from its might they originate, and they are flexible limbs while it is their single self.
>
> (b) The particular activities and agencies of the state are its essential moments and therefore are proper to it. The individual functionaries and agents are attached to their office not on the strength of their immediate personality, but only on the strength of their universal and objective qualities.
>
> The idealism which constitutes sovereignty is the same characteristic as that in accordance with which the so-called parts of an animal organism are not parts but members, moments in an organic whole, whose isolation and independence spell disease. The principle here is the same as that which came before us in the abstract concept of the will … The fact that the sovereignty of the state is the ideality of all particular authorities within it gives rise to the easy and also very common misunderstanding that this ideality is only might and pure arbitrariness while sovereignty is a synonym of despotism.[62]

Hegel considered the sovereign as a self-subsistent and independent being based on a concept of ideality. Following the metaphor of Hegel, this ideal existence and self-subsistence protects itself like an animal when something or someone threatens its life. The self-protection is through violence, plain brutal violence. At an early stage the sovereign uses constitutional violence to maintain its hegemonic power, but later the constitution itself becomes the sovereign, as Kelsen described.

Another feature of sovereignty that must be stressed in view of the subject of this book is *ipseity* or self-definition. Derrida, quoting Benveniste, states that sovereignty is characterised by ipseity (*lui soi même*):[63]

l'ipséité de l'ipse implique l'exercice du pouvoir par quelqu'un qu'il suffit de désigner comme lui-même, ipse. Le souverain, au sens le plus large du terme, c'est celui qui a le droit et la force d'être et d'être reconnu comme lui-même, le même, proprement le même que soit.[64]

The concept of sovereignty always implies the possibility of this self-imposition of he who appears as *ipse*, *le même*, and this characteristic is valid for all sovereigns.[65] Sovereignty is a self-attributed condition. The sovereign has the right, but also the force, to be and to be recognised as a sovereign.[66] Unlike Derrida, I contend that force is the nuclear and exclusive characteristic of sovereignty. The right to be defined as a sovereign will be provided by force, not the other way round. There seems to be little chance of finding an entity with the power and competence to become a sovereign which decides not to implement this right. In my understanding, sovereignty means power and not right, and power is based on violence or threat. Law without force is not worthy of this name.[67] The right of the sovereign is based on this violent law, on its power to enforce political decisions and laws.

Another important feature of sovereignty highlighted by Derrida and related to violence is *mortality* as a characteristic that is common to both the beast (*la bête*) and the sovereign: '*En tant que vivants, c'est d'être exposés à la mort*'.[68] Sovereignty cannot only be destroyed, it can also be created and transformed. The possibility of transforming the sovereign power provides hope for democracy in our constitutional systems. It seems feasible to enable mechanisms in order to restore power to the real and only legitimate sovereign, the people, even though the main doctrine is based on a distinction between these two notions. The first step is to avoid this starting premise. On the subject of the destruction of the sovereign we find many modern examples, such as Yugoslavia, the Soviet Union or post-Second World War Germany and Japan.

The traditional division of the sovereignty of the state is twofold: internal and external. Internal sovereignty is the exclusive authority of a people to enact and enforce laws. Therefore, internal sovereignty consists in the people giving itself its own legal order. No other entity determines the form of government or its representatives. These elements arise as an expression of popular sovereignty. On the other hand, external sovereignty predominantly involves the freedom of a nation and its equality with other nations in the international arena. The most important consequence of this aspect of sovereignty is the nation's independence. This can be understood as the international projection of internal sovereignty. This twofold division has been developed by authors such as Hegel and Jellinek, who have both referred to this distinction. In an external sense, the state is the sovereign personality. Popular sovereignty expresses an idea that is true only when one regards the state externally as one among others, as when one refers to the people of

Great Britain as sovereign. Internally, the people are sovereign in a very general sense by which the 'people' are understood as the whole state, including monarch and what is ordinarily meant by 'people'.

It is not the subject of this book to analyse carefully the definitions of the concept of internal and external sovereignty, but to analyse how the sovereign was obliged to cede part of its monopolistic power both internally and externally. In this respect, if we consider and correct the Derridian image, sovereignty will not correspond to the philosophical monotheistic theology of the first stationary engine, but rather to a political polytheistic theology, according to which the pantheon is but a series of unstable fights among gods, that is, a struggle among sovereignties. The European constitutions have established different mechanisms to cede and transfer sovereignty not only to entities different to 'the people'.

Kelsen also recognises that the supreme existence designated as 'sovereignty' is habitually understood in two different senses, internal and external, arguing that it should always be the same. This is a central aspect of his theory.[69] This typographic refers to two different functions of the same structure.[70] This book is interested mainly in internal sovereignty, and the internal and external violence associated with law. Therefore, this typology has only a limited significance, namely, how this type of sovereignty has been implemented against the people. Taussig-Rubbo defines as a dimension of sovereignty the capacity to exercise violence with legal impunity.[71] Sovereignty is this dimension and the only possibility of legitimating this sort of violence is not legally, but democratically.

FROM CONSTITUTIONAL SOVEREIGNTY TO POPULAR SOVEREIGNTY

The present section attempts to demonstrate some of the main characteristics of sovereignty: openness, contingency and instability. On the basis of an ancient Athenian experience of the fifth century BC in which there was a change from popular sovereignty to the sovereignty of law, I intend to obtain valid premises and conclusions applicable to the notion of sovereignty nowadays. The main conclusions drawn are that: (a) there is a real possibility of altering the sovereign from aristocracy to democracy, or from the constitution to the people and vice versa; (b) this alteration occurs gradually over time and not necessarily traumatically; (c) popular sovereignty functioned fully for centuries in Athens; (d) the Athenian experience can be studied as an example of democratic establishment and to learn about the events that led to regression through the sovereignty of law.

All these conclusions and the fact that new technology outweighs the main fears of the Founding Fathers qualifies this ancient experience as a good source from which to obtain premises and conclusions in order to enable a popular sovereignty today. The main thesis is not to abolish the constitution, but to give sovereignty progressively to the people. The fact of expounding this real and ancient experience of popular sovereignty does not mean as Ostwald claims that:

> 'Democracy' was for all the Greeks more restricted than it is for us; it did not imply the potential participation of all adult citizens in every aspect of political life. To exclude women from active participation in politics is not as puzzling in this respect as is the fact that even in the heyday of democracy noble birth and wealth remained important criteria for eligibility to some high offices ... that it is nevertheless correct to use terms such as 'democracy' and 'popular sovereignty' in describing the government of Athens in the fifth century.[72]

Some doctrine has underestimated Athenian democracy because of these fundamental deficiencies, but these anachronistic conclusions are not valid premises when assessing democracy in the fifth century BC. Is it not in our modern democratic republics, where all adult citizens have access to minimum democratic and human rights, that economics, visas and citizenship cards condemn millions of people to a new version of slavery? As Habermas states, the modern conception of democracy differs from the classical conception by virtue of its relation to a type of law that displays three characteristics: modern law is positive, compulsory and individualistic.[73] But some of the ancient definitions and experiences of *demos-kratos* can be applied to enlighten the modern relationship between the two spheres.

The ancient experience consisted of various proposals that aimed to democratise the Athenian political system. As quoted above, the consolidation of popular sovereignty was the result of a gradual process. None of these democratic reforms tried to implement a preconceived ideological pattern that made the rule of the people by the people a desirable political end for its own sake. All were responses to historical situations that, as a by-product, led to the increase in popular power to the point at which the sovereignty of the people in all public affairs came to be a recognised principle, which could then become an ideology.[74]

Since time immemorial the concept of 'caste' had been rooted in politics. The political leadership of Attica was in the hands of men whose claim to social prominence rested on a combination of landed wealth and membership of old and distinguished families and clans. Membership was conferred by birth, to the extent that the governing class was referred to as 'nobility' or 'aristocracy', as differentiated from the commoners.[75] This situation, which already existed in the fifth century BC, has continued in different forms throughout history until the present. In this respect the Founding Fathers of the United States were concerned about the role that aristocracy and democracy played in Athens through the works of Plato, Aristotle, Plutarch, Cicero and Polybius. Tocqueville, for instance, focused his interest on the role that aristocracy and democracy developed in the young American democracy. Nowadays the intellectual and economic aristocracy and their constitution adapt a 'reality' generated and maintained by themselves.

In relation to the subject of this section, the first historical lesson to observe is the capacity for mutation and adaptation of the aristocracy in different political systems. In the particular example of the fifth century BC, the elite introduced several mechanisms (constitution, polarisation, political conflicts, the sycophants, etc.) to achieve the breakdown of popular sovereignty.

Solon applied the first of the procedures that initiated the growth of popular sovereignty. The measure affected the administration of justice. Solon contributed to the establishment of popular power by opening membership of the law courts to all.[76] Solon's main contributions to the judicial system of Athens affected the jurisdiction of the Areopagus in public cases, since its membership consisted of ex-archons, all of whom belonged to the upper classes, and since it was believed to be the oldest and most venerable political body in Athens even before Solon, it had considerable and presumably undefined powers, which are usually described in the ancient sources as the guardianship of the laws (*nomophylakein*).[77]

The role of the guardians of the constitution and their relationship with the democratic institutions has been one of the most analysed subjects from Plato until today. Any serious analysis regarding the relationship between constitutionalism and democracy has to address the undemocratic role of the judiciary and the enormous significance of their actions in the political system. Whereas the object of interest of this book is really related to this literature, at its heart it focuses on a different premise: textual and enforced constitutional violence.

The democratising political reform of Solon that affected the guardians of the constitution and its undemocratic character is a good example of the struggles between aristocracy and democracy. A search for harmony between these two clashing commitments – the ideal of government constrained by law ('constitutionalism') and the ideal of government by act of the people ('democracy') – has eternally hounded, if not totally consumed, American constitutional history.[78] Solon anticipated the routes of this eternal debate. After the 'democratic' transitions in Greece, Portugal and Spain, or lately in Argentina and Chile or in the Colour Revolutions in Eastern Europe, the pre-revolutionary aristocracy did not disappear, but was self-relocated and constitutionally legitimised. Who really thinks that the Egyptian aristocracy will disappear with Mubarak?

Solon's second contribution to the judicial system of Athens was the right to hold magistrates accountable for their conduct in office.[79] Accountability of constitutional guardians is limited or null in the vast majority of our modern constitutional systems. Constitutions and magistrates' statutes exclude judges from liability and accountability for their decisions and actions in court.

Cleisthenes took the second step to achieving popular sovereignty in ancient Athens. This statesman and Athenian noble reformed the legislative procedure, considering that the empowerment of 'the people' was the only way to counterbalance the aristocracy and its political and economic power. Solon's reform of the administration of justice was left untouched by Cleisthenes, whose contribution to the growth of popular power was a by-product of the solution to a different set of fundamental problems.[80] The origins themselves, as described by Herodotus and Aristotle, show that Cleisthenes' aim was not to place the decisive power of governing the state (*kratos*) into the hands of the *demos*, but rather to ameliorate conditions that had first brought about tyranny in Athens. Cleisthenes was, in other words, no ideological democrat, but a practical statesman and politician concerned with eliminating the roots of internal conflict from the society in which he lived.[81] The mixing process that Aristotle saw at the centre of Cleisthenes' reforms applies in an even wider sense than he recognised to the blend of aristocratic and democratic elements in the constitution those reforms produced. Cleisthenes created in the Council and the Assembly a counterweight to break the monopoly of the political power that birth and wealth held through its control of the electorate, which had been responsible for the dynastic rivalries that had characterised the politics of sixth-century Athens.[82] The elimination from political life of the four kingship tribes, dominated by the *genē*, which Solon had made the electoral units for his constitution, and the substitution of ten new tribes, each composed from each of the three regions of Attica, was regarded as a democratic measure already in antiquity.[83]

The idea of a mixing process is the best example to follow at the present time to achieve a feasible greater democratic sovereignty. The people will apply the same argument used by the aristocracy in order to obtain more participation and political decision-making power. In this respect an actual mixing process will consist in introducing mechanisms to allow citizen involvement in the undemocratic institutions of the US republican democratic system, such as the Supreme Court or the Senate. The people's participation can involve the system of election, appointment, nomination, etc. The only requirements needed to achieve this participation are trust in the people and popular will. The main improvement with a mixing process is that the aristocrats will remain in power, but second-class citizens will progressively be included in political and juridical affairs. 'We the people' is a very strong fiction with which citizens need to identify. By allowing a sort of mixed involvement, the fiction becomes more real.

The next reform was the establishment of the jury courts (*dikasteria*) by Ephialtes. In the democratic city-states the *dikasteria* were the most important democratic organ of the state, alongside the Assembly (*ekklesia*). Aristotle defines the citizen in a democracy as one who has the right to be a juror and a participator in the Assembly;[84] this coincides neatly with the specific analysis of the Athenian democracy in the *Constitution of Athens*, where, in the introduction to the systematic description of the constitution, he classifies the Athenian democracy as one 'where power is wielded (by the Assembly), which passes decrees, and the People's Court'.[85]

By way of example, the debate about the jury was reproduced in recent Spanish history with the approval of the Organic Law on Jury Courts. The explanatory memorandum of this law was a clear political expression of the debate. It began by citing the constitutional mandate established by Section 125 of the Spanish Constitution: 'Citizens may engage in popular action and participate in the administration of justice through the institution of the jury, in the manner and with respect to those criminal trials as may be determined by law, as well as in customary and traditional courts.' The Spanish Constitution links the institution of the jury to two fundamental rights: citizen participation in public matters and the right to a judge predetermined by the law. The debate clearly polarised the aristocrats and the people of the country, as occurred in the Athens of Ephialtes.

The last contribution to the consolidation of the political development in Athens is attributed to Pericles. This was the citizenship law of 451 BC, by which citizens' rights were bestowed only on those who could prove that both of their parents were citizens of Athens. The minimum effect will have been to give the people as a whole the power to determine who was and who was not to enjoy citizenship and the privileges that went with it instead of leaving the final decision to the demes.[86] This historical experience evidences that migration issues are closely related to democracy. Democracy cannot be built on despair and the enslavement of millions of people.

The historical example analysed here ended with the breakdown of popular sovereignty and the subsequent birth of the sovereignty of law. But the Athenian experience remains as an example of democratic establishment and shows that democratic reforms are possible and suitable.

UNCONSTITUTIONAL 'CONSTITUTIONAL SOVEREIGNTY'

The last section of this chapter focuses on constitutional sovereignty. The starting point is a brief and updated definition of the notion of the constitution and the role that this important law plays in terms of sovereignty. The constitution is also discussed from a multidisciplinary standpoint, as the meaning of the constitution varies according to the approach. From a strict jus-positivistic point of view, the constitution is analysed as a set of norms, principles and structures. In this sense, most of the US constitutional law doctrine completely ignores the definition of the Constitution in its works. This literature simply attaches the US Constitution to the main text or the book starts with the judicial review.[87] The reason for this omission is not only because law schools focus on absolute pragmatism, but also because the American system is built downwards, from case law to the constitutional meaning, and the Continental system is the opposite: from the constitution to case law. Certainly, some American scholars have analysed the unconstitutionality of some constitutional amendments or contents,[88] but none of these authors deal with the constitutional allocation of sovereignty as unconstitutional.

But the meaning of a constitution is much more than a text and case law, not only because, being a text, it requires interpretations and the existence of a *meta-constitution*, or because the constitution's drafters, interpreters and enforcers are the real sovereigns, but also because the constitution has different notions and meanings.[89]

Using the Schmittian constitutional categorisation, which divides the constitution into relative, positive and absolute senses, the US doctrine mentioned earlier will be limited to the first and second types.[90] The relative sense considers the constitution as a multitude of individual laws:

> Every substantive and factual distinction is lost due to the dissolution of the unified constitution into a multitude of individual, formally equivalent constitutional laws. Whether the constitutional law regulates the organization of the state will or has any other content is a matter of indifference for this formal concept. It is no longer generally asked why a constitutional provision must be fundamental ... In other words, it makes everything equally relative.[91]

The positive concept of the constitution approaches the constitution as the whole decision about the type and form of the political unity:

> A concept of constitution is only possible when one distinguishes constitution and constitutional law. It is not acceptable to first dissolve the constitution into a multitude of individual laws and then to define constitutional law in reference to some external characteristic or theory even according to the method of its alteration ... The constitution in the positive sense originates from an act of the constitution-making power. The act of establishing a constitution as such involves not separate sets of norms. Instead, it determines the entirety of the political unity in regard to its peculiar form of existence through a single instance of decision. This act constitutes the form and type of the political unity, the existence of which is presupposed.[92]

The last (first in appearance) category of constitutional concept is relevant in order to figure out the significance of constitutional sovereignty. The concept of absolute constitution is the concrete manner of existence that is given with every political unity. In an absolute sense the state does not *have* a constitution, the state *is* a constitution; the state would cease to exist if the constitution, more specifically, this unity and order, ceased to exist. The constitution is its soul, its concrete life and its individual existence.[93] Unlike Schmitt, I contend that the constitution (as an institution and symbol) is not the state, but the sovereign, regardless of what the constitutional text itself states. Along these lines, Lindsay found that:

> if the sovereign is the one that with his recognized authority makes possible the government of the nation and the right sustained by force, therefore the constitution is the sovereign, because the Constitution contains and retains the unity, indivisibility and the supremacy that constitute the essence of the sovereignty.[94]

Then the constitution is not only the juridification of the state, but also the sovereign.

The constitution is not limited to a text (written or otherwise); it has an absolute and omnipresent transcendence. No one can act against the constitutional empire, including the people. Constitutional sovereignty is divided into two different realities: in a symbolic sphere the constitutional text, shielded by a sacred discourse, is absolute reason; and in a pragmatic sphere, the drafters, enforcers and interpreters of the text (none of whom is chosen by the people) are the real sovereigns.

The usurpation of the sovereign power in favour of the constitution provokes a legal paradox. Constitutional sovereignty is unconstitutional because it is against what is prescribed in the text. In this respect, Article 1.2 of the Italian Constitution of 1947 states: 'Sovereignty belongs to the people and is exercised by the people in the forms and within the limits of the Constitution'; Article 3.1 of the Portuguese Constitution of 1976 states: 'Sovereignty shall be single and indivisible and shall lie with the people, who shall exercise it in the forms provided for in this Constitution'; Article 1.2 of the Spanish Constitution of 1978 states: 'National sovereignty belongs to the Spanish people, from whom all state powers emanate'; but also the preambles of 'we the people' of the United States, the Republic of South Africa, India, Korea, etc.

According to all these texts there is only one legitimate sovereign, the people, and therefore constitutional sovereignty is unconstitutional. In these concrete examples the usurpation of sovereignty will clearly violate not only the preamble (politically, but not juridically, binding), but also the juridically binding body of the constitution. Then the aristocracy introduces new juridical concepts, new rules and theories to disable a possible appliance of these articles and principles, such as the notion of the 'programmatic' and the not juridically enforceable character of some constitutional articles.

The real sovereigns interpret the constitution in order to have the last word on all constitutional issues. Literacy threatens the guardians of the law with *ad hoc* techniques in Continental or common law systems. If a constitutional text declares *we the people*, from which all powers come, this *de facto* relocation of the sovereign power is against the text. Consequently, the next amendment should shape this fiction, and instead of *we the people* it should state *I the Constitution* or *we the elite*.

Constitutional sovereignty is a different way of saying Schmitt's 'constitutional supremacy'. The main arguments for building this supremacy are positivistic; the constitutional text itself and jurisprudence are the main sources. United States' doctrine has analysed these influences thoroughly, but it is necessary to note that the actual juridical and political interpretation of the constitution provides arguments to ground this sort of undisputed and unconstitutional sovereignty. Different constitutional meanings build up this theoretical supremacy.

As Schmitt shows, the word constitution often had the sense of order in Greek philosophy.[95] The first example that Schmitt expounds to define the conception of constitution as order is based on Aristotle:

> the state is an order of the naturally occurring association of human beings of a city or area. The order involves governance in the state and how it is organized. By the virtue of this order, there is a ruler. However, a component of this order is its living goal, which is contained in the actually existing property of the concrete political formation. If this constitution is eliminated, the state is as well; if a new constitution is founded, a new state arises ... It is perhaps best to clarify this idea of the constitution through a comparison. The song or musical piece of a choir remains the same if the people singing or performing change or if the place where they perform changes.[96]

The constitution in this sense is separated from the popular will and becomes an independent being. This new 'creature' determines the order to be respected, and it configures the new authority. Ruler and ruled are differentiated from the origin, as of the appearance of the constitution. The second sense to be discussed is supremacy. This supremacy is induced on a strict textual basis (there is not a single constitution that does not declare its supremacy; no law, act or fact can contradict the constitution), from a theoretical jus-positivistic point of view (Kelsen), but also as a special type of political order.

Plato has been regarded from antiquity as one of the first expounders, if

not the originator, of the theory of the mixed constitution, although the
term occurs nowhere in the *Laws*.[97] Plato considered that:

> Of constitutions there are, so to speak, two mother forms from which we
> can rightly say that the others have been derived. One of these we may
> properly call monarchy, the other democracy ... A constitution must
> necessarily partake of them both, if there is to be freedom and friendship,
> together with wisdom.[98]

The extreme terms in Plato's political proportion – the two 'mother forms'
of constitution, which every rightly ordered state must have – are mentioned
later in an incidental reaffirmation of the general principle: 'Our
constitution must always keep the middle path between the monarchical
and the democratic constitutions.'[99] Aristotle, who quotes this formula,
objects that there seems to be no monarchical element at all in Plato's state;
its features seem rather to be taken from oligarchy and democracy.[100]
Obviously, we have to find Plato's monarchical element in some more
general feature of political constitutions. As a first approximation we can
say that what Plato means is some recognised centre or source of authority
in the state.[101] This antagonism evolves in two other forms of constitution:
oligarchy and aristocracy.

The Platonic division is the pattern of other constitutional forms.
Aristotle stated:

> the words constitution and government have the same meaning, and the
> government, which is the supreme authority in states, must be in the hands
> of one, or of a few, or of many. The true forms of government (*politeia* and
> therefore *rei publicae*), therefore, are those in which the one, or the few, or
> the many, govern with a view to the common interest; but governments
> which rule with a view to the private interest, whether of the one, or of the
> few, or of the many, are perversions ... Of forms of government in which
> one rules, we call that which regards the common interests, kingship; that in
> which more than one, but not many, rule, aristocracy; and it is so called,
> either because the rulers are the best men, or because they have at heart the
> best interests of the state and of the citizens. But when the many administer
> the state for the common interest, the government is called by the generic
> name – a constitution.[102]

Therefore, the term constitution is polysemic. Aristotle, distinguishing the
different meanings, stated: 'we have to describe the so-called constitutional
government, which bears the common name of all constitutions, and the
other forms, tyranny, oligarchy, and democracy'.[103] The term *politeia* is related
to the nature of men as a political being, *zoon politikon* (ζ ον πολιτικόν).
Therefore, the word constitution in its general sense means the form of
government of the political animal.

Cicero considered the best constitution for a state to be that which is a balanced combination of the three forms: when supreme authority is in the hands of one man, we call him king, and the form of state is a kingship (*regnum*); when selected citizens hold this power we say that the state is ruled by an aristocracy (*civitas optimatium*). But a popular government (*civitas popularis*) (for so it is called) exists when all the power is in the hands of the people.[104]

It is illuminating in several ways to carry out an etymological analysis of the language used by Cicero in his constitutional classification and how these words are understood nowadays. The word *politeia* was translated to the Latin as *rei publicae*. The Founding Fathers (*The Federalist Papers* and also Tocqueville) brought a polysemic meaning to the term *res publica* that included not only a general form of government (Cicero and Polybius), but also a concrete one, the new form of mixed constitutionalism. However, the *res publica* had never before been defined as a mixed democratic system; *res publica* means commonwealth and not a balanced democracy. The new meaning of the term seeks to encompass in a single term a mixed form of government, a full opposition to kingship and the legitimacy of aristocratic rule.

The other etymological analysis concerns the modern use of the terms *optimum* and *popularis*. *Optimum* evolved as *òptim* in Catalan, *ottimale* in Italian and optimal in English. Optimal means the most favourable or desirable. Popular (the same word in Catalan and English and *populare* in Italian) is related to ordinary or vulgar; ordinary people, taste or intelligence. Therefore, the codification of the language evidences which is the best system and also normalises the fact that there are optimal and vulgar people. Optimal has a widespread use in our languages and it is not restricted to a form of government or social class like aristocracy (ριστοκρατία). Polybius also classified polities into kingship, aristocracy and democracy, concluding that they are neither the only ones nor the best. 'For it is plain that we must regard as the best constitution that which partakes of all these three elements.'[105]

Thomas Aquinas also distinguishes among state forms: (a) optimal state (*status optimatum*) or aristocracy, in which a minority with exceptional excellence rules the government; (b) *status paucorum*, oligarchy in Aristotle (Skinner),[106] but also in Cicero and Polybius, in which a minority without an extraordinary excellence rules; and (c) *status popularis* (popular state), democracy in Aristotle, Cicero and Polybius, in which the multitude of farmers, craftsmen and workers rule.[107] Bodin, also adopting this pattern, distinguishes the popular state, monarchical state and aristocratic state.[108]

All these classifications are crucial to the subject of this book because mixed constitution and democracy are clearly differentiated as dissimilar forms of government or constitutions. To define our systems as constitutional democracies makes no sense, even when we use new meanings such as republic.

These classifications inspired the drafters and Founding Fathers of the US Constitution – and therefore the rest of the modern constitutional systems – to adopt a mixed constitutional form. As Biondi mentions, during the eighteenth century the American founders, some of whom explicitly reached back to Aristotle (but also Plutarch, Polybius and Cicero), also struggle, especially in *The Federalist Papers*, with these thorny issues of constitutional design. They created the US Constitution in part to address these issues.[109]

Another important conclusion to be drawn is the clear division between two opposite poles. These poles subsist today, even though the constitution mutes their existence. This antagonism is reflected and consolidated in our modern constitutions, where the *we the people* (Plato's democracy) remains illiterate and poor, and the usurpers are the centre of authority in the state (Plato's monarchy). The constitution as a juridical and political device has been created to maintain and consolidate this separation.

The single exclusive valid constitutional rationality and juridical violence are tools to keep the illiterate, the poor and other 'subnational' identities or peoples controlled and submitted. Therefore, the constitution is not only used to impose a particular logic, but also to begin the normalisation of the outlaw.

The last and probably the most refined feature of the constitution in an absolute sense was defined by Hegel:

> The constitution is rational in so far as the state inwardly differentiates and determines its activity in accordance with the nature of the concept. The result of this is that each of these powers is in itself the totality of the constitution, because each contains the other moments and has them effective in itself, and because the moments, being expressions of the differentiation of the concept, simply abide in their ideality and constitute nothing but a single individual whole.[110]

The constitution is the only legal and political rationality possible. Everything that is out of its empire is not only considered as unlawful, but also as irrational. Consequently, when there is a conflict between the will of the people and the constitution or a particular consolidated constitutional interpretation, the latter prevails. To violate this empire means to become a *furiosus*, in the sense of *furiosus absentis loco est*[111] (the insane is compared with the absent), which means that being unconstitutional or extra-constitutional is tantamount to not being. There is no totalitarianism more powerful than reason. This sole valid reason is enforced with all the state's means and force, and the main goal is to dilute the possible 'insane' tendencies in this exclusive rationality. The consequences of this sole rationality are set forth in Chapters 4 and 5, below. The constitution and its reason sweep aside everything and everybody, even if this means the juridi-fication of genocide. The only way to tinge constitutional totalitarianism is to enable a reattribution of the people's sovereignty to achieve a real democratic system, in which the constitution is understood as a living constitution, adapted to allow government of the people, by the people and for the people, as Article 2.1 of the French Constitution states.

The last issue analysed in this section is the concept of the democratic constitution. There is a sort of irremediable conflict between the two notions democracy and constitution. Their impossible conciliation is based on the following aspects: (a) the constitution participates in a rebirth of the *mikte* by mirroring the socio-economic classes in the community, constituting a balancing of interests.[112] It is a matter of fact that the constitution as a basic institutional structure has been used to consolidate the influence and sover-eignty of the few, the *optimals*; (b) the constitution (drafters, interpreters and enforcers) are the *de facto* sovereign instead of the people; (c) a real popular sovereignty will threaten the privileged and the official *nomos*.

Therefore, the *mikte* as a mixture disappears when the people's power is usurped or limited to electing representatives, and the constitution becomes a tool to eternise these socio-economic differences. These socio-economic differences are the main issue to be controlled in order to bring stability to the state, not only in Plato, Aristotle, Cicero and Polybius, but also in the US Founding Fathers, Jefferson and also Tocqueville. Democracy cannot be restricted to a system of election and the only possibility of cohabitation between democracy and constitution is to enable popular sovereignty and popular involvement in constitutional affairs. The fiction of representation of the people is analysed in Chapter 3, below, with a definition of democracy.

As a sort of conclusion, the relationship between sovereignty and constitution is based on the supreme power that the constitution has over all other political powers and juridical norms. In modern constitutional states sovereignty cannot belong only to the constitution, which is the sole framework of all the activities of all the citizens of the state. There is a relocation of power from the people to the constitution. Constitutional supremacy is material, that is, the entire state juridical system is based on it, but it is also formal, related to the specific creation and amendment processes of the supreme norm that determines its highest rank in the hierarchy. Consequently, all that is within the constitution is hierarchically supreme. Nor can we forget supra-legality, which is the quality provided to a norm according to the source of creation and amendment. Supremacy can be seen as a kind of quality that affects all political constitutions. In Kelsen the constitution must be the highest point of the normative pyramid: the whole system of regulations is under the constitutional empire. While the supremacy of law is essential in the legal and liberal system, the 'living constitution', as Ackerman claims, must be linked to some democratic radicalism to prevent a prettification of the status quo.

Notes

1. Luke 20:25.
2. J. M. Balkin, *Constitutional Redemption: Political Faith in an Unjust World*, Cambridge, MA: Harvard University Press, 2011.
3. Hamilton, J. Madison and J. Jay, *The Federalist Papers*, p. 148, 1787–1788, available at: http://Avalon.law.yale.edu/18th_century/fed02.asp, accessed 20 December 2010.
4. Ferejohn, J, K. Rakove and J. Riley (eds), *Constitutional Culture and Democratic Rule*, Cambridge: Cambridge University Press, 2001, p. 67.
5. S. Levinson, *Constitutional Faith*, Princeton, NJ: Princeton University Press, 1989, p. 11.
6. See Article VI, Section 1, Clause 3. Oath of Office: 'The Senators and Representatives before mentioned, and the members of the several state legislatures, and all executive and judicial officers, both of the United States and of the several states, shall be bound by oath or affirmation, to support this Constitution; but no religious test shall ever be required as a qualification to any office or public trust under the United States.'
7. J. M. Balkin, 'Original meaning and constitutional redemption', *Constitutional Commentary*, 24(2), 2007, 427–532.
8. B. Ackerman, 'The living constitution', *Harvard Law Review*, 120, 2007, 1737–93.
9. The United States declared its independence in 1776. The Constitution was not drafted until 1787, and it was ratified in 1789. There was no governing document until 1783, when the Revolution formally ended with the Treaty of Paris. From 1783 to 1789 the country was governed by the ill-fated Articles of Confederation.
10. T. C. Grey, 'The constitution as scripture', *Stanford Law Review*, 37, 1984, 1, 1–24.
11. L. Kramer, *The People Themselves: Popular Constitutionalism and Judicial Review*, Oxford: Oxford University Press, 2004.
12. A. Hamilton, J. Madison and J. Jay, *The Federalist Papers*, p. 148, 1787–1788, available at: http://Avalon.law.yale.edu/18th_century/fed02.asp, accessed 20 December 2010.
13. J. Ferejohn, J. K. Rakove and J. Riley (eds), *Constitutional Culture and Democratic Rule*, Cambridge: Cambridge University Press, 2001, p. 67.
14. *Ibid.*, p. 42.
15. H. Arendt, *On Revolution*, London: Faber & Faber, 1963, pp. 125–6.

16. A. Marmor, *Positive Law and Objective Values*, New York: Oxford University Press, 2001.
17. H. Kelsen, *General Theory of Law and State*, New York: Russell & Russell, 1961.
18. A. Abat i Ninet, 'Playing at being gods', *Philosophia Quarterly of Israel*, 38(1), 2009, 2.
19. T. Honoré, 'The basic norm of a society', in S. L. Paulson and B. Litschewski Paulson (eds), *Normativity and Norms: Critical Perspectives on Kelsenian Themes*, Oxford: Clarendon Press, 1998, pp. 89–113.
20. H. Kelsen, *General Theory of Law and State*, New York: Russell & Russell, 1961, p. 116.
21. *Ibid.*, p. 116.
22. *Ibid.*
23. E. Bulygin, 'An antinomy in Kelsen's pure theory of law', in S. L. Paulson and B. Litschewski Paulson (eds), *Normativity and Norms, Critical Perspectives on Kelsenian Themes*, Oxford: Clarendon Press, 1998, pp. 297–317.
24. E. A. Kleinhaus, 'History as a precedent: the post original problem in constitutional law', *Yale Law Journal*, 110, 2000, 121–53.
25. H. Arendt, *On Revolution*, London: Faber & Faber, 1963, pp. 125–6.
26. R. S. Kay, 'American constitutionalism', in L. Alexander (ed.), *Constitutionalism: Philosophical Foundations*, Cambridge: Cambridge University Press, 1998.
27. *Ibid.*, p. 2.
28. A. Abat i Ninet, 'Playing at being gods', *Philosophia Quarterly of Israel*, 38(1), 2009, 41–55; for the doctrinal sector denying the concept of mixed constitution, see also A. H. J. Greenidge, *A Handbook of Greek Constitutional History*, London: Macmillan, 1928, p. 74.
29. *Ibid.*, p. 2.
30. A. H. J. Greenidge, *A Handbook of Greek Constitutional History*, London: Macmillan, 1928, p. 76.
31. A. Hamilton, J. Madison and J. Jay, *The Federalist Papers*, p. 148, 1787–1788, available at: http://Avalon.law.yale.edu/18th_century/fed02.asp, accessed 20 December 2010.
32. To analyse some of the main influences of these authors on the US drafters, see A. C. Biondi, 'Aristotle on the mixed constitution and its relevance for American political thought', *Social Philosophy & Policy Foundation*, 24, 2007, 184; H. A. Clough, *Plutarch's Lives: The Translation Called Dryden's*, Boston, MA: Little, Brown, 1885; G. Stourzh, *Alexander Hamilton and the Idea of Republican Government*, Stanford, CA: Stanford University Press, 1970; G. Hart, *The Restoration of the Republic: The Jeffersonian Idea in 21st-Century America*, New York: Oxford University Press, 2004; H. Taylor, *Cicero: A Sketch of his Life and Works*, Chicago, IL: A. C. McClurg, 1918.

33. K. von Fritz, *The Theory of the Mixed Constitution in Antiquity: A Critical Analysis of Polybius Political Ideas*, New York: Columbia University Press, 1958, preface.

34. K. Kelsen, *General Theory of Law and State*, New York: Russell & Russell, 1961.

35. G. Scholem, *The Messianic Idea in Judaism, and other Essays on Jewish Spirituality*, New York: Schocken Books, 1971; J. Taubes, *Religionstheorie und politische Theologie, vol. I: Der Fürst dieser Welt, Carl Schmitt und die Folgen, vol. II: Gnosis und Politik, vol. III: Theokratie*, Paderborn: Wilhelm Fink Verlag/Ferdinand Schöningh, 1983, pp. 595–600.

36. Available at: http://www.merriam-webster.com/dictionary/messianism, accessed 11 January 2011.

37. J. Taubes, *Religionstheorie und politische Theologie, vol. I: Der Fürst dieser Welt, Carl Schmitt und die Folgen, vol. II: Gnosis und Politik, vol. III: Theokratie*, Paderborn: Wilhelm Fink Verlag/Ferdinand Schöningh, 1983.

38. D. Ohana, 'J. L. Talmon, Gershom Scholem and the price of Messianism', *History of European Ideas*, 34(2), 2008, 169–88.

39. L. Strauss, *Introduction of Moses Maimonides, Guide of the Perplexed*, Chicago, IL: University of Chicago Press, 1963, p. xiv.

40. *Ibid.*, p. xv.

41. J. L. Kraemer, 'Moises Maimonides: the intellectual portrait', in K. Seeskin (ed.), *The Cambridge Companion to Maimonides*, Cambridge: Cambridge University Press, 2005, p. 34.

42. H. Kreseil, 'Maimonides political philosophy', in K. Seeskin (ed.), *The Cambridge Companion to Maimonides*, Cambridge: Cambridge University Press, 2005, p. 218.

43. M. Maimonides, *Mishneh Torah (Book 14, The Book of Judges)*, New Haven, CT: Yale University Press, 1949.

44. *Ibid.*, p. 113.

45. G. Scholem, *The Messianic Idea in Judaism, and other Essays on Jewish Spirituality*, New York: Schocken Books, 1971, p. 30.

46. J. Derrida, *Séminaire La Bête et le Souverain, I (2001–2002)*, Paris: Galilée, 2008, p. 19.

47. F. H. Hinsley, *Sovereignty*, Cambridge: Cambridge University Press, 1986.

48. J. Chopra and T. G. Weiss, 'Sovereignty is no longer sacrosanct: codifying humanitarian intervention', *Ethics & International Affairs*, 6, 1992, 103.

49. J. Bartelson, *A Genealogy of Sovereignty*, Cambridge: Cambridge University Press, 1995, p. 2.

50. P. W. Kahn, *Sacred Violence, Torture, Terror and Sovereignty*, Ann Arbor, MI: University of Michigan Press, 2008.

51. G. Briguglia, *Il corpo vivente dello Stato*, Milan: Mondadori, 2006.

52. P. W. Kahn, *Sacred Violence, Torture, Terror and Sovereignty*, Ann Arbor, MI: University of Michigan Press, 2008.

53. J. Derrida, *Séminaire la Bête et le Souverain, I (2001–2002)*, Paris: Galilée, 2008, p. 278.
54. Constitution of the República Bolivariana de Venezuela, 20 December 1999.
55. J. Derrida, *Séminaire la Bête et le Souverain, I (2001–2002)*, Paris: Galilée, 2008.
56. J. Rawls, *Lectures on the History of Political Philosophy*, Cambridge, MA: Belknap Press of Harvard University Press, 2007, p. 77.
57. *Ibid.*, p. 80.
58. *Ibid.*, p. 80.
59. *Ibid.*, p. 73.
60. *Ibid.*, p. 80.
61. J. Chopra and T. G. Weiss, 'Sovereignty is no longer sacrosanct: codifying humanitarian intervention', *Ethics & International Affairs*, 6, 1992, 103.
62. G. W. F. Hegel, *Philosophy of Right*, Oxford: Clarendon Press, 1942, p. 179.
63. J. Derrida, *Rogues: Two Essays on Reason*, Stanford, CA: Stanford University Press, 2005, p. 23.
64. J. Derrida, *Séminaire La Bête et le Souverain, I (2001–2002)*, Paris: Galilée, 2008, p. 105.
65. *Ibid.*, p. 23.
66. *Ibid.*, p. 278.
67. *Ibid.*, p. 191.
68. *Ibid.*, p. 191.
69. V. Frosini, 'Kelsen y las interpretaciones de la soberanía', *Revista Española de Derecho Constitucional*, 31, 1991, 61.
70. *Ibid.*, p. 62.
71. M. Taussig-Rubbo, 'Outsourcing sacrifice: the labor of private military contractors', *Yale Journal of Law & Humanities*, 21(1), 2009, 110.
72. M. Ostwald, *From Popular Sovereignty to the Sovereignty of Law: Law, Society, and Politics in Fifth-Century Athens*, Berkeley, CA: University of California Press, 1986, p. 22.
73. J. Habermas, 'Constitutional democracy: a paradoxical union of contradictory principles?', *Political Theory*, 29(6), 2001, 766.
74. *Ibid.*, p. 20.
75. *Ibid.*, p. 3.
76. Aristotle, *Politics: A Treatise on Government*, Seattle, WA: Create Space, 2010, p. 12.
77. M. Ostwald, *From Popular Sovereignty to the Sovereignty of Law: Law, Society, and Politics in Fifth-Century Athens*, Berkeley, CA: University of California Press, 1986, p. 8.
78. F. I. Michelman, *Brennan and Democracy*. Princeton, NJ: Princeton University Press, 1999, p. 4.
79. M. Ostwald, *From Popular Sovereignty to the Sovereignty of Law: Law, Society, and Politics in Fifth-Century Athens*, Berkeley, CA: University of California Press, 1986, p. 12.

80. *Ibid.*, p. 15.
81. *Ibid.*, p. 16.
82. *Ibid.*, p. 16.
83. *Ibid.*, p. 21.
84. Aristotle, *Politics: A Treatise on Government*, Seattle, WA: Create Space, 2010.
85. M. H. Hansen, *The Athenian Democracy in the Age of Demosthenes: Structure, Principles and Ideology*, Norman, OK: University of Oklahoma Press, 1999, p. 179.
86. M. Ostwald, *From Popular Sovereignty to the Sovereignty of Law: Law, Society, and Politics in Fifth-Century Athens*, Berkeley, CA: University of California Press, 1986, p. 183.
87. D. A. Farber, W. N. Eskridge and P. P. Frickey, *Constitutional Law*, St Paul, MN: Thomson West, 2003; R. Rotunda, *Modern Constitutional Law*, 9th edn, St Paul, MN: Thomson West, 2009; J. C. Foster and S. M. Leeson, *Constitutional Law: Cases in Context*, Upper Saddle River, NJ: Prentice Hall, 1998; K. M. Sullivan and G. Gunther, *Constitutional Law*, St Paul, MN: Foundation Press, 2004; V. Cohen and A. R. Amar, *Constitutional Law*, 12th edn, St Paul, MN: Foundation Press, 2006; A. Roddey Holder and T. J. Roddey Holder, *The Meaning of the Constitution*, Happauge, NY: Barron's Educational Series, 1997.
88. In this respect, see A. R. Amar, 'The consent of the governed: constitutional amendment outside Article V', *Columbia Law Review*, 94, 1994a, 457–508; A. R. Amar and A. R. Hirsch, *For the People*, New York: Free Press, 1998; A. R. Amar, 'The constitution versus the court: some thoughts on Hills on Amar', *Northwestern University Law Review*, 94, 1994b, 205–10; J. M. Balkin and S. Levinson, 'Constitutional dictatorship: its dangers and its design', *Minnesota Law Review*, 94, 2010, 1789–1865.
89. See M. Tushnet, *Why the Constitution Matters*, New Haven, CT: Yale University Press, 2010, where the author explains that the US Constitution matters not because it structures governments or fundamental rights, but because it structures US politics.
90. C. Schmitt, *Constitutional Theory*, Durham, NC: Duke University Press, 2008, p. 59.
91. *Ibid.*, p. 67.
92. *Ibid.*, p. 75.
93. *Ibid.*, p. 75.
94. A. D. Lindsay, *The Modern Democratic State*, Oxford: Oxford University Press, 1943, p. 224.
95. C. Schmitt, *Constitutional Theory*, Durham, NC: Duke University Press, 2008.
96. *Ibid.*, p. 60.
97. G. R. Morrow, *Plato's Cretan City*, Princeton, NJ: Princeton University Press, 1993, p. 521.

98. *Ibid.*, p. 521.
99. *Ibid.*, p. 521.
100. *Ibid.*, p. 525.
101. *Ibid.*, p. 526.
102. Aristotle, *Politics: A Treatise on Government*, Seattle, WA: Create Space, 2010, p. 71.
103. *Ibid.*, p. 93.
104. Cicero, *De Re Publica, De Legibus*, Cambridge, MA: Harvard University Press, 1961, p. 67.
105. Polybius, *The Histories of Polybius*, vol. I, Bloomington, IN: Indiana University Press, 1962, p. 459.
106. Q. Skinner, *Visions of Politics, vol. II: Renaissance Virtues*, Cambridge: Cambridge University Press, 2002, p. 375.
107. St Thomas Aquinas, *Summa Theologica and Doctoris Angelici*, Grand Rapids, MI: Christian Classics, 1981.
108. J. Bodin, *On Sovereignty*, Cambridge: Cambridge University Press, 1992.
109. *Ibid.*, p. 177.
110. A. C. Biondi, 'Aristotle on the mixed constitution and its relevance for American political thought', *Social Philosophy & Policy Foundation*, 24, 2007, 177.
111. Dig. 50, 17, 24, 1.
112. S. Gordon, *Controlling the State: Constitutionalism from Ancient Athens to Today*, Cambridge, MA: Harvard University Press, 1999, p. 80.

3

Democracy

This chapter asks whether the disjunction between democracy and sovereignty might have its roots in the vagueness of the concept of democracy. Democracy is a concept that has had various meanings throughout history. Despite this difficulty it is essential to pin down the meaning of democracy because of its relationship with the main object of this book. If democracy is the only way to legitimise constitutionalism then we need to know what democracy means. The chapter starts by discussing an etymological and historical definition of democracy in an attempt to specify the semantic indeterminacy (Derrida) that affects the notion. The second section the chapter with an important issue related to the foundation of popular sovereignty: who are 'the people'? And who determines who the people are? We will then discuss who the *optimum* are. From a positive-law perspective each legal system answers these questions, but this issue affects many other disciplines of thought, and gives rise to a wide variety of answers depending on each discipline's particular casuistry. The section deals with these two questions by starting with a reference to the American Constitution and by extension to other constitutional documents. Once the people and the *optimum* are defined, I examine the legitimisation of the role of the judiciary – the subject of ongoing analysis by Anglo-American jurisprudents. I develop this section by analysing the work of Michelman, Ackerman and Tushnet, but also Raz and Kutz, in an attempt to define the role of the judiciary from various perspectives.

The chapter addresses a central question regarding the considerable tensions existing between constitutionalism and democracy. This section focuses on various approaches to enhancing constitutional legitimacy: contractualism (or contract-based legitimacy); consensualism (acceptance-oriented legitimacy); procedural-dialogical legitimacy; constitutional authorship, and, finally, the rule of recognition. In the exposition of these theoretical approaches I stress the attribution of legitimacy to the role of the *demos*. The main point is an analysis of the lack of democratic legitimacy in the 'founding moment', the approval of the basic norm or the first constitution. I contend that the undemocratic and violent founding (eighteenth-century France) has had consequences for the development of democratic legitimacy in our current constitutional systems. Where does constitutional legitimacy originate if a constitution is approved without democratic legitimacy?

DEFINING DEMOCRACY

Democracy is a concept that has had multiple meanings throughout history. Today it is still an indeterminate concept. Even knowing this difficulty, it is essential to define the meaning of democracy because of its relationship with the main object of this book. If democracy is the only way to provide constitutionalism with legitimacy, we need to know what democracy means. Democracy is probably one of the most defined and redefined concepts. We can quote a thousand works and definitions, complementary and contradictory conceptualisations of the term. Democracy, like the eternal return, reappears periodically at the centre of the political discourse.

But before attempting to define the concept of democracy in relation to the object of this book, a prior question arises: is it democratic to define democracy?[1] The answer to this question lies in the philosophy of language and not in political philosophy, and specifically in the nature of the meaning and the relationship between the signifier, the process of codification and the signified. What democracy means and does not mean has changed from generation to generation, especially in countries afflicted by totalitarian regimes.

Every word has a meaning, and democracy is no exception. With a different approach the same ostensible notion can be taught and understood quite differently. Each generation has redefined democracy; in our modern era we find various different examples, for example, in Greece, Portugal and Spain in the 1970s, also in Argentina and Chile in the 1980s; the Colour Revolutions of the former USSR in the 2000s; and in the 2011 revolutions in the Arab countries.

It is necessary to distinguish between word and meaning. That is to say, we must bear in mind Saussure's well-known distinction between signifier (the codification of a word, its phonic component, D E M O C R A C Y), signified (the ideational component, the concept that appears in our mind when we hear or read the signifier) and the word codification process that links the two spheres.[2] The signifier (phonemic structure) democracy, δημοκρατία or הַיְטָרְקוֹמֵד is the result of the codification process, and bears no relation to the concept at all. The meaning (signified) of democracy and other words cannot be democratic, because meanings are attributed to words regardless of political ascriptions. All the more so when we take into consideration that the description of the use of the word 'democracy' (the ideational concept) cannot be reduced to the statement that this word signifies this object.

Finally, the codification process of a word – democracy, freedom, laptop, etc. – is a matter of language and philosophy of language, where democratic or tyrannical legitimacy or participation plays no role. In an ancient notion such as democracy, where the signified must include more than twenty-five centuries of meanings and variations, this fact is even more evident. Trying to apply a political conception to the language codification process is a sort of unfeasible acculturation that has nothing to do with the meaning itself. Should the concept of freedom be left uncodified in order to be consistent?

Although in this section democracy is going to be analysed as the political orientation of those who favour government by the people, the definition has other meanings concerning collective decision making, covering different kinds of groups that may be called democratic. Again, the definition is not intended to carry any normative weight to it. So the definition of democracy does not settle any normative questions. The equality required by democracy may be deeper or less so. It may be the merely formal equality of 'one person, one vote' in an election for representatives to an assembly where there is competition among candidates for the position.[3]

Because of its ancient origins and conceptualisation it is necessary to define the work of Plato to understand the essential characteristics of the term democracy. Plato considered democracy as one of the two 'mother forms' of constitution from which we can rightly say that the others have been derived. One of these we may properly call monarchy, the other democracy.[4] Democracy was regarded as fatally flawed in that it allowed the ignorant masses to determine public policy – which in his view was a specialised function that could be properly performed only by the few men of philosophic talent who had been selected in youth and trained for the task.[5] Plato argues that democracy tends to undermine the expertise necessary to properly governed societies. In a democracy, he argues, those who are expert at winning elections and nothing else will eventually dominate democratic politics.[6] Democracy tends to emphasise this expertise at the expense of the expertise that is necessary to properly governed societies. The reason for this is that most people do not have the type of talents that enable them to think well about the difficult issues that politics involves.[7] The seeds of mistrust and fear of the people are found in this work. Plato's arguments have been reproduced over time. The ignorant masses need the rule and government of the philosopher, who knows what we need. Using Plato's distinction, democracy is the government of opinion (*doxa*) instead of that of knowledge (*episteme*). As Havelock states: 'the realm of absolute knowledge, opposed to the realm of the visible, imperfectly and confusedly apprehended by opinion'.[8] Plato supplies a mathematical reinforcement by proposing a straight line divided into two equal parts, one to represent the visible order, the other the intelligible, each part divided again in the same proportion, symbolising degrees of comparative clearness or obscurity.[9] This dichotomy raises several questions that are important in order to overcome ghosts that haunt the concept of democracy.

The first question is whether is possible to apply mathematical knowledge to social sciences. Plato brings to bear this sort of exact knowledge to differentiate between philosophers and the rest of the citizens. This infallible cognizance was possible through education. For this reason the Platonic system required fifteen years of mathematics and dialectics to be followed by fifteen years of service in subordinate administrative posts before the candidate for guardianship was fully trained.[10]

The well-known accusation of Popper and Havelock comes from the fact that the Platonic theories of education, law and social justice are inquiries carried on not merely for their speculative interest, but for the purpose of finding solutions to the problems of the statesman and the educator. As Morrow states, when we view Plato's work as a whole, we see that he was more concerned with practice than with theory.[11] The *episteme* does not exist in law or politics; even the justices of the Supreme Court have dissenting opinions, and so the rule of our guardians is based on other grounds. Furthermore, the key factor in the failure to put into practice a sort of Platonic theory is the betrayal of philosophers rather than the unfeasibility of popular sovereignty. The guardians of the law are not the guardians of Plato's ideal state. At this point, someone might say that nowadays we are in a situation of government of the aristocracy with the approval of the people, a sort of legitimate mixed constitutionalism. In order to follow this theoretical construction I assume this 'approval', although as I argue later in this book I think there is no such 'approval', but compliance is forged through rationalisation, violence and coercion.

Once we have presupposed this approval, the Platonic ideal state needs to keep evolving, and the guardians of the law (philosophers) should show the light and the way for the people to access knowledge. *Philosophers* should not obstruct the light, denying the people access. This position of privilege, even if it is based on a clear *ipseity* (the guardians will consider you as one of them), has as a counterpart the annihilation of democracy and the impossibility of a citizen's self-determination. In other words, our philosophers should work to provide the means for the people's self-determination and critical sense. Therefore, it is not that a democracy cannot work for pragmatic reasons, but that the rulers in this intermediate form of state must apply the way to enable the citizen's self-determination.

Derrida highlights the need for self-determination of the self when defining democracy:

> Democracy would be precisely this, a force (*kratos*), a force in form of sovereign authority (sovereign, that is, *kurios* or *kuros*, having the power to decide, to be decisive, to prevail, to have reason over or win out over and to give the force of law, *kuroō*), and thus the power and ipseity of the people (*dēmos*).[12]

Derrida remarks about democratic man:

> An arraignment brings forward for judgment, in crisis, the democratic man, his character, his way of being and acting, his turns of speech and his bearing, quite literally, his turn or his turns. The *krisis* makes a judgment, and the critique is devastating: with democratic man comes a general abdication, a complete loss of authority, a refusal to correct by means of the law ...[13]

In the worst case scenario self-determination will be based on *doxa* instead of *episteme*, as occurs with our guardians. If we admit that there is no pure knowledge in law and politics, why is the opinion of one citizen superior to the opinion of another? Why do we assume the inexistence of the *ethos* in the people? Why do we not want to listen to what the people thinks about same sex marriage, abortion or immigration, for example? Our fears may be justified, but the solution to overcome this eternal situation lies in a progressive individual self-determination promoted by education and social justice. In this respect, this progressive individual self-determination must be based on different elements such as 'the strengthening of critical sense' in democracy.[14] Proudhon defined this critical sense as a highly motivated and long debated judgement that requires basically a high degree of impartiality. Critical sense in Proudhon was the essence of democracy and liberty in this kind of judgement must be considered the first political right. This critical sense in a strict individual sphere is the way to achieve self-determination in our societies and the best way to enable a real democracy. Three initial questions can be formulated about this individual self-determination, this *ipseity* in each member of 'we the people'. The first question is whether citizens in our current society can acquire this degree of critical judgement. Proudhon considers that to be able to answer in an affirmative way, our societies need a long-term preparation in citizenship; this preparation must be grounded on equality and freedom. In other words, Proudhon revives the old statement and leitmotif of Cicero, *ars discursi et diserendi*, applied to law and politics.

Another question is whether our fellows want to assume this critical judgement. What happens if after all they prefer to get on their Playstation, watch movies or think about what sort of season the Buffalo Bills are having?

This question can be answered with Fromm's escape from freedom.[15] But not to be involved in political affairs is a consubstantial right of democracy.

In any case, people are not so far removed from political issues as some want to suppose. In this respect, think of how the population reacts in Ackerman's *constitutional moments* or how democracy is entreated in the Arab world. An element that must be taken into consideration in order to implement the necessary critical sense and therefore the individual self-determination of democratic man is the concept of dialogue.

It is important to define 'equality', 'freedom' and 'critical sense' as the main portraits of democracy, and also the relationship between the three elements. The relationship between equality and freedom characterised democracy in Aristotle's literature. The well-known theory of justice is conceived as equality for equals. And inequality is thought to be, and is, justice; neither is this for all, but only for unequals.[16] Among the different types of democracy, Aristotle first defines the democracy based on strict equality: 'in such a democracy the law says that it is just for the poor to have more advantage than the rich; and that neither should be masters, but both equal.'[17] This is the sort of democracy that Proudhon thinks about when defining his system (*Mon Système*): he states that the right to equality, equilibrium, harmony must be everywhere, a strict equality that will mean a balance of roles, balance of fortunes, balance of rights, balance of properties and prerogatives, etc.[18] This equilibrium or balance, the basis of the whole political system in ancient Athens and also in Proudhon's definition of democracy, must be the rule between democracy and constitution.

Schmitt defines democracy as a form of state as well as a governmental or legislative form; it is the identity of ruler and ruled, governing and governed, commander and follower.[19] Equality is so extreme and strict in democracy that it becomes identity. As I will show in the last chapter, when defining the example of French constitutional violence, equality has been confused with complete unity. Equality does not mean uniformity.

Schmitt states:

This definition results from the substantial equality that is the essential presupposition of democracy. It precludes the possibility that inside the democratic state the distinction of ruler and being ruled, governor and governed expresses or produces a qualitative difference. In democracy, dominance or government may not rest on inequality, therefore, not on the superiority of those ruling or governing, nor on the fact that those governing are qualitatively better than the governed. They must agree substantively in terms of democratic equality and homogeneity … Consequently, the power or authority of those who rule or govern may not be based on some higher qualities that are not obtained by the people, but rather only on the will, on the commission from and confidence of those who are being ruled or governed and thereby actually rule themselves. Thus the turn of phrase that democracy is the rule of the people over itself receives its sense as an idea. All democratic tendencies and institutions like equality and equal rights in the most diverse areas ... arise from this striving to realize the identity of governing and governed.[20]

Schmitt continues:

In democracy, state power and government derive from the people. The problem of government internal to democracy lies in the fact that those governing and those governed may differentiate themselves only inside the comparability of the people, which remain equal with one another.[21]

Finally, Schmitt argues that a democracy must not permit the inevitable *factual difference* between governing and being governed to become a qualitative distinction and to distance governing persons from those governed.[22] This sense of equality is also stressed by other authors, such as Tocqueville when defining democracy in America. Tocqueville introduces his well-known work emphasising the equality of conditions by stating that:

I saw the equality of conditions that, without having reached its extreme limits as it had in the United States, was approaching them more each day: and the same democracy reigning in American societies appeared to me to be advancing rapidly toward power in Europe.[23]

Tocqueville knew perfectly well the difference between democracy and 'democratic republic', as he demonstrates in his work, but he uses both terms vaguely. The political system of the United States is defined indiscriminately as a democracy and as a 'democratic republic' (Madison), but these terms are not synonyms.

The French author also considers that equality and freedom are the main causes of the establishment and maintenance of a democratic democracy in the United States.[24] As Mansfield and Winthrop state, Tocqueville does not put much stock in representative institutions in *Democracy in America*, yet for him representative institutions are democratic; they have been designed to hold democracy at bay, yet at the same time they are an expression of democracy.[25, 26] This confusion disregards Aristotle's distinction between democracy and constitutional democracy. The inclusion of representatives as a full democratic institution is a contradiction in Tocqueville's work. If equal opportunities were the pre-eminent feature of American democracy, representation fractures the notion of equality as identity and therefore the required homogeneity among ruled and rulers. Representation allows the *factual difference*. This conceptual identity between democracy and republic has been used lately to institute a fake idea of democracy to calm the masses.

The second main element to be highlighted is freedom. Where Schmitt considered that the difference in democracy is a question that concerns equality, Aristotle argued that it is an issue related to liberty:

> democracy is the form of government in which the free are rulers, and oligarchy in which the rich are the rulers; it is only an accident that the free are the many and the rich are the few. Thus the difference between those governing and those governed cannot be displaced.[27]

Plato, Aristotle and Cicero seem to emphasise that democracy is freedom when analysing the best forms of government.

Derrida studied the effects of freedom (*eleuteuria* or *exousia*) at the core of democracy by developing his concept of *ipse*. The author stated that:

> Before even determining demo-cracy on the basis of the minimal though enigmatic meaning of its two guiding concepts and the syntax that relates them, the people and power, *dēmos* and *kratos* – or *kratein* (which also means 'to prevail', 'to bring off', 'to be the strongest' ... 'to be right' ...) – it is on the basis of freedom that we will have conceived the concept ... from Plato's Greece onward ... Freedom is essentially the faculty or power to do as one pleases, to decide, to choose, to determine one's-self, to have self-determination, to be master, and first of all master of one-self (*autos, ipse*) ... There is no freedom without *ipseity* and vice-versa, no *ipseity* without freedom.[28]

Derrida argued that in political philosophy the dominant discourse about democracy presupposes freedom as a power, faculty or power to act, the force or strength, in short, to do as one pleases, the energy of an international and deciding will.[29] This sort of freedom means that in Derrida's terms democracy may be impossible.

As Derrida notes, Plato had already announced that 'democracy' is in the end neither the name of a regime nor the name of a constitution. It is not a constitutional form among others. And yet there have in fact been, in addition to the monarchic, plutocratic and tyrannical democracies of antiquity, so many so-called modern democratic regimes, regimes that at least present themselves as democratic, that is, under and in the name of, the always Greek name, let us never forget, of democracy: democracy at once monarchic (what is called constitutional monarchy) and parliamentary (found in a large number of European nation-states), popular democracy, direct or indirect democracy, parliamentary democracy (whether presidential or not), liberal democracy, Christian democracy, social democracy, military or authoritarian democracy, and so on.[30] To achieve a progressive 'democratic democracy' in our societies it is necessary to foment individual self-determination through strict equality and freedom. This required self-determination must be completed with education, social justice and human rights enforcement. These elements are essential requirements to enable a feasible 'democratic democracy'. The failure to meet these requirements cannot vitiate the definition of democracy on an abstract level. Nor can it legitimise a democratic-aristocratic system or serve as an argument to confuse republic (Madison) with democracy.

Part of the criticism that the concept of democracy has received is due to the disregard of the distinction between democracy and mob rule. Polybius' differentiation between democracy and its degeneration into mob rule is extremely important in order to clarify the concept of democracy. The Founding Fathers (Madison, *The Federalist Papers* 10) and also Tocqueville (*Democracy in America*) were frightened by the atrocious effects of mob rule, not by democracy itself. The awful effects of mob rule had more weight in the Founding Fathers' thought than the favourable effects of democracy. Nevertheless, stability was the main goal sought in 1776. I understand that democracy has been confused with mob rule until the present, but if mob rule exists it is because a non-degeneration of democracy is possible and suitable. Is mob rule what happened in Ukraine, Georgia, Tunisia and Egypt? Would not the fear of the *demos* be preferable to the rule of the tyrants, even when the latter is justified on economic grounds, as in China with its new friends in the Western world?

I claim the existence of a non-degenerated democracy as the goal to be implemented progressively. As Polybius quotes, the main causes of the transmutation from democracy to mob rule is the lack of equality and freedom. I contend that both terms are the two faces of the same coin, democracy. There is no real equality or freedom outside democracy, and there is no equality without freedom and vice versa.

DEMOCRATIC DEMOCRACY

Who are 'we the people' and who are 'we the *optimum*'?

This section deals with the theoretical foundations of popular sovereignty. The starting point is a core question: who are 'the people'? Furthermore, who determines who the people are? This question leads to a new interrelated one: who are the *optimum*? From a positivist perspective each legal system will answer these questions, but this issue affects many other disciplines of thought, giving rise to a wide variety of answers depending on each discipline's particular discourse. This section answers these two questions starting with close reference to the US Constitution and by extension to other constitutional documents.

The concept of 'the people' shares some fundamental characteristics with the notion of sovereignty, such as its fictitious nature and its *ipseity* or self-defined nature. 'We the people' is a strong fiction that has persisted since the draft of the American revolutionary constitution in the unconscious of natural and naturalised US citizens. This amazing technique of legislative building has been the essence and core of the American condition and evidences some of the main features of US revolutionary constitution making. The statement 'we the people' is the best consolidation of the democratic sovereignty fiction.[31] The drafters of the first modern constitution decided to affirm 'we the people' and not 'we the delegates and representatives of Virginia, New York, etc.', because they knew the strong meaning of this statement. It included not only the entire present population, but also future generations. Its immense inclusive strength has effective consequences in terms of national identity and popular involvement. If we assume that 'we the people' and the concept of sovereignty are fictitious, the consequence of this assumption is that democratic sovereignty has also been a fiction.

The second feature is *ipseity*: it is the actual people who define themselves as such. Constitutional texts around the world, for example, state: 'we the people of the United States of America'; *nosotros los representantes de las provincias unidas de Sudamérica, el pueblo de Ecuador*, 'we the people of South Africa' and 'whereas the people of New South Wales, Victoria, South Australia, Queensland, and Tasmania', etc. They do not need another people, entity or authority to define them as a people. Therefore, the main characteristic of the people's definition is its *volitive* nature, built on the will to be considered as such. In other words, a people's conscious desire for recognition constitutes its legal-formal aspiration, with its own distinct personality and identity from other peoples. The first element of the conceptual answer to the question 'who are the people?' would be: the people who want to be 'the people'.

The locution 'the people' enhances a constitutional text and not the opposite. No constitution determines who 'the people' are, but the opposite, a people defines and creates a constitution. This statement only appears once the act of national self-definition has been invoked in the constitutional text. This strengthens the concept of 'the people' as something unitary, as a single entity without divisions, in which the institutions should not be assigned to groups or sectors of the whole, but individuals acting on behalf of the ideal 'people'.[32] This vision transcends the Greco-Roman tradition according to which the city was formed by several groups competing among each other.[33]

Some authors are sceptical of claims that portray 'we the people' as an organic whole capable of collective action.[34] This scepticism rests on several grounds, such as 'methodological individualism' or the denial of a real empirical way to express collective will. I agree that collective action is always the result of interaction among individuals, and that we can find several problems to configuring a 'common will', but is it impossible? If so, has it always been impossible? I do not really think so. I offer as examples the actors of self-determination processes in all the nations of the Americas, and the fight against slavery. Democracy is already conceived of and based on a common will and collective action. Once this fundamental issue is clarified, the concept of the people covers other elements, such as belonging to a territory, culture, religion, etc. It is not the subject of this book to analyse well-known objective and subjective theories of nations, but to emphasise that no sort of authorisation is needed to be constituted as a people. Who but its own citizens asked the United States for its definition as a people? At this point an interesting analogy is possible between the concept of 'we the people', as a democratic organ, and the people as a 'national' or plural identity. In this respect, Ackerman recognises this sort of *volitive* (will-based) element.

To answer the question 'are we a nation?', Ackerman starts by highlighting that 'we [Americans] understand ourselves today as Americans first and Californians second'.[35] This volitive element is a common characteristic of both senses of people, people as a democratic institution and people as identity.

The second feature that seems basic to determine who 'the people' are is the notion of present time, because as Ackerman correctly states, America's political identity 'is at war with the system of constitutional revision' left by the framers; the amendment system was written for people who thought of themselves primarily as New Yorkers or Georgians. 'We have become a nation-centered People stuck with a state-centered system of formal amendment.'[36] The disjunction between state-centred form and nation-centred substance serves as a dynamic force behind the living constitution. Since the Civil War, Americans have given decisive and self-conscious support to national politicians and their judicial appointees as they have repeatedly adapted state-centred institutions, and constitutional texts, in order to express national purposes. The great challenge for constitutional law is to develop historically sensitive categories for understanding these developments. Ackerman concludes that the constitution has been the juridification of the identity of a people and the starting point of their consideration as a people. The author recounts moments that created and consolidated the common sense of identity of the United States. Further, he analyses whether the US Constitution has been adapted to meet emerging needs and, consequently, whether this constitution can be defined as a living constitution.

Ackerman affirms that Americans have lost the ability to write down new constitutional commitments in the old-fashioned way. They are now in the midst of great debates about abortion and religion, about federalism and the war powers of the presidency, but nobody expects a constitutional amendment to resolve any of these issues; instead, we see symbolic gestures on matters like flag burning and gay marriage.[37] Consequently, the feature of keeping up to date should be a permanent concern in constitutional practice if we are to be able to define the constitution as a living constitution. In fact, there is no confusion between the emancipation process understood as 'independence' and the emancipation process understood as a 'liberal revolution'.

Ackerman goes on to define the unconventional foundational process of the United States, because fifty-five men went to Philadelphia, but only thirty-nine signed the document. Compared with the average citizen, they were revolutionary nationalists, and they proved it when they came out of their secret sessions in Philadelphia to propose a new constitution in the name of 'We the People of the United States'.[38] I do not concur with the characterisation of the foundational process of the United States as unconventional.[39] With his statement, Ackerman contributes to the well-known idea of 'American exceptionalism'. To be able to make this statement, it is necessary to consider the existence of a sort of 'conventional emancipation process', and the model of the first modern constitution and the juridification of a new political unit by a new people is the most commonly followed form in the world.

If the United States is not a conventional process, which one can be defined as such? For instance, the proclamation of independence of the state of Israel pronounces:

> Accordingly we, members of the People's Council, representatives of the Jewish Community of Eretz-Israel and of the Zionist Movement, are here assembled on the day of the termination of the British Mandate over Eretz-Israel and, by virtue of our natural and historic right and on the strength of the resolution of the United Nations General Assembly, hereby declare the establishment of a Jewish state in Eretz-Israel, to be known as the State of Israel.

The declaration of the political constitution of the United States of Mexico states that it is based on the first constitutionalist army. Moreover, the constitutions in the New World established a new identity.

The new US identity replaced the old British one in the subconscious of the people, who remained New Yorkers but became Americans, rather than British. The same process of constitution of new identities, new peoples and therefore new sovereigns happened in the new states of Latin America. After emancipation processes new identities are constituted. In all these cases constitutions created new identities. Before the independence of these states there was not an 'Argentinean people': they were representatives of the *Provincias Unidas de Sudamérica, del Virreinato del Río de la Plata*, as the declarations of independence demonstrate. The people and the sovereign were Spanish or Portuguese, since the people who predated the arrival of the first Europeans also existed there before the formation of national states, which is why they are called 'Indians'[40] Possibly, if the constitutional drafters and founding fathers of the Latin American states had been indigenous representatives, the sovereigns would be another people, but as happened in the United States, the signers of the independence acts of Chile and Uruguay were revolutionary nationalists who proposed a new constitution and created a new 'people' and a new sovereign. But can we extract a general rule from the constitutional experience of the United States? What happens if a constitution creating an identity does not garner the same results?[41]

The United States provided an example and a baseline for future cases, but each case is adapted according to the events and the people that each new constitution juridifies. The content of the constitution (as a legal rule) would not necessarily generate a new reality or create a new social-political framework. It could be limited simply to confirming a fact, to responding to a given pre-existing legal-political reality. Thus, certain modern European constitutions of multinational states have tried to build a new reality, but without taking into consideration who is really 'the people' of those states, or whether other pre-constitutional peoples existed. Paradoxically, these constitutions have seen that this fiction could not survive in the 'living constitution' itself as events evolved. The same democratic foundation that Ackerman uses in his paper should be applied to these multinational states, which cannot impose who the 'people' are, because, if republican principles are observed, the constitution will clash with democracy and/or human rights. In this sense, legal-constitutional denial of the right to self-determination of a people or other nation is a clear example of constitutional violence.

The second issue of this section is to define who 'the *optimum*' are. Who occupies the position of the monarch in modern 'constitutional republics'? This second question is also relevant in identitarian terms, because the *optimum* also have the power to affect the *ipseity* required to be defined as a people. The answer to this question has evolved over time and, depending on each author, a different characterisation has been attributed to this undemocratic balancing factor.

Plato described this undemocratic element as kingship, this social stratum being represented by the guardians of the law in the Republic. Aristotle speaks of aristocracy, and Cicero and Polybius also use Aristotle's terminology in reference to this privileged class.[42] Polybius characterises this undemocratic element with aristocracy – oligarchy – and with the Gerusia:

> The people in their turn were restrained from a bold contempt of the kings by fear of the Gerusia: the members of which, being selected on grounds of merit, were certain to throw their influence on the side of justice in every

question that arose; and thus the party placed at a disadvantage by its conservative tendency was always strengthened and supported by the weight and influence of the Gerusia.[43]

We can use other signifiers (Saussure) to characterise the '*optimum*', but all significance will be linked with a social class that has a privileged economic status or a greater intellectuality. This '*White*', using Donahue's terminology,[44] will defend his privileges at the expense of everything, including, of course, a feasible democratic development. It is important to differentiate between the sovereign (constitution) and the organs that exercise sovereignty in the name of the constitution. This sort of constitutional aristocracy forms the *optimum*. Tocqueville develops in his work how lawyers and the spirit of the lawyer serve as a counterweight to democracy.[45] The French author considered that the authority that the Americans had given to lawyers and the influence that they were allowed to have over the form of government was the most powerful barrier against the lapses of democracy.[46] Tocqueville continues by stating that:

> the special knowledge that lawyers acquire in studying the law assures them a separate rank in society; they form a sort of privileged class among (persons of) intelligence. Each day they find the idea of this superiority in knowledge in the exercise of their profession; they are masters of a necessary science, knowledge of which is not widespread; they serve as arbiters between citizens, and a habit of directing the blind passions of the litigants toward a goal gives them a certain scorn for the judgment of the crowd.[47]

Tocqueville recognises this sort of 'intellectual' aristocracy in the body of lawyers, when he openly affirms that:

> hidden at the bottom of the souls of lawyers one therefore finds a part of the tastes and habits of aristocracy ... In all free governments, whatever their form may be, lawyers will be found in the first ranks of all parties. This same remark is also applicable to aristocracy.[48]

In fact, Tocqueville identifies from the time of birth of the modern democratic republic the *body* that is going to monopolise the type of intellectual aristocracy that serves to counterbalance democracy. The author does not consider this influence as negative, but as necessary, when stating that he doubts that democracy could long govern society and that he cannot believe that in our day a republic could hope to preserve its existence if the influence of lawyers in its affairs did not grow in proportion with the power of the people.[49] Although Tocqueville does not cover the concept of representation in his work he establishes the sources to locate the modern aristocracy, and on this point Carl Schmitt correctly states that the political form of aristocracy rests on the idea of representation.[50] The Founding Fathers also pointed out the core essence of representation in the new Republic. Therefore, the first manifestation of Tocqueville's lawyers in our democratic system is guided by representation. Our representatives are the first aristocratic counterbalance of democracy. These representatives, like the lawyers in *Democracy in America*, belong to the people by their interest and birth, and to the aristocracy by their habits and their tastes; it is like a natural liaison between two things. It is not simply a coincidence that the majority of our representatives in parliaments around the world are lawyers. '*Optimum*', 'lawyers', 'aristocracy' are different terms to refer to the same thing: the group of individuals who are ruling without democratic legitimacy, but in a republican form.

DEMOCRATIC RULE AS AN ORIGINAL INTERPRETATION OF CONSTITUTIONALISM

The second manifestation of Tocqueville's lawyers is in the form of the members of constitutional courts. The author stated:

> The courts of justice are the visible organs by which the legal profession is enabled to control the democracy. The judge is a lawyer who, independently of the taste for regularity and order that he has contracted in the study of law, derives an additional love of stability from the inalienability of his own functions. His legal attainments have already raised him to a distinguished rank among his fellows; his political power completes the distinction of his station and gives him the instincts of the privileged classes. Armed with the power of declaring the laws to be unconstitutional, the American magistrate perpetually interferes in political affairs. He cannot force the people to make laws, but at least he can oblige them not to disobey their own enactments and not to be inconsistent with themselves.[51]

While judicial review and judicial activism are not the objects of this book, doctrine has proved the undemocratic character of this institution. The legitimisation of the role of the judiciary has been the subject of ongoing analysis by Anglo-American jurisprudents. In relation to the undemocratic nature of the judicial review of constitutional affairs, the work of Kramer is extremely enlightening.[52]

Kramer wants to counter the idea that the US Constitution was, first and foremost, an instrument of reaction designed to blunt democratic politics by channelling authority to an elite removed as far as possible from popular control.[53]

Kramer continues by stating that the people's options for changing those rules, for establishing a different interpretation, are said to be limited to amending the text (i.e., making a new constitutional law), importuning the justices to chart a different course, and waiting for one or more of them to die or tire of the job so we can (hopefully) appoint new justices with views more to our liking. Anything else is unlawful and unconstitutional.[54]

Kramer then affirms that:

> Constitutionalism in the Founding era was different. Then, power to interpret (and not just the power to make) constitutional law was thought to reside with the people. And not theoretically or in abstract, but in an active, ongoing sense. It was the community at large – not the judiciary, not any branch of the government – that controlled the meaning of the Constitution and was responsible for ensuring its proper implementation in the day-to-day process of governing. This is the notion I labeled 'popular constitutionalism' – to distinguish it from "legal constitutionalism" or the idea that constitutional interpretation has been turned over to the judiciary and, in particular, to the Supreme Court.[55]

Consequently, the usurpation of popular sovereignty in constitutional matters is not only unconstitutional, but is also contrary to an original interpretation of the Constitution.

This 'turning over to the judiciary' is contrary to the intentions of Madison and Jefferson. As Kramer affirms, Madison believed in popular government and believed that the people must control the government and laws at all times: he was someone for whom an idea like judicial supremacy was and could only be anathema, a selling out of the very *raison d'être* of the American Revolution that was his life's passion.[56] Kramer contends that the Founding Father conceived the position and role of constitutional sovereignty as belonging to the people. The 'democratic' conception of constitutionalism that Kramer attributes to Madison and Jefferson makes sense with these distinguished jurisprudents of constitutionalism and democracy.[57] Kramer's theory of popular constitutionalism departs from a modern distinction between two different domains: a domain of politics, where the author considers that the people rules; and a domain of law, where law is understood as set aside for lawyers in Tocqueville's sense.[58] The Stanford scholar adds that popular constitutionalism rests and relies on a political culture in which public officials, community leaders and ordinary citizens believe in the above-mentioned distinction, and also share a set of conventions about how to argue within each domain, and take seriously the role difference it produces. In popular constitutionalism, participants respond to different arguments in each setting and treat questions of constitutional interpretation as 'legal' problems that can be settled only by resort to the 'law' as understood through interpretative norms like text, history and precedent.[59] Nevertheless, the main point related to the subject of this book is that this modern distinction that places the role of the people in a residual sphere (at least in the field of law) is based on a non-original interpretation of American constitutionalism.

Kramer also clarifies:

> The modern constitutional system thus draws a distinction between interpreting an existing Constitution and making new constitutional law and does its best to confine popular control to the latter, nearly impossible task. The community at large has no formal authority to interpret. On the contrary, resisting popular views about the meaning of the Constitution is considered a judicial virtue, which is why battles over the new Supreme Court appointments have grown so fierce in recent years.[60]

Kramer affirms that the Constitution, in this modern sense, is a species of law – special only inasmuch as it sets the boundaries within which politics takes place. As law, the Constitution is part of the set brought before the elite to handle, subject to the paramount supervision of the US Supreme Court. He continues by stating that constitutionalism in the Founding era was different.

Then, power to interpret (and not just the power to make) constitutional law was thought to reside with the people. And not theoretically or in abstract, but in an active, ongoing sense. It was the community at large – not the judiciary, not any branch of the government – that controlled the meaning of the Constitution and was responsible for ensuring its proper implementation in the day-to-day process of governing. This is the notion that Kramer labels 'popular constitutionalism'.[61] Popular constitutionalism means that final authority to control the interpretation and implementation of constitutional law resides at all times in the community in an active sense.[62]

Popular constitutionalism is not mere politics, but is in fact a legal concept that treats the constitution as law in its proper sense. Kramer's theory is conciliatory and dualist. The author does not want to exclude the judiciary from its current task and power, which is why he insists that where popular constitutionalism differs from present-day understandings is that it does not assume that authoritative legal interpretation can take place *only* in courts, but rather supposes that an equally valid process of interpretation can be undertaken in the political branches and by the community at large.[63] Following the conciliatory trend between democracy and the judiciary of the constitution as a legal norm, he states that the constitution remains 'law' in a system of popular constitutionalism in that *whoever* is doing the interpreting is bound by the constitution's legal content and must ascertain and enforce whatever limits the text imposes on political actions and political actors. Where popular constitutionalism differs from present-day understandings is that it does not assume that authoritative legal interpretation can take place only in courts, but rather supposes that an equally valid process of interpretation can be undertaken in the political branches by the community at large.[64]

Kramer formulates a theoretical historical exercise without analysing how to develop a mixed constitutional–democratic system. He points to the original idea of the United States constitutional system in Madison's works, trying to conciliate Supreme Court and *demos*. Kramer's point is that constitutionalism in its 'modern' origins was a different conception. Unlike Kramer, I believe that democracy and constitution are not reconcilable. Both notions demand their empire. The struggle between sovereigns can be mediated, but finally the nature of the relationship is always hierarchical and not jurisdictional. In short, someone has the last word. Although democracy and constitution are irreconcilable, the following propositions are designed to mediate between the two spheres, as popular constitutionalism endeavours.

A possible practical proposal is to analogise an application of the Swiss constitutional system to other constitutional structures. I try to encourage a 'Swiss democratisation effect'.[65] The Swiss constitutional system provides a model to be followed, solving some of the concerns voiced by Kramer,[66] Tushnet[67] and Michelman.[68] Article 113 of the Swiss Constitution of 1848 defined the Federal Court Public Law Jurisdiction; in its last point (3) it stated that: 'In all aforementioned instances, the Federal Court shall apply the laws and generally binding decree adopted by the Federal Assembly, as well as the international treaties approved by this Assembly.' In 1999, Switzerland adopted a new constitution, which became effective in 2000. The new constitution was understood not as a radical change, but as designed to incorporate into a single text the original constitution with accumulated amendments.[69] An analogous application of the Swiss constitutional system is not an easy enterprise. Not only because juridical acculturation is always complicated, but also because the common constitutional systems never adopted a real democratic culture. The Swiss constitutional system does not provide any constitutional jurisdiction over federal laws. Laws proclaimed by Parliament or by a popular majority may not be barred by the Federal Court on the grounds of unconstitutionality. This singular feature of the Swiss Constitution is evidence of how democratic principles are held to outweigh the principles upon which the constitutional state is built. Laws proclaimed by the Federal Assembly are not to be taken out of force by a court not chosen by the people. The Swiss system is consistent with the constitutional texts when they affirm that sovereignty resides in the people. This system represents the best solution for the defence of democracy against undemocratic actions of the constitutional/supreme courts. The restriction of constitutional/supreme court jurisdiction is legally feasible in our constitutional systems. This simple proposal would cause a political tsunami in most of our political systems and would demonstrate the enormous distrust in the people. I believe that separation of powers does not necessarily mean judicial supremacy.

Perhaps our societies are not ready to achieve the Swiss degree of democracy and they need a group of Platonic philosophers to guide the system. A second proposition is a democratisation and universalisation of the constitutional/supreme court system of election to obtain a novel interpretation of the responsive democracy theory. One of the main principles highlighted by comparative constitutional law studies is the relativity of texts, formulas and dogmas. Men and ideas, parties and principles, mysticism and slogans, customs and traditions, are the determinant factors of a determinate regime.[70] But if we define the constitution as the juridification of democracy,[71] it is necessary to adapt the constitutional content to the reality that governs each moment; the definition of juridification is a phenomenon that appears to regulate and codify new legal fields emerging in society.[72] Otherwise the constitution will be a juridification of 'partitocracy'.

This proposal seeks to develop Nino's statement: 'that it is essential to widen the ways of direct participation of the people whose interest are at stake, by general procedures such as plebiscites or popular consultations, or by decentralizing decisions into smaller ambits in which the people concerned can affect them ...'[73] It is essential to democratise the judicial system and bring the judiciary closer to the people to define our political system as a democracy. This variant of democratic electoral system is based on a novel interpretation of the theory of responsive democracy.[74]

This theory is not directed specifically at systems of representation, election arrangements and interest groups, but I would like to point out a possible application of the theory's essence. The theory lies in the hermeneutical apprehension of the meaning of our democratic institutions.[75] While the constitutional court is not a democratic institution,[76] its actions affect the *demos* directly, occasionally against the democratic will. Therefore, constitutional courts have to be affected by this popular apprehension. A major practical objective of responsive democracy is to inculcate in its citizenry a sense of participation, legitimacy and identification.[77] This idea of democracy is linked with the citizens' self-determination and self-government. Promoting citizen's self-determination implies the necessary inclusion of citizens in the duties of the highest interpreter of the constitution. The possible role developed by the people would strengthen a system of dualist democracy instead of the monist tendency dominated by partisan interests as happens nowadays in the majority of our constitutional democracies. Popular initiatives, types of referendums, polls and Internet forums can be adapted to encourage and facilitate public access to constitutional court issues and debates. A practical way of enabling the performance of citizenship is by linking the professional and legal bar councils, civic organisations, attorneys, judges and law schools. These sorts of institutions can provide the infrastructure and professional organisation needed to implement citizen participation. In federal or quasi-federal states, the subnational units can also afford some kind of participation, through local entities such as boroughs or counties. Directly democratic, but strictly applied to the constitutional court.

One benefit of this people's approach is a decrease in the crisis of confidence in high courts over decisions against the legislative branch or the popular will. Direct democracy mechanisms will encourage citizens to become partners in the functioning of the court. People will appear to be co-responsible for this institution, the legitimacy issue thus being resolved. In this respect, the US federal experience is an important example to consider when implementing mechanisms of direct democracy regarding the judiciary. The US constitutional system is an example because the Constitution provides for absolutely no direct involvement by the people in any matter of governance,[78] but individual states' constitutions adopt various possibilities to enable popular participation, even in judiciary matters. An item of proposed legislation or a proposed constitutional amendment is submitted to the voters' approval by referendum.[79] Nineteen states presently provide for initiative measures. Twelve state constitutions, for example, provide a recall procedure under which the terms of sitting elected officials can be ended prematurely by popular vote. Forty-three states provide for the election of at least some judges. The greater scope of direct electoral accountability to the people provides various tools to ensure that state government is conducted according to the people's wishes.[80] Why not enable popular participation at a national level?

Democracy and constitutionalism seem irreconcilable notions, and the only way to deal with this antinomy is through checks and balances. But mediation is necessary between these two defining notions of modern states. Constitutions have evolved, encoding their relationship with the people. They have juridified the will of the people, adapting state characterisations to the evolution of the relationship between democracy and constitutionalism. Article 1 of the Swedish Constitution of 1975 states:

> 1. All public power in Sweden proceeds from the people; 2. Swedish democracy is founded on freedom of opinion and on universal and equal suffrage. It shall be realized through a representative and parliamentary polity and local self-government; 3. Public power shall be exercised under the law.[81]

Article 1 of the Austrian Constitution of 1945 defines Austria as a democratic republic, and its law emanates from the people.[82] In turn, Article 1 of the Italian Constitution of 1947 defines Italy as a democratic republic based on labour.[83]

In all these constitutional examples the state is defined as a democracy without mention of the law. This trend changes in the constitutions of the late 1970s because of the evolution of the relationship and the definitions of constitutionalism and democracy. Thus, the Portuguese Republic is defined as a democratic state based on the rule of law in Article 2 of the Portuguese Constitution of 1976. Spain in its first constitutional article of 1978 is defined as a social and democratic state of law, and also Romania in Article 2 of its Constitution of 1991 is defined as a democratic and social state governed by the rule of law.[84] These constitutional texts are recognising a new reality, a new situation where democracy has been redefined and subordinated to the law. A following stage in the constitutional 'recognition' between constitution and democracy is represented by the constitutions of the late 1990s. The Hungarian Constitution of 1949, amended in 1997 and 2003, defines Hungary in its Article 2 as a democratic constitutional state.[85]

My main thesis is not the suppression of the rule of law, *Gesetzmäßigkeit* or *principe de légalité* as the duty imposed on any person, institution or public office to submit their acts to the mandate of law. The *Gesetzmäßigkeit* (rule of law) means the supremacy of the constitution as an expression of the general will. But if the constitution does not represent the general will, the will of the *demos*, the rule of law is perverted. The rule of law as guarantor of discretionary power and the separation of powers requires a mechanism to involve the people. This sort of participation should affect judicial review and also the codification of laws. In constitutional issues the people's involvement is necessary to avoid the perception that the supreme norm and the rule of law reflect only the will of the aristocracy.

DEMOCRACY AND CONSTITUTIONALISM

Modern constitutional scholars have analysed the relationship between constitution and democracy since the appearance of the first modern constitutions. Madison's *Federalist Papers* 10, 37 and 50 (Hamilton or Madison), 'Jeffersonian democracy' and Toqueville's *Democracy in America* are good examples of this concern.[86] The Founding Fathers and drafters of the first modern republican constitution were aware of the tension between the *demos* and the constitution and its apparatus. In this regard, Thomas Jefferson was emphatic on the considerable tensions of constitutionalism and democracy, arguing that constitutions should be amended by each generation in order to ensure that the dead past would not constrain the living present. Many contemporary observers echo the Jeffersonian position, claiming that constitutional constraints often amount to unjustified, anti-democratic limits on the power of the present and future.[87]

The Declaration of the Rights of Man and of the Citizen, approved by the National Assembly of France on 26 August 1789, also addresses this issue in Articles 3, 6 and 14. An excellent example of the tension between constitution and democracy is Article 16 of this transcendent declaration, which states: 'A society in which the observance of the law is not assured, nor the separation of powers defined, has no constitution at all.' This article has been used as a starting definition of what a (modern) constitution is, but it does not impose a democratic requirement to the constitutional definition. In other words, a constitution has been considered as such even if the *demos* does not have an essential role in its legitimacy.

This section focuses on different methods to achieve 'constitutional legitimacy': contractualism (or contract-based legitimacy); consensualism (acceptance-oriented legitimacy); procedural-dialogical legitimacy; and, finally, the rule of recognition and constitutional authorship.

In the exposition of these four theoretical ways to attribute legitimacy, the role of the *demos* and how 'we the people' act is going to be a central issue. 'Contractualism' and 'consensual acceptance' are symbolic ways to bestow legitimacy on the constitution, while 'procedural-dialogical legitimacy', 'rule of recognition' and 'constitutional authorship' focus on constitutional processes and discourse, and the role that citizens may play in the approval and amendment of a constitution. The analysis of these theories is necessary in order to conclude that against the will of the people there is no constitutional legitimacy, but constitutional enforcement.

The first theory reviewed is the metaphor of the social contract applied to the field of law. Certain doctrinal sectors consider that the required legitimacy of all constitutional texts comes from a tacit constitutional contract ratified by all the citizens. Contractarians argue a sort of metaphorical analogy of the social contract theory to the field of constitutionalism. They presume that social contract theory can be applied to constitutional theory, where the constitution is a contract. But this analogy is against a basic right of the citizenry. A tacit constitutional contract diminishes the people's rights, affecting the real possibilities of amending the constitution. How can the most important political and juridical norm be tacitly and supposedly approved by the parties? The theoretical explanation of these authors is subjected to the ultimate goal of this section, which is to clarify the failures of the metaphorical application.

After reviewing the social contract theories and the analogous application of this source of theoretical legitimacy to the constitutional field, this section goes on to analyse other theories of constitutional legitimacy. Dialogue, procedure and constitutional authorship are proposed as ways to enhance the legitimacy of the constitution and the constitutional process. The application of dialogue to the field of law is not uncontroversial. Several authors have introduced dialogue into the sphere of law, but Bruce

Ackerman's neutral concept of dialogue applied to the constitutional sphere is the best example to take in this work because of its clear link with the issue under analysis. Procedural and dialogical doctrines allow the people and future generations to express and ratify the constitutional text, something which is unfeasible in the contract theories. The last theories developed are Michelman's constitutional authorship and Hart's rule of recognition. The last part of this section is not only a conclusion to this chapter, but also an introduction to the next chapter of the book.

Contract-based Legitimacy

The metaphor defended by constitutional contractarians is a clear example of the shortcomings that constitutionalism has if it abandons democracy as a source of legitimacy. Contractarianism names both a political theory of the legitimacy of political authority and a moral theory about the origin or legitimate content of moral norms.[88] Because of the scope of this book the analysis of contractarianism is focused strictly on the political theory that seeks to confer legitimacy on the constitution. The analysis is structured around the goal of this section, the study of the analogous application of the contractarian metaphor as a source of legitimacy for a constitutional text. To speak of the social contract necessarily implies quoting the work of Rousseau, who stated in his well-known work *The Social Contract* that:

> Man is born free; and everywhere he is in chains. One thinks himself the master of others, and still remains a greater slave than they. How did this change come about? I do not know. What can make it legitimate? That question I think I can answer. If I took into account only force, and the effects derived from it, I should say: As long as a people is compelled to obey, and obeys, it does well; as soon as it can shake off the yoke, and shakes it off, it does still better; for, regaining its liberty by the same right as took it away, either it is justified in resuming it, or there was no justification for those who took it away.[89]

The first concern of Rousseau was legitimacy. What can make the government legitimate? At this point, I contend that this express mention of violence in Rousseau's first statement of his social contract was not gratuitous. Rousseau analysed violence in terms of legitimacy. The author had in mind how to avoid illegitimate violence by his contemporary government, which is why he analysed in detail the right of the strongest (among the different components of society) and the role of violence as a source of *de facto* legitimacy. Rousseau considered that the metaphor of a social contract was the way to give legitimacy to governments, but he expressly excluded any sort of analogy of his theory to other fields: 'There is only one contract in the

State, and that is the act of association, which in itself excludes the existence of a second. It is impossible to conceive of any public contract that would not be a violation of the first.'[90] For this reason there is a single ruler and not two heads in our 'constitutional democracies'. It can be said that constitutional contractarians have applied the theory of the social contract in two different ways: the first, consists in replacing the social contract with the constitutional contract. Rousseau created a contract between the people and the state; in this first analogy constitutional contractarians replaced the new body (the state) with the constitution. Therefore, citizens are tacit parties to a contract that creates a new legal entity (beyond the text itself). In this case, the constitution creates the state, and not the opposite; the constitution becomes the real social, juridical and political contract.

The second constitutional contractarian analogy considers the constitutional text as a contract, regardless of the relationship with the state. This issue is crucial when analysing the relationship between national identity and constitutionalism. Rousseau continued by stating that:

> 'The problem is to find a form of association which will defend and protect with the whole common force the person and goods of each associate, and in which each, while uniting himself with all, may still obey himself alone, and remain as free as before.' This is the fundamental problem to which the social contract provides solutions.[91]

To obtain legitimacy the social contract requires a full alienation of the citizens, a sort of alienation without reserve, yet what sort of democracy, dialogue or freedom is possible with this sort of alienation? Rousseau stated:

> If the individuals retained certain rights, as there would be no common superior to decide between them and the public, each, being on one point his own judge, would ask to be so on all ... At once, in place of the individual personality of each contracting party, this act of association creates a moral and collective body ... This public person, so formed by the union of all other persons formerly took the name of city, and now takes that of the Republic or body politic; it is called by its members State when passive, Sovereign when active, and Power when compared with others like itself. Those who are associated in it take collectively the name of people, and severally are called citizens, as sharing in the sovereign power, and subjects, as being under the laws of the State.[92]

The constitutional contract theory aims to save the lack of democratic legitimacy within a similar type of obedience, a submission without reserve. Thus, every constitutional article or every decision of the constitutional court must be applied and accepted without discussion. This sort of alienation is excessive; it kills the liberal condition of citizenship. This liberal condition is a necessary quality to develop a democratic legitimacy process, a dialogue between real political members of a society (citizens), and also requires a critical sense through dialogue. Rational alienation also means totalitarianism. The constitution as the real sovereign found arguments to legitimate its empire in social contract metaphor. Rousseau, when defining democracy, stated: 'He who makes the law knows better than anyone else how it should be executed and interpreted.'[93] Rousseau continues by stating, and herein lies my criticism: 'It seems impossible to have a better constitution than that in which the executive and legislative powers are united.'[94] And where is the people? And the judiciary? The contractarian answer to this second question can be defined in Gaus: that constitutionalism is not a *demos* business.[95] Therefore, there is no possible relationship or collision between democracy and constitution because the two notions and realities are placed in different spheres.

A third social contract theory is Bell's contractualist interpretation of constitutionalism. Bell includes more variants to the 'constitutional contract', stating that:

> we interpret the US Constitution as a form contract written, judged, and offered by a government services provider. That adhesion contract binds citizens to the extent that they objectively manifest consent to the federal government's proposed bargain ... A contractual constitution can claim justifiability only relative to certain parties, such as one who signs a promise to obey the Constitution. A hierarchy of justifications applies to the constitutional contract, running from the ideal of a negotiated and express agreement between equals, through a form of contract imposed from on high, down to consent implied by conduct, bottoming out at hypothetical consent. Greater justifications trump lesser ones. An express disavowal of allegiance, for instance, typically negates an argument for implied consent. Constitutional contractualism thus suggests that the US Constitution binds government agents very tightly, while binding the government's subjects only loosely, at most.[96]

Michelman's response to the contractualist doctrine is also interesting. This author affirms that the conditions for thinking in a quasi-contractual way about a country's constitution may be stringent, but they are far from unimaginable.[97] The constitutional contractual approach treats the higher-law body of constitutional rules and standards as, in effect, a contract between oneself and the government, or among all the people respecting the government's powers over any of them.[98] Michelman goes on to state that, roughly and intuitively, the constitutional contractual proposition would appear to be this: a governmental system whose performance is, with few and minor exceptions, guaranteed to comply with the substantive constitution's requirements can be known, by that fact alone, not to be so awful as to merit denial of its respect-worthiness or hence of the legitimacy of whatever laws it makes.[99]

The idea that every legal act is valid in our legal system can safely be deemed legitimate. This is what makes the constitutional contract idea so appealing – its apparent ability to supply us with a clean, clear, objective basis for justification to others of our collaboration in the subjection of everyone to compulsion to comply with every valid legal act be it right or wrong.[100]

Michelman's argument against the possibility of constitutional contractualism – of treating a constitution as a legitimation contract – is avoidable by anyone willing to stand forth and embrace, as normatively warranted, a strictly content-independent conception of the binding virtue for constitutions, or the grounds of constitutional respect-worthiness.[101] To function as a 'legitimacy contract' that makes the entire legal system worthy of respect, the constitution must include only certain content that grounds its moral bindingness.[102]

The main conclusion of this section is that a constitution is not a (social) contract, and this metaphor has been used to feign the legitimacy of a text, to avoid debates and challenges to the juridification of the ruling nation or social group of the state.

Acceptance-oriented Legitimacy

Another doctrinal sector considers that the legitimacy of our constitutional texts comes from its acceptance by the population. In other words, we the people consent to the constitution and therefore it is legitimate. This conception has its origins in Hume's formulation of the original contract. Hume stated:

> the one party, by tracing up government to the Deity, endeavour to render it so sacred and inviolate, that it must be little less than sacrilege, however tyrannical it may become, to touch or invade it in the smallest article. The other party, by founding government altogether on the consent of the people, suppose that there is a kind of original contract, by which the subjects, have tacitly reserved the power of resisting their sovereign, whenever they find themselves aggrieved by that authority, which they have, for certain purposes, voluntarily entrusted him ... we must assert that every particular government which is lawful, and which imposes any duty of allegiance on the subject, was, at first, founded on consent and a voluntary compact.[103]

Consent appeared as a necessary element in the original contract. Therefore, Hume recognises the consent of the people as the best and most sacred foundation of government.

Hume (like Rousseau) relates violence to political legitimacy. He considers that the original establishment was formed by violence, and submitted to from necessity.[104] In other words, violence is the origin of and alternative to consent, just as it is for constitutional foundation. Hume goes on to analyse this 'truest tacit consent' that is observed. In constitutional discourse this tacit consent is also applied as a source of legitimacy. It is said that constitutions obtain this tacit consent because 'the people' does not alter the constitution or does not disobey the emperor. Jackson and Tushnet define consent as a plastic concept.[105] Even if we agree on what consent truly means, how do we know when a people have in fact consented to a political system or to a constitution? These authors define the possible arguments for consent as the legitimator of a constitution. Barnett affirms that the most common answer to the question why, more than two hundred years later, legislators or judges need to follow the constitution, is the 'consent of the governed'. It is said that 'we the people' established this constitution and the people are therefore bound to it until it is changed.[106] Barnett rightly considers that this answer is not only inaccurate, but as an ideal may even prove to be dangerous in practice, and may nurture unwarranted criticism of the constitution's legitimacy.[107] Barnett also challenges the idea that the US Constitution was or is legitimate because it was established by 'we the people' or by the consent of the people.[108]

The author continues by stating that though the people can surely be bound by their consent, this consent must be real, not fictional and unanimous.[109] This last characteristic (unanimity) places Barnett in the realm of ideas. Unanimity is impossible and non-desirable in modern plural, multi-cultural and globalised societies.

Consent has been understood not only as 'no contrary action', but also as derived by voting. Barnett explains perfectly the differences between voting and consent. If consent is a message we communicate to others – 'I consent to be bound by the outcome' – it is not clear that voting conveys such a message.[110] First, we are speaking about two different spheres, two different realities, voting for a representative or a lawmaker and consenting to a law; to enact a law depends on several factors, such as political opportunity, majorities, etc. Second, voting is not a blank cheque to the lawmaker; we do not consent to all the laws. Imagine that I voted for President Obama because I was concerned about the need for universal social security, a law granting residence and nationality to all immigrants within the US borders and a law decriminalising abortion. If President Obama finally approves the social security budget, and the decriminalisation of abortion, does that mean that my vote consents to a law extending the Iraqi occupation? I do not really think so. But if we speak about consent on constitutional issues the presumption is even bigger because normal citizens cannot amend the constitution. Did the citizens of the US consent to slavery and racial or gender discrimination until the consequent amendments of the US constitutional text?

Procedural-dialogical Legitimacy

Another theory that seeks to grant constitutional legitimacy is what doctrine calls procedural legitimation.[111] A valid law could be illegitimate and a legitimate law could be unjust. A law may be valid because it was produced in accordance with all the procedures required by a particular law-making system, but illegitimate because these procedures were inadequate to provide assurances that the law is just.[112] According to my usage, a juridical and political system ruled by a constitution that clearly states that *we the people* are the sovereign means that a law, to be considered legitimate, must involve the people. Barnett concludes that when consent is lacking, a constitution is legitimate only when it provides sufficient procedures to ensure that the laws enacted pursuant to its procedures are just.[113]

Legitimacy and justice are not synonyms in juridical terms. Barnett answers this question by stating that a constitution is legitimate if it provides adequate procedural assurances that enacted laws properly respect the rights of those on whom they are imposed and are necessary to protect the rights of others.[114] Therefore, Barnett establishes a kind of extra-constitutional and extra-democratic legitimacy. That is, the legitimacy of the constitution is dependent on the respect of rights in a procedure. Legitimacy does not depend on the involvement of the *demos* in the constitutional process. These procedural rights have a higher hierarchical status than democracy. Consequently, Barnett switches from constitution (as a whole sovereign) to certain procedural rights that will bring legitimacy to the constitutional text, without taking into consideration the final content of the text, but only how the constitution is approved. Barnett's procedural legitimacy does not affirm who is the final sovereign, who will enforce the procedural rights and who legitimises these sovereigns. I understand that Barnett's positivistic legitimacy does not solve the conflict between constitution and democracy, nor grants sovereignty to the people, but tries to avoid the conflict with the submission of legitimacy to a third concept, these procedural rights. Regardless of what has been said, Barnett should explain who legitimises these rights, the *demos*, the Constitution or neither. If the answer is neither, who then?

Barnett, discussing the legitimacy of constitutional construction, consistently affirms that to be legitimate the law-making processes must provide assurances that both the enumerated and unenumerated rights of those who are governed will not be violated.[115] This assumption could work if we were not talking about the creation of the first law, the first constitution. In this respect, I see a clear coincidence with the criticism of Kelsen's basic norm legitimacy that I expound in Chapter 2, above.

The second procedural theory of constitutional legitimacy that I want to discuss is based on Habermas' work.[116] When this author comes to the matter of constitutional law, he is expressly committed both to bottomless procedural democracy and to liberal justice.[117] 'The democratic procedure for the production of law,' Habermas declares, 'forms the only ... source of legitimacy' for our post-metaphysical age.[118] Certain components of the largely forgotten theoretical part of Habermas' work are positive, and worth reviving, especially the possibility of applying democratic processes to the codification of laws without necessarily excluding morality from the system. I understand that in *Faktizität und Geltung*, a work that is basically legal in content, Habermas introduces a radical change in his conception of positive and natural law that modifies the process of legitimation of legal norms and alters the relationship between legal norms, on the one hand, and moral and ethical norms, on the other. In spite of the affirmations of certain positivistic authors, self-proclaimed defenders of democracy applied to the law, Habermas' normative theory actually predates the publication of his *Faktizität und Geltung*.[119] In my opinion, the normative contents of works such as *Theorie und Praxis*, in which Habermas defines the concepts of natural law, positive law and the process of codification of legal norms, cannot be rejected on positivist grounds or on the contention that Habermas had a negative vision of law. In *Theorie und Praxis*, the author dedicates a whole chapter to natural law and to revolutionary declarations of natural rights, placing special emphasis on the process of positivisation of these kind of rights from a philosophical perspective.[120] Nor should we ignore the legal and normative importance of Habermas' *Theory of Communicative Action*,[121] in which he develops the Weberian concept of rationalisation, and explores how this process affects the law and defines juridification.

Although *Theory of Communicative Action* is not only a legal work and its legal concepts and theories are developed alongside social and philosophical theories, it deals with important legal definitions, such as natural law, positive law and modern law. Habermas affirms that modern law is a concept that is still in need of a moral justification able to gauge the validity of its legal norms; modern law, whether understood as a means or as an institution, has a need for moral justification. Therefore, a hierarchical parity between ethical, juridical and moral norms is clear. Habermas distinguishes between positive legal norms and norms that are not already positivised; the latter are norms of natural law, located at the top of the hierarchical scale of norms. Habermas' third work that deals with normative issues is *Die nachholende* Revolution,[122] in which he introduces for the first time the concept of the legitimation of law, which he goes on to develop later, and discusses the political consequences that the procedure of legitimation entails. *Die nachholende Revolution* continues the conceptual criticism of positivism that Habermas maintained throughout his work. Though *Die nachholende Revolution* is a kind of bridge between the two main parts of Habermas' normative theory, it defends the same position on legal rationalism and the need for a relationship between law and morality, conceiving morality as a necessary component of the legitimation of specific legal norms. Codification, which was considered as something that limited freedom and was always in need of ethical support and moral norms in order to legitimate legal norms, is finally seen as the only procedure capable of doing so; all the connotations and relations between law and ethics and morals are removed. Habermas eliminates any external relation of the law, which allows us to qualify the theory as a positivist one. The main goal of Habermas in *Faktizität und Geltung* is to reconcile the concept of law with that of justice, and to reconcile democracy with law.

Habermas contends the law's legitimation as a source of self-imposition and obligation. The law is a bridge that unites democracy and legal norms. The legal norms that are the result of this sort of self-imposition and obliga-tion must successfully reconcile legal and *de facto* equality.[123] Habermas seems to confuse the concept of right (*Recht*) with the concept of law (*Gesetz*), and the concept of justice with legality.

Habermas' formulation of the legitimation procedure is inconsistent in several essential aspects, and needs to be examined. Habermas considers that the source of every legitimate law lies in the democratic process of the production of the law linked to the principle of popular sovereignty.

Despite this criticism, the stimulation of direct citizen participation in the *res publica* and the assumption of responsibilities by citizens in the public sphere are not only very positive, but necessary in democratic terms. The central premise of Habermas' theory of law and democracy is the principle of discourse. This principle implies that norms will be legitimate when free and equal citizens deliberate and make decisions, in such a way that all can agree to them without coercion or distorted beliefs. According to this principle, the validity of a decision is related to a 'rational consensus'; norms are valid only if those affected can agree to them as participants in a rational consensus.[124] For Habermas, the introduction of this principle pre-supposes that practical questions can be impartially and rationally decided.[125] The legitimacy of the law, therefore, will be based in the final instance on a communicative mechanism. This is the point where the communicative action theory and the procedure of the legitimation of norms presented in *Faktizität und Geltung* are linked. Habermas recognises that his principle of discourse supposes an increase in rationalisation, and this new overdose of rationality is justified by the theory of argumentation. It would seem, then, that Habermas finally understands the law's rationality as unavoidable and, because of the magnitude of his project, something that he is ready to accept.

The other principle that Habermas introduces in his normative theory in *Faktizität und Geltung* is the principle of democracy, which consists in the uniting of the wills of citizens in acceptance of a legal norm that will be applied on their behalf. As Habermas states, the main idea is that the principle of democracy is due to the link of the principle of discourse with a legal content, understanding this fusion as a logical genesis of rights, which must continue their gradual reconstruction. In my view, the implantation of a foreign discourse in the legal sphere raises problems for the theory. Habermas defines the purpose of the principle of democracy as establishing a legitimate procedure for the production of laws. We can only claim legitimate validity for legal norms on the basis of a legally articulated discourse, to which all the members of the juridical community affected by the norm give their consent.[126] The principle of democracy presupposes the possibility of deciding rationally on practical questions, and of making all kinds of possible discourses from which laws derive their legitimacy. Consequently, the resulting legal norm will be considered as a law because of the procedure by which it has been approved, and not as a result of its final content.

Ackerman's division between constitutional and normal politics is of paramount importance at this point. Ackerman's theory in relation to the dialogue used by citizens when participating in law is the distinction he makes between constitutional moments and normal moments. Constitutional moments occur very rarely, at times when 'we the people' speak using extra-constitutional means to make fundamental changes in the constitution.[127] These situations are characterised by the fact that an unusually large number of citizens are convinced of the seriousness of the matter under discussion (far greater than in the case of decisions to be taken in normal times), by the fact that all citizens have the opportunity to express their own views on the question, and finally by the fact that a majority supports a specific way of solving the question.[128] Unlike other authors, Ackerman considers that constitutional moments arise only at times of political upheaval, and in fact only very rarely: he sees only three important constitutional moments in the history of the United States. Ackerman establishes a kind of formal criterion to determine whether a particular moment should be defined as constitutional or normal. This formal criterion is decisive.

The distinction between normal and constitutional moments turns out to be (at least) three distinctions mapped onto each other. Normal moments are managed by elected representatives, while constitutional moments are managed by the people; normal politics are not particularly reflective, whereas constitutional politics are; normal politics involve the pluralist pursuit of group interests, while constitutional politics involve principles and the common good.[129]

Constitutional politics also play a role in altering the framework in which normal politics develop: that is, constitutional moments not only differ from the periods of normality that precede and follow them, but must also ensure that the two phases of normal politics, before and afterwards, are totally different. The constitutional moment is thus marked by discontinuity and transformation. Constitutional moments are extremely rare, occurring only at key political moments; they have long-lasting constitutional effects (even though the constitutional moment is only temporary) and, most importantly for the present study, the citizens who aim to effect a constitutional transformation act directly. The other kind of political moment is the normal moment. In normal moments we include the everyday decisions taken by the government; there is no debate or popular mobilisation. The electorate entrusts the management of legal matters to the government, and the government, legitimated by this mandate, takes the decisions that it believes to be most appropriate. In normal moments, a 'united' population allows democratically elected groups to take political decisions. For Ackerman, we should treat normal moments – that is, the situation in which the people decide to withdraw from politics – with the greatest respect. The people delegate power to their representatives, who may be substituted through the appropriate democratic procedures. Therefore, normal politics is as important as constitutional politics for the stability and necessary continuity that every legal system needs. As noted above, the purpose of the constitutional moment is to affect a specific normal moment in a direct way, and to produce a different new normal moment. In normal politics Ackerman stresses that the lack of debate and popular participation does not necessarily vitiate the legitimacy of the decisions taken by the government if specific institutional conditions are satisfied. These conditions are, first, that the representatives of the people are responsible for their decisions. This statement is a sort of responsive democracy applied to the people. The best way to construct a complete responsive democracy is to start with the representatives. Second, that the institutional structure obliges the people's representatives to take decisions with regard to a broad vision of the public interest. Third, that a legislation should be established that stops interest groups from entering government in order to obtain unfair advantages.

These conditions demonstrate that it is possible to make a theory that is less utopian than Habermas', when introducing more democratic contents into political life in general, even if they are aimed at the representatives. In my view, the theory and experience of constitutional and normal politics should be studied carefully if we want to enable citizenship in constitutional affairs. The differentiation between the two types of political moments is part of the analysis of the concept of dualist democracy. Dualist democracy distinguishes between the decisions taken by the government and those taken directly by the people. Therefore, the concept of dualist democracy rests on the difference between constitutional and ordinary politics introduced above. The opposite of the dualist theory of democracy is the monist theory. Ackerman describes these two contradictory approaches in order to provide a synthesis. Monism sees the task of constitutional theorising as the reconciliation of the authority of unelected life-tenured judges to invalidate legislation with the United State's primary and fundamental commitment to democracy. The usual monistic solution is the assumption of legislative validity.[130]

Monist democracy consists in the basic idea that democracy requires government by the representatives chosen by the people. These representatives have been conceded full power to pass laws, insofar as the choice has been freely made. The most important institutional consequence of the theory of monism is that in the period between elections any attempt to reduce the government's powers is seen as anti-democratic. The idea of monism is very simple and attractive to anyone who believes in democracy and popular representation and, therefore, in the anti-majority nature of judicial resolutions. For monism there is no democratic authority other than a democratically chosen parliament.

For this theory, the basic distinction that dualism makes between the decisions of the people and the decisions of the people's representatives makes no sense.[131] Ackerman reminds us that democracy has been conceived for citizens and that the system must allow their direct participation. Throughout history, and especially in the last two centuries, society has adopted the term 'democracy', but has reduced it to banality. The transformation took place after a radical reconceptualisation: the image of the Athenian polis has been removed from the centre of democratic thought and practice.

Other critical elements that we should highlight with respect to Habermas' formulations are the need for unanimity in the approval of legal norms, in addition to the ideal demands of universality and timelessness. In this regard Habermas' proceduralist theory of legitimation depends largely on the concept of dialogue between citizens legislating. The impossible unanimity may be reached through dialogue between citizens. Here the first thing that we must clarify is the peculiarity of legal language. Jurists themselves have traditionally regarded language as the primary means for the formulation and interpretation of legal concepts. Jackson remarks upon a number of characteristics of legal language, notably including the following two: (1) the diversity of forms of legal language; and (2) the much-discussed problem of comprehensibility of legal writing, and the solutions which have been proposed to improve it. Written legal language may be considered a particular register of the 'grapholect': 'it shares the grammar of the standard form of the language, and is capable of utilizing any part of its lexicon'.[132] In the autopoietic theory of Luhmann, law is understood as a self-referential, self-reproducing system, rather than a form of social integration.[133]

According to Hutton, *autopoiesis* is a term derived from evolutionary biology, referring to systems that reproduce themselves autonomously: 'law produces by itself all the distinctions and concepts which it uses'. This author goes on to say that one of the main practical issues related to this paper is how to overcome the 'operative closure' that is law. Closure does not mean total isolation, but refers to the autonomy of the internal self-referring, communicative order that Luhmann terms 'informational' or 'semantic' closure.[134] There is an absolute boundary between law and non-law that we need to overcome to enable a feasible public sphere (Arendt) where citizens will be able to participate in legal issues.[135] This legal semantic closure may have direct repercussions for procedural constitutional legitimacy. However, there is no unanimity about this 'radical objectivism'. Habermas does not establish any type of speciality for legal language because he reduces the concept simply to language in general, without taking into account the fact that legal language has a series of characteristics of its own.[136] Consequently, as Pattaro asserts, Habermas reduces the concept of legal discourse to linguisticity. Constitutional authorship overcomes this point, since the people becomes the author of the law.[137] At this point Ackerman's notion of neutral dialogue may be an excellent contribution to achieve the needed unanimity. Ackerman concedes a special role to the concept and functions of dialogue in his work. For this author dialogue is the first obligation of citizenship. 'As a citizen I had an especially strong obligation to participate in the dialogic search for the moral truth ... a refusal to talk simply disqualifies her [a liberal citizen in dialogue] as a participant in a liberal state unless she is willing to participate.' Dialogue is therefore a core element of liberal societies. Ackerman considers that these sorts of societies must create places where dialogue between citizens can be developed. Dialogue has a fundamental social function, but it is also a compulsory element for our moral self-definition, since it is the mechanism through which we take into consideration the rest of the citizens.

Ackerman assumes that dialogue between citizens of a liberal society is constrictive, that is, through the dialogue the citizens attempt to convince the other members of the society competitively and not neutrally. The Yale professor highlights among the functions of dialogue the fact that it serves to control in a sensitive way the power of repression. The establishment of moral truth at both individual and collective levels is crucial when implementing the legal framework that regulates the state or certain rules that should serve as general principles of law. Ackerman affirms that the best way to understand the liberal tradition is precisely through the effort to define and justify a great force in the power of dialogue. The notion of constrained conversation should serve as the organizing principle of liberal thought. Ackerman considers that in undertaking this exercise in liberal conversation, citizen P does not try to convince fellow citizens P2 to change their minds and see, at long last, the compelling truth of P. Instead, the conversation has a more pragmatic intention. Therefore, as Ackerman states, in a liberal dialogue citizens do not feel free to introduce moral arguments into the field of conversation, but they try to reach a conversational win far away from the dialogical ideal situation.

The definition of constrained dialogue is applicable to the communication between legal operators. Dialogue between parties in a court of justice is constrictive, as Ackerman characterises. The main objective is to convince the jury or mediator about one's own claims. After analysing the importance of dialogue in modern societies, Ackerman introduces the concept of neutrality, which should rule modern liberal societies. Ackerman affirms: in these sorts of societies (liberal ones) a sort of purification of 'constrictiveness' is performed. A political community of diverse individuals can organise its power struggle consistently with neutral discourse if it takes steps to assure that: (a) *No citizen genetically dominates another.* One of the basic requirements in order to be able to define dialogue under conditions of neutrality is to prove that there are no differences based on genetics. In this regard, I extend the concept to other aspects such as race, religion or language; (b) *Each citizen receives a liberal education.*[138] Education has a fundamental role in Ackerman's work. It must provide the basis to establish liberal principles. Regarding education, I want to emphasise the risk of normalisation and standardised education; liberal education may be aimed at generating self-determined citizens in the sense that Derrida gives to the term.[139] (c) *Each citizen begins adult life under conditions of material equality.*

The last classification departs from the characterisation of law as a social practice. In this context, Adler accurately states:

> The law within each legal system is a function of the practices of some social group. In short, law is a kind of socially grounded norm. This is a point of consensus for modern jurisprudents in the Anglo-American tradition: not just Hart and his followers in the positive schools, most prominently Raz and Coleman, but also Dworkin, who argues that law necessarily synthesizes moral considerations with social facts.[140]

Consequently, Adler continues:

> A social rule, for Hart, is more than a shared habit. Rather, a social rule is practiced by a group if its members conform to some behavioural regularity,

believing that they ought to do so. More precisely, the Concept of Law explains that group acceptance of a social rule involves 'a critical reflective attitude to certain patterns of behaviour as a common standard, (which attitude) display(s) itself in criticism (including self-criticism), demands for conformity, and in acknowledgements that such criticism and demands are justified'.[141]

There are abysmal differences in the determination, significance and scope of this role. The two doctrines 'constitutional authorship' and 'rule of recognition' vary depending on how the question should be answered. Adapting Adler's statement to the subject of this chapter, the main question will be: which group grounds the constitution?

Adler, defining the relationship between popular constitutionalism and the rule of recognition, states that positivists since Hart have universally pointed to either officials or judges as the 'recognitional community' (Adler's term): the group whose rules, conventions, cooperative activities or practices in some other sense are the social facts from which the law of a given legal system derives, and popular constitutionalists assert that judges and officials should be responsive to the constitutional views expressed by citizens in elections, demonstrations and other political activities.[142] The link between the rule of recognition and constitutional authorship is simply structural. At this point I am not trying to solve the problem, but I believe that neither theory closes the door to the people's role, which is my aim. The main problem that I face is that without democratic involvement in constitutional (legal) affairs, Hart is right: the legal power of the sovereign (the constitution) cannot be explained simply by noting that others are in a habit of obeying him. This obedience is based on several aspects (normalisation and legal violence) that will be analysed in the last two chapters of this book.

Rule of Recognition

Hart told us that law is a kind of norm ultimately grounded in official practice.[143] The author considered a community that does not have a legal system and then invites the reader to ponder the various social problems that would arise in that group, and how the introduction of certain rules would resolve these difficulties.[144] Legal rights, duties, liberties, powers, liabilities, immunities and disabilities that exist in each legal system are just those putative rights, duties, etc., that are validated by what Hart called the rule of recognition: the rule for identifying law that is accepted as the ultimate rule by officials in the legal system, particularly judges.[145] Hart suggested that the fundamental rules of legal systems solve the various defects of pre-legal, customary societies.[146] Legal systems address the problem of uncertainty by providing a rule that determines which rules are binding.[147] Then, as Green assumes for Hart, the only consensus necessary for law is a consensus of elites.[148] In Hart's account, citizen's beliefs about the role of voting and other forms of popular political expression in constitutional decision making are necessarily legally irrelevant, in the absence of some validation of those beliefs by officials.[149] Citizens have no legal role in constitutional decision making unless officials come to believe that they do or at least come to accept other rules from which a citizen role is derivable.[150] Raz's and Kutz's account of the rule of recognition implies, therefore, that the ultimate criterion of legal validity is constituted by judicial practice, and so all of the possible limitations on judicial supremacy must ultimately be legally justified by appeal to judicial practice. Judges might be legally required to defer to Congress (or to the people) on certain issues, but only if judges agree that deference is required or at least accept the axiom from which deference is derivable.[151]

Assuming that this is true, the main unresolved question raised in this book reappears: who legitimates these officials (Hart), judges (Raz and Kutz) or lawyers (Tocqueville) to have such a power? Then Adler wonders if popular constitutionalism is possible under the rule of recognition, quoting the variant forms of 'popular constitutionalism' of Neal Katyal, Larry Kramer, Robert Post, Reva Siegel, Mark Tushnet, Jeremy Waldron and Keith Whittington, enabling some inclusion of popular views about the constitution in constitutional decision making.[152] To do so, he states that the 'popular constitutionalist' authors claim either: '(1) that the legal status of citizen involvement in constitutional decision making hinges on, and is delimited by, officials' views about what the fundamental legal principles of our system are', or alternatively: '(2) that citizen views have a larger role in shaping the legal system, perhaps a coequal or dominant role'. This doctrinal sector in relation to the rule of recognition points to citizen practices as the foundation of law.[153]

Popular constitutionalists would insist that citizen practices trump or at least have co-equal status with official or judicial practices in determining what the US Constitution requires as a matter of law, not merely in determining what constitutional law ought to be as a matter of morality or political theory. Adler cleverly puts the problem of the *recognitional community* on the agenda of constitutional theory, as a way to clarify which source of legitimacy the constitution has in practice. It seems clear to me that at the starting point both doctrines – 'rule of recognition' and 'constitutional authorship' – need to answer an equivalent question: who recognises? or who is the author? The first assumes categorically that the *demos* need the 'filter' and interpretation of public officials to validate the legal concept, to understand the meaning of all these concepts. Democratic constitutional authorship presumes that the *demos* do not need this 'translation' to be able to decide on legal-constitutional issues. Through the exercise of summarising popular constitutionalism in two main claims, Adler limits the doctrinal arguments and real possibilities of implementation of these theories.

Certainly, if the direct participation of the citizenry in constitutional affairs is sought, the intermediary role of public officers should be limited if not suppressed. If we consider valid the rule of recognition theory, the *demos* can never free themselves from the public officials who determine the content and scope of the constitution and all other legal concepts. Hence, the question would no longer be whether public officials are democratically legitimated, but whether their activity cannot be transferred to the people. One of the main differences between these two doctrines is the impossibility of applying the 'rule of recognition' to the basic norm, the 'first constitution'. Probably the lack of a possible application of this essentially positivistic doctrine is related to the doctrinal inconsistency that we observe in Kelsen's doctrine on this same issue. Hart suggests a theory of law as 'interplay of primary and secondary rules, where primary rules impose obligations and secondary rules confer powers'.[154] Hart develops his picture of law by indulging in some fictions concerning a hypothetical community governed by primary rules and containing a single rule which sets out the text of validity for the whole system. The most salient property of Hart's rule of recognition is a *secondary rule*, that is, a rule of recognition of other rules (i.e., the 'primary' rules).[155]

In a constitutional regime, the secondary rules will typically limit the supreme and independent powers of the sovereign.[156] Then, Shapiro introduces that the American people are sovereign in the United States and have the power to amend the Constitution, yet the Constitution nonetheless limits their power to do so, both making certain provisions unalterable and prescribing an extremely onerous procedure that must be followed before the amendment is ratified.[157] Shapiro goes on to contend that:

> Because the rule of recognition is a social rule, it is capable of being an ultimate rule. It is ultimate in the sense that it does not exist in virtue of any other rule. Its existence is secured simply because of its acceptance and practice. The primary rules of the legal system, by contrast, are not ultimate because they exist in virtue of the rule of recognition. The rule of recognition validates, but is not itself validated.[158]

As I have mentioned throughout this book, it is necessary to overcome the status quo that petrifies the question of legitimacy addressed to constitutional issues and keeps the *demos* away from their legitimate constitutional powers. In this direction, the main thing is to overcome the *de facto* monopoly of judges (Hart/Kutz), officials (Hart) or lawyers (Tocqueville and others), and thus enable a universal rule of recognition or a democratic constitutional authorship. Otherwise, as is the case today, the legitimacy of these bodies is undemocratic and, as I will try to demonstrate in Chapters 4 and 5, violent.

Constitutional Authorship

The last theory explained in this chapter is Michelman's interpretation and innovation of constitutional authorship. I agree with Ming-Sung Kuo when he states that the 'presentist' view of legitimacy introduced by Michelman into constitutional democracy bolsters constitutional authorship.[159] The theoretical exercise must be considered the theory to be followed to achieve the needed constitutional legitimacy. The main attraction of this theory is the involvement of the people as such in constitutional affairs. This main fact relates, in a plane of abstraction, Michelman's work with other constitutional democratic theories, and works such as Kramer's popular constitutionalism or Tushner's constitutional populism. At the centre of constitutional authorship is the idea that the legitimacy of the constitution is built on the nature of the relationship between us, who live under a constitutional regime, and the authors of the regime.[160] According to Michelman, the 'we–they' relationship is one of 'allegiance', in which 'you and I might consider ourselves and the country bound to [the authors'] word by communal ties'.[161] Michelman brings some meaning and realism to the aphorism 'we the people' as authors of the constitution. With his definition of 'normative authority' and the authorship syndrome, Michelman grounds in a legitimate way the strong linkage between us (the people) and the text. In this regard, he states that:

> by the internal act of basing allegiance to the Constitution on its having been authored by whom it was, we set aside, if only momentarily, whatever concerns we may also have with either the bare facticity or the rational necessity of society's acceptance of it as the basic law of the country ... The issue here is the connection we draw between perceived historical facts of the textual 'Constitution's' authorship and the current normative authority for us, as law, of a body of practical political principles that we take this text to express or represent. By the 'normative authority' of a political directive I mean its serious impingement on our feelings and judgments about what is required and permitted in the conduct of the political affairs. The connection we draw between normative authority and perceived historical facts of authorship ... I sometimes refer to ... as the authority–authorship syndrome ... Something strong must be motivating the connection – the syndrome – because, as we shall soon start to notice, linkage of the Constitution's authority to its authorship is a sitting duck for critique.[162]

Therefore, the author affirms that social acceptance of the constitution as supreme law is a very different matter from acceptance of someone's entitlement to make the constitution be supreme law by legislating it as such. The latter sort of acceptance still traces legal bindingness to facts about someone's exercise of a legislative will; the former does not.[163]

What is the relationship between us and the drafters of the constitution that makes us owe allegiance to their opus?[164] The answer, Michelman holds, is that the allegiance is based on who the constitutional authors are, not on what they have authored. Thus, in order to conceive of a relationship of allegiance based on the identity of the constitution's authors, rather than on its contents, and, at the same time, to take seriously the 'burden of judgement' concerning the legitimacy of the constitutional order, the author-based conception of legitimacy centres on the conceit that we, the observant citizen-readers, are 'identical' to those constitutional authors. The idea of constitutional authorship and the whole author-based concept of legitimacy. The 'presentist' or *generation problem* links Michelman's theory with Ackerman's (*second generation*). Both authors are concerned about the need to link constitutional legitimacy with presentness, safe-guarding all the same rights of all generations alike.

According to Michelman, any justification of constitutionalism as practice must be based on *presentist* first-person judgement; thus, he resists the notion of the constitution as a set object of the common project of interpretation.[165] Like Michelman, I consider that we cannot accept a conception that can be justified only by faith and not by works or by reason.

The theory of constitutional authorship can be adapted to the constitutional crowd-sourcing that is happening in Iceland and other countries. In the case of Iceland, the Constitutional Council presented the Speaker of the Althingi (the National Parliament), with the bill for a new constitution. The bill was unanimously approved by all delegates at the last meeting of the Council, and assumes that from now on changes to the constitution will be submitted to a vote by all who are eligible to vote in Iceland, for either approval or rejection. All delegates agree that the population should be given the chance to vote on the new constitution before the Althingi's final vote on it. In the case of ideas arising to make changes to the bill prepared by the Constitutional Council, the delegates of the Council declare themselves ready to revert to the matter before a national referendum is held.[166] This new constitutional experience engages a complete new sphere of 'mediation' though IT and opens the door to a popular constitutional drafting focus on the 'constituent moment', in the first stage of the basic norm (Kelsen), where the people are going to be the authentic constitutional author. The Internet and IT create a new system, a new reality, with huge possibilities for implementing democratic tools. The Internet is the new system. Through social networks, mobile technology and other IT devices, the Internet is beginning to impose its rule and logic on the constitutional domain, on the drafting of a *magna carta*. These technological tools allow political and constitutional crowd-sourcing, where laymen will have the possibility to opine and decide on constitutional contents.

The possibility of switching constitutional authorship from a few enlightened men to millions of persons can redefine the relationship between constitutionalism and democracy. Mediation between constitution and democracy is achieved with this popular constitutional drafting. Tamanaha states that: 'the possible role developed by the people would strengthen a system of dualist democracy instead of the monist tendency dominated by partisan interests as happens nowadays in the majority of our constitutional democracies'.[167] Popular constitutional drafting means not only popular constitutional authorship, but more participation and fewer opportunities for partisan interests or domination by the elite.

CONCLUSION

This chapter develops a fundamental issue of the book: democracy. An exercise of popular constitutionalism necessarily has to deal with a definition of the concept of democracy and whether the *demos* can be involved in legal and constitutional affairs. The first section deals with the semantic indeterminacy that affects democracy, considering that this lack of determination cannot be used to limit the potentialities of a democratic system and the necessary involvement of the *demos* in constitutional legitimacy affairs. The best way to increase the sense of 'engagement' or 'attachment' is to give to the *demos* and not only to one small social group a decisive role in government acts, or in our subject analysed, in constitutional matters. The people's participation in constitutional affairs must be channelled through a concept of individual autonomy or self-government, which in turn is an instrument to challenge normalised – constitutional – violence.

Defining democracy necessarily entails specifying what and who the *demos* is, and who is included in or excluded from the *demos*. This question is related to the scope of the legitimating theories of constitutionalism, 'constitutional authorship' and 'rule of recognition', and, depending how the question is solved, the legitimation will be considered democratic or not. Analysing the main Anglo-American theories of constitutional legitimation, a quasi-exclusive topic emerges: the role of the judiciary. Raz and Kurz consider the US rule of recognition as the ultimate criterion of legal validity in our systems, and this rule is constituted by judicial practice. The undemocratic role of the judiciary becomes a central issue in the work of Michelman, Kramer, Tushnet, Levinson, Ackerman and others when these prominent jurisprudents analyse the relationship between democracy and the Supreme Court. Certainly, these authors deal with the amendments to the constitutional text, but as Kelsen contended, to amend is not equivalent to creating a new constitution.

My aim has been to fix the lack of democratic legitimacy in the 'founding moment', in the approval of the basic norm, the first constitution. I consider that this undemocratic founding has consequences for the development of the potentialities of a democratic legitimacy of our current constitutional systems. Once the constitution is approved without democratic legitimation, I wonder where the undemocratic constitutional legitimacy comes from. The answer to this question is complex and involves elements of a very diverse nature. The first element is psycho-social: legal normalisation (what is to be considered valid, normal and legal). At this point, I will link Sarat's theory of 'habit of obedience' with this process of normalisation and juridification. The second element is an economic one: the aristocracy or ruling class cannot allow the *demos* in general terms to participate in its quasi-monopolistic business of ruling.

These elements are related to each other and benefited by constitutional-legal violence, since the constitution and its aristocracy determines what is valid, legal, legitimate and normal. I consider that the only way to disable the violent source of constitutional legitimation is to gradually introduce democratic mechanisms. I am not asking for a transformation of laymen into Platonic philosophers but, as is happening now in Iceland, the possibility for the people, the only sovereign, not only to participate, but also to decide in constitutional matters.

Notes

1. I want to thank my colleague at the SUNY at Buffalo Guyora Binder, who asked me this question when we were discussing various possible and feasible definitions of democracy.
2. F. de Saussure, *Ecrits de linguistique générale*. Paris: Gallimard, 2002.
3. Available at: http://plato.stanford.edu/entries/democracy/#DemDef, accessed 15 December 2011.
4. G. R. Morrow, *Plato's Cretan City*, Princeton, NJ: Princeton University Press, 1993, p. 525.
5. S. Gordon, *Controlling the State: Constitutionalism from Ancient Athens to Today*, Cambridge, MA: Harvard University Press, 1999, p. 76.
6. Plato, *The Republic*. New York: Penguin, 2006.
7. Available at: http://plato.stanford.edu/entries/democracy/#DemDef, 15 December 2011.
8. E. Havelock, 'Plato's politics and the American Constitution', *Harvard Studies in Classical Philology*, 93, 1990, 22.

9. *Ibid.*, p. 22.
10. G. R. Morrow, *Plato's Cretan City*, Princeton, NJ: Princeton University Press, 1993, p. 5.
11. *Ibid.*, p. 4.
12. J. Derrida, *Rogues: Two Essays on Reason*, Stanford, CA: Stanford University Press, 2005 p. 13.
13. *Ibid.*, p. 21.
14. P. J. Proudhon (Manuscrits – Documents Inedits), *De la critique et des idées dans la démocratie française, à propos d'un ouvrage sur la Guerre et la Paix (vers 1861)*, Paris: Éditions Tops/H. Trinquier, 1999.
15. E. Fromm, *Escape from Freedom*, New York: Henry Holt, 1941.
16. Aristotle, *Politics: A Treatise on Government*, Seattle, WA: Create Space, 2010, p. 73.
17. *Ibid.*, p. 98.
18. P. J. Proudhon (Manuscrits – Documents Inedits), *De la critique et des idées dans la démocratie française, à propos d'un ouvrage sur la Guerre et la Paix (vers 1861)*, Paris: Éditions Tops/H. Trinquier, 1999.
19. C. Schmitt, *Constitutional Theory*. Durham, NC: Duke University Press, 2008, p. 264.
20. *Ibid.*, p. 264.
21. *Ibid.*, p. 265.
22. *Ibid.*, p. 266.
23. A. Tocqueville, *Democracy in America*, Chicago, IL: Chicago University Press, 2002, p. 3.
24. *Ibid.*, p. 267.
25. *Ibid.*, p. 267.
26. *Ibid.*, p. xxvi.
27. Aristotle, *Politics: A Treatise on Government*, Seattle, WA: Create Space, 2010, p. 95.
28. J. Derrida, *Rogues: Two Essays on Reason*, Stanford, CA: Stanford University Press, 2005, p. 22.
29. *Ibid.*, p. 44.
30. *Ibid.*, p. 26.
31. R. Barnett, 'Restoring the lost constitution, not the constitution in exile', *Fordham Law Review*, 75, 2006, 669–73.
32. J. G. A. Pocock, *El momento maquiavélico. El pensamiento político florentino y la tradición republicana atlántica*, Madrid: Tecnos, 2006, p. 623.
33. P. López Borja de Quiroga, *Imperio legítimo. El pensamiento político en tiempos de Cicerón*, Madrid: Machado Libros, 2004, p. 92.
34. A. Larry and B. L. Solum, 'Popular? Constitutionalism?', 2004, p. 1606, available at: http://papers.ssrn.com/sol3/papers.cfm?abstract_id=692224.
35. B. Ackerman, 'The living constitution', *Harvard Law Review*, 120, 2007, 1743.
36. *Ibid.*, p. 1743.

37. *Ibid.*, p. 1744.
38. *Ibid.*, p. 1744.
39. B. Ackerman and N. Katyal, 'Our unconventional founding', *University of Chicago Law Review*, 62, 1995, 475, 514.
40. Constitution of the República Bolivariana de Venezuela, 20 December 1999.
41. For an excellent exercise on the relationship between constitutions and collective identities, see G. J. Jacobsohn, *Constitutional Identity*, Cambridge, MA: Harvard University Press, 2010.
42. Cicero, *De Re Publica, De Legibus*, Cambridge, MA: Harvard University Press, 1961, p. 461.
43. Polybius, *The Histories of Polybius*, vol. I, Bloomington, IN: Indiana University Press, 1962, p. 467.
44. T. Donahue, 'The scope of justice and global dark oppression', 2010, available at: http://papers.ssrn.com/sol3/papers.cfm?abstract_id=1483241, accessed 15 January 2011.
45. A. de Tocqueville, *Democracy in America*, Chicago, IL: Chicago University Press, 2002, p. 251.
46. *Ibid.*, p. 252.
47. *Ibid.*, p. 252.
48. *Ibid.*, p. 252.
49. *Ibid.*, p. 254.
50. C. Schmitt, *Constitutional Theory*, Durham, NC: Duke University Press, 2008, p. 318.
51. A de Tocqueville, *Democracy in America*, Chicago, IL: Chicago University Press, 2002, p. 257.
52. L. Kramer, '"The interest of the man": James Madison, popular constitutionalism, and the theory of deliberative democracy', *Valparaiso University Law Review*, 41(2), 2006, 697–754 and L. Kramer, *The People Themselves: Popular Constitutionalism and Judicial Review*, Oxford: Oxford University Press, 2004.
53. L. Kramer, '"The interest of the man": James Madison, popular constitutionalism, and the theory of deliberative democracy', *Valparaiso University Law Review*, 41(2), 2006, 697.
54. *Ibid.*, p. 689.
55. *Ibid.*, p. 699.
56. See L. Kramer, '"The interest of the man": James Madison, popular constitutionalism, and the theory of deliberative democracy', *Valparaiso University Law Review*, 41(2), 2006 to delve into the arguments on which he bases Madison's commitment to popular government and the people's control of government and laws.
57. L. Kramer, '"The interest of the man": James Madison, popular constitutionalism, and the theory of deliberative democracy', *Valparaiso University Law Review*, 41(2), 2006.
58. *Ibid.*, pp. 7–8.

59. *Ibid.*, pp. 7–8.
60. *Ibid.*, p. 699.
61. *Ibid.*, p. 699.
62. *Ibid.*, p. 702.
63. *Ibid.*, p. 700.
64. *Ibid.*, p. 700.
65. A. Abat i Ninet, 'Demagogy and democratic loyalty instead of oligogy and constitutional patriotism', *Vienna Journal of International Constitutional Law*, 2/10, 2010, 641–62.
66. See L. Kramer, *The People Themselves: Popular Constitutionalism and Judicial Review*, Oxford: Oxford University Press 2004, and L. Kramer, '"The interest of the man": James Madison, popular constitutionalism, and the theory of deliberative democracy', *Valparaiso University Law Review*, 41(2), 2006, 697–754.
67. See M. Tushnet, *The New Constitutional Order*, Princeton, NJ: Princeton University Press, 2003; M. Tushnet (ed.), 'Introduction', *I Dissent: Great Opposing Opinions in Landmark Supreme Court Cases*, Boston, MA: Beacon Press, 2008a; M. Tushnet, *Weak Courts, Strong Rights: Judicial Review and Social Welfare Rights in Comparative Constitutional Law*, vol. II, Princeton, NJ: Princeton University Press, 2008b.
68. F. I. Michelman, *Brennan and Democracy*, Princeton, NJ: Princeton University Press, 1999; F. I. Michelman, 'Suspicion, or the new prince', in C. Sunstein and R. A. Epstein (eds), *The Vote: Bush, Gore and the Supreme Court*, Chicago, IL: Chicago University Press, 2001; F. I. Michelman, 'The problem of constitutional interpretative disagreement: can "discourses of application" help?', in M. Aboulafia, M. Bookman and C. Kemp (eds), *Habermas and Pragmatism*, New York: Routledge, 2002; F. I. Michelman, 'Is the constitution a contract for legitimacy?', *Review of Constitutional Studies*, 8(2), 2003, 101–18; F. I. Michelman, 'The integrity of law. Ida's way: constructing the respect-worthy governmental system', *Fordham Law Review*, 72, 2003–4, 345–62.
69. V. C. Jackson and M. Tushnet, *Comparative Constitutional Law*, New York: Foundation Press, 2006, p. 478.
70. G. Vergotinni, *Derecho Constitucional Comparado*, Barcelona: Espasa Calpe, 1983, p. 28.
71. M. Aragón Reyes, *Teoría del Neoconstitucionalismo, Ensayos escogidos, AAVV*, Madrid: Trotta, 2007, p. 39.
72. J. Habermas, *Theorie des kommunikativen Handelns, vol. 1: Handlungsrationalität und gessellschaftliche Rationaliserung*, Frankfurt am Main: Suhrkamp Verlag, 1981, p. 455.
73. As quoted in V. C. Jackson and M. Tushnet, *Comparative Constitutional Law*, New York: Foundation Press, 2006, p. 259.
74. R. C. Post, *Constitutional Domains: Democracy, Community, Management*, Cambridge, MA: Harvard University Press, 1995.

75. *Ibid.*, p. 187.
76. F. I. Michelman, *Brennan and Democracy*, Princeton, NJ: Princeton University Press, 1999, p. 4.
77. *Ibid.*, p. 273.
78. J. A. Gardner, *Interpreting State Constitutions: A Jurisprudence of Function in a Federal System*, Chicago, IL: University of Chicago Press, 2005, p. 175.
79. *Ibid.*, p. 176.
80. *Ibid.*, p. 176.
81. Available at: www.servat.unibe.ch/icl/sw00000_.html, accessed 5 April 2010.
82. Available at: www.servat.unibe.ch/icl/au00000_.html, accessed 5 April 2010.
83. Available at: www.servat.unibe.ch/icl/it00000_.html, accessed 5 April 2010.
84. Available at: www.servat.unibe.ch/icl/pt00000_.html; www.servat.unibe.ch/icl/sp00000_.html; www.servat.unibe.ch/icl/ro00000_.html.
85. Available at: www.servat.unibe.ch/icl/hu00000_.html, accessed 5 April 2010.
86. Madison, *The Federalist Papers* 10, 37, 50. Thomas Jefferson to James Madison, in J. P. Boyd (ed.), *The Papers of Thomas Jefferson*, Princeton, NJ: Princeton University, 1950. I consider in this paper that American constitutionalism started in 1787 as a sort of big bang of the American constitutionalist experiment. Other authors might suggest that the American constitutional tradition is more critically tied to the events and moral-religious-legal context leading to the execution of Charles I in 1649; in connection with this, see D. L. Holmes, *The Faiths of the Founding Fathers*, New York: Oxford University Press, 2006 and D. Lutz, *The Origins of American Constitutionalism*, Baton Rouge, LA: Louisiana University Press, 1988.
87. V. C. Jackson and M. Tushnet, *Comparative Constitutional Law*, New York: Foundation Press, 2006, p. 213.
88. See *Stanford Encyclopedia of Philosophy*, available online at: plato.stanford.edu.
89. J.-J. Rousseau, *The Social Contract or Principles of Political Right*, ed. R. Maynard, Great Books of the Western World, 38, Montesquieu, Rousseau, Chicago, IL: Encyclopaedia Britannica, 1954, p. 387.
90. *Ibid.*, p. 423.
91. *Ibid.*, p. 391.
92. *Ibid.*, p. 392.
93. *Ibid.*, p. 410.
94. *Ibid.*, p. 410.
95. G. F. Gaus, *Justificatory Liberalism: An Essay on Epistemology and Political Theory*, Oxford: Oxford University Press, 1996, p. 204.
96. W. T. Bell, 'Graduated consent theory, explained and applied', 2009 available at: http://works.bepress.com/tom_bell/2, accessed 20 September 2010.
97. F. I. Michelman, 'Is the constitution a contract for legitimacy?' *Review of Constitutional Studies*, 8(2), 2003, 120.

98. *Ibid.*, p. 120.
99. *Ibid.*, p. 121.
100. *Ibid.*, p. 121.
101. *Ibid.*, p. 127.
102. *Ibid.*, p. 127.
103. D. Hume, *Essays, Moral, Political, and Literary (Of Civil Liberty)*, Indianapolis, IN: Liberty Found Books, 1985, p. 154.
104. *Ibid.*, p. 155.
105. V. C. Jackson and M. Tushnet, *Comparative Constitutional Law*, New York: Foundation Press, 2006, p. 292.
106. R. Barnett, 'Restoring the lost constitution, not the constitution in exile', *Fordham Law Review*, 75, 2006, 669.
107. *Ibid.*, p. 9.
108. *Ibid.*, p. 11.
109. *Ibid.*, p. 11.
110. *Ibid.*, p. 15.
111. J. Habermas, *Between Facts and Norms: Contributions to a Discourse Theory of Law and Democracy*, Boston, MA: MIT Press 1998.
112. *Ibid.*, p. 86.
113. R. Barnett, 'Restoring the lost constitution, not the constitution in exile', *Fordham Law Review*, 75, 2006, 12.
114. *Ibid.*, p. 86.
115. *Ibid.*, p. 122.
116. A. Abat i Ninet and J. Monserrat Molas, 'From popular sovereignty to constitutional sovereignty?' Workshop paper, AAPS, Texas A&M, 22–4 October 2009, pp. 510–31.
117. F. I. Michelman, *Brennan and Democracy*, Princeton, NJ: Princeton University Press, 1999, p. 87.
118. J. Habermas, *Between Facts and Norms: Contributions to a Discourse Theory of Law and Democracy*, Boston, MA: MIT Press, 1998, p. 87.
119. *Ibid.*, p. 87.
120. J. Habermas, *Theorie und Praxis*, Berlin: Hermann Luchterland Verlag, 1969.
121. J. Habermas, *The Theory of Communicative Action, vol. II: Lifeworld and System: A Critique of Functionalist Reason*, Boston, MA: Beacon Press, 1985.
122. J. Habermas, *Die Nachholende Revolution*, Frankfurt am Main: Suhrkamp Verlag, 1990a.
123. M. Rosenfeld and A. Arato, *Habermas on Law and Democracy: Critical Exchanges*, Berkeley, CA: University of California Press, 1998, p. 5.
124. J. Habermas, *Between Facts and Norms: Contributions to a Discourse Theory of Law and Democracy*, Boston, MA: MIT Press, 1998, p 138.
125. J. Habermas, 'Three problems of social organisation: institutional law and economics meets Habermasian law and democracy', *Cambridge Journal of Economics*, 26, 2002, 501–20.

126. J. Habermas, *Between Facts and Norms: Contributions to a Discourse Theory of Law and Democracy*, Boston, MA: MIT Press, 1998, p. 175.

127. J. Nedelsky, 'The puzzle of modern constitutionalism', *Ethics*, 104, 1994, 500–15.

128. B. Ackerman and C. Rosenkrantz, *Fundamentos y alcances del control judicial de constitucionalidad*, Madrid: Centro de Estudios Constitucionales, 1991, p. 15.

129. D. Herzog, 'Democratic credentials', *Ethics*, 104(3), 1994, 467–79.

130. R. A. Posner, 'Democracy and dualism', *Transition*, 56, 1992, 68–79.

131. B. Ackerman and C. Rosenkrantz, *Fundamentos y alcances del control judicial de constitucionalidad*, Madrid: Centro de Estudios Constitucionales, 1991, p. 15.

132. B. S. Jackson, *Making Sense in Law: Linguistic, Psychological and Semiotic Perspectives*, Liverpool: Deborah Charles Publications, 1995.

133. N. Luhmann, *Die Wirtschaft der Gesellschaft*, Frankfurt am Main: Suhrkamp Verlag, 1988.

134. C. Hutton, *Language, Meaning and the Law*, Edinburgh: Edinburgh University Press, 2009.

135. H. Arendt, *On Revolution*, London: Faber & Faber, 1963, pp. 125–6.

136. J. Habermas, *Between Facts and Norms: Contributions to a Discourse Theory of Law and Democracy*, Boston, MA: MIT Press, 1998.

137. E. Pattaro, *A Treatise of Legal Philosophy and General Jurisprudence*, Heidelberg: Springer Verlag, 2009, p. 9.

138. B. Ackerman, *We the People: Foundations*, Cambridge, MA: Belknap Press of Harvard University Press, 1993.

139. J. Derrida, *Rogues: Two Essays on Reason*, Stanford, CA: Stanford University Press, 2005; J. Derrida, *Séminaire la Bête et le Souverain, I (2001–2002)*, Paris: Galilée, 2008.

140. M. D. Adler, 'Popular constitutionalism and the rule of recognition: whose practices ground US law?', *Northwestern University Law Review*, 100(2), 2006, 719–806.

141. H. L. A. Hart, *The Concept of Law*, Oxford: Clarendon Press, 1986, as quoted in M. D. Adler, 'Popular constitutionalism and the rule of recognition: whose practices ground US law?', *Northwestern University Law Review*, 100(2), 2006, 719–806.

142. M. D. Adler, 'Popular constitutionalism and the rule of recognition: whose practices ground US law?', *Northwestern University Law Review*, 100(2), 2006, 721–805.

143. H. L. A. Hart, *The Concept of Law*, Oxford: Clarendon Press, 1986, as quoted in M. D. Adler, 'Popular constitutionalism and the rule of recognition: whose practices ground US law?', *Northwestern University Law Review*, 100(2), 2006, 719–806.

144. S. J. Shapiro, 'What is the rule of recognition (and does it exist)?', *Yale Law School, Public Law & legal Theory Research paper series*, Research

paper No. 181, 2008, available at: papers.ssrn.com/abstract#1304645, accessed 20 September 2011.

145. M. D. Adler, 'Popular constitutionalism and the rule of recognition: whose practices ground US law?', *Northwestern University Law Review*, 100(2), 2006, 721.

146. S. J. Shapiro, 'What is the rule of recognition (and does it exist)?', *Yale Law School, Public Law & legal Theory Research paper series*, Research paper No. 181, 2008, p. 3, available at: papers.ssrn.com/abstract#1304645, accessed 20 September 2011.

147. *Ibid.*

148. L. Green, 'The concept of law revisited', *Michigan Law Review*, 94, 1996, 1687, 1691–2.

149. M. D. Adler, 'Popular constitutionalism and the rule of recognition: whose practices ground US law?', *Northwestern University Law Review*, 100(2), 2006, 722.

150. *Ibid.*, p. 722.

151. *Ibid.*, p. 725.

152. As quoted in Adler, 'Popular constitutionalism and the rule of recognition', and Kramer, *The People Themselves*.

153. M. D. Adler, 'Popular constitutionalism and the rule of recognition: whose practices ground US law?', *Northwestern University Law Review*, 100(2), 2006, 727.

154. H. L. A. Hart, *The Concept of Law*, Oxford: Clarendon Press, 1986; D. Gerber, 'Levels of rules and Hart's concept of law', *Mind*, 81(321), 1972, 102–5.

155. S. J. Shapiro, 'What is the rule of recognition (and does it exist)?', *Yale Law School, Public Law & legal Theory Research paper series*, Research paper No. 181, 2008, p. 4, available at: papers.ssrn.com/abstract#1304645, accessed 20 September 2011.

156. *Ibid.*, p. 10.

157. *Ibid.* See, for example, US Constitution, Article V.

158. S. J. Shapiro, 'What is the rule of recognition (and does it exist)?', *Yale Law School, Public Law & legal Theory Research paper series*, Research paper No. 181, 2008, p. 5, available at: papers.ssrn.com/abstract#1304645, accessed 20 September 2011.

159. M. S. Kuo, 'Cutting the Gordian knot of legitimacy theory? An anatomy of Frank Michelman's presentist critique of constitutional authorship', *International Journal of Constitutional Law*, 7(4), 2009, 683–714.

160. *Ibid.*, p. 687.

161. F. I. Michelman, 'Constitutional authorship', in L. Alexander (ed.), *Constitutionalism: Philosophical Foundations*, Cambridge: Cambridge University Press, 1998, as quoted in M. S. Kuo, 'Cutting the Gordian knot of legitimacy theory? An anatomy of Frank Michelman's presentist critique of constitutional authorship', *International Journal of Constitutional Law*, 7(4), 2009, 683–714.

162. F. I. Michelman, 'Constitutional authorship', in L. Alexander (ed.), *Constitutionalism: Philosophical Foundations*, Cambridge: Cambridge University Press, 1998, pp. 66–7.

163. *Ibid.*, p. 70.

164. P. W. Kahn, *The Reign of Law: Marbury v. Madison and the Construction of America*, New Haven, CT: Yale University Press, 1997, as quoted in M. S. Kuo, 'Cutting the Gordian knot of legitimacy theory? An anatomy of Frank Michelman's presentist critique of constitutional authorship', *International Journal of Constitutional Law*, 7(4), 2009, 683–714.

165. *Ibid.*, p. 710.

166. Available at: http://www.stjornlagathing.is/english, accessed 20 September 2011.

167. B. Z. Tamanaha, *Law as a Means to an End: Threat to the Rule of Law*, New York: Cambridge University Press, 2006.

4

Legal Violence

INTRODUCTION

> Constitutional violence is violence nonetheless; it crushes and kills with
> a steadfastness equal to a violence undisciplined by legitimacy.[1]

This chapter analyses the relationship between violence, legitimacy and law, and constitutionalism from a theoretical perspective. The first issue that arises in the study of this question is why the people obey the law, and the role that legitimacy plays in voluntary compliance. The doctrine answers this question with various theories, such as the 'habit of obedience', 'risk of punishment' or the role of authority. After considering this issue, the chapter deals with the intimate and long-standing relationship between violence and law. The starting point is a definition of legal violence and the role that legitimacy plays in order to convert plain into legal, and therefore, legitimate violence. The open debate between Cover, Derrida, Benjamin and Sarat on one side, and Kelsen, Ross and Hart on the other, will initiate this section. Is violence part of the legal content or is it only a way to enforce or apply law? Is it an internal feature of law or an external phenomenon?

The description of the violent character of law begins with a historical analysis, starting from Hebrew law and going on to the role that violence played in the law's understanding and conceptualisation in Athens and especially in Rome. I contend that it is necessary to analyse the evolution of law and violence to achieve a comprehensive description of legal violence. Concepts such as *vis* and *vindicatio* help us to understand what law was and what law is now, and how our norms are conditioned by violence. Because the final object of this book is constitutional violence, it is also necessary to pay special attention to the eighteenth and nineteenth centuries, when modern constitutionalism was born, conditioned by revolutions, blood and extreme violence. Since its origins, the constitution has been closely related to violence, and nowadays there is little or no exception, although violence is manifested in different conducts.

This chapter is built on the symbioses of constitution/violence, how legal violence is used by constitutionalism, why a constitution without legitimacy means plain violence, and how this violent implementation is considered 'legitimate' by the enforcers and those within the law. What happens when there is a clear lack of people's consent or will? What happens if a judicial decision clearly contradicts the will of the people or their representatives?

As we will see, violence affects law in different manners, in different spheres, internally as a feature of law, but also externally in the process of codification or the determination, interpretation and enforcement of legal meaning. This chapter analyses these different influences and stages. The key point of the structure lies in the need to classify violence depending on how this phenomenon acts and affects law. This differentiation will help us to analyse how violence interacts in the *nomos* of constitutionalism, and also to define and isolate concrete constitutional violent practices.

The conceptual study of legal violence is segmented into four main groups: (a) conceptual legal violence, focusing on the theoretical construction of law and its violent nature; (b) legal meaning, dealing with how legal violence affects the process of codification; (c) interpretative violence; and, finally, (d) law enforcement, examining how legal violence affects the law's enforcement process.

The modern nation-state has successfully linked law to violence not because government managed to monopolise the legitimate means of coercion, but because the modern nation-state rests on the oldest form of realising meaning in the West: sacrifice.[2] This monopolisation does not tend to protect just and legal ends, but instead it protects the law itself.[3] All these elements together, violence, force and sacrifice, affect decisively the collective subconscious of the people. One of the effects of this sort of normalisation is to believe the convictions of constitutional law, which considers popular politics by nature dangerous and arbitrary; that 'tyranny of the majority' is a pervasive threat, that a democratic constitutional order is therefore precarious and highly vulnerable, and that substantial checks on politics are necessary lest things fall apart.[4]

LEGAL VIOLENCE: CONCEPTUAL APPROACH

Fitzpatrick contends that:

> in its narrow perhaps popular sense, violence is equated with unrestrained physical violence. A standard history of the West would connect a decline in violence with an increase in civility. Others would see civility itself as a transformed violence, as a constraining even if not immediately coercive discipline. The dissipation of simple meaning is heightened in recent sensibilities where violence is discerned in the denial of the uniqueness or even existence of the other.[5]

Legal Compliance

> There are two great dangers in the use of violence which, if not guarded
> against may easily defeat the ends, no matter how exalted ... Unless very
> stringent control is exercised by representative organs of the community
> over the forces and instruments of violence, the latter may set themselves
> up as the ruling power and oppress the community in the name of their
> ultimate interests.[6]

Prior questions concerning the analysis of the relationship between legitimacy, violence and law include: why do people obey the law?; do the people
comply with the law voluntarily?; is legitimacy a normative question, and
does legality necessarily assume legitimacy?[7]

The question of legitimacy may be resolved if we implement legislative
policies allowing people to feel that they are real authors or participants in
the codification process. Tyler states correctly that social control refers
specifically to altering the behaviour of citizens by manipulating access to
valued social resources or by delivering or threatening to deliver sanctions.
Legal authorities attempt to modify behaviour by rewarding compliance with
the rules and punishing or threatening to punish the violation of rules.[8]

Constitutional authorities are not an exception. A norm without compliance is not a valid norm, and a constitution without enforcement is not a
constitution. In this respect, the state needs to enforce constitutional dispositions and principles, and nobody can escape constitutional domination.
The point is that our system presumes that a constitution is legitimate and,
therefore, any attempt to demonstrate the opposite is to set oneself up as a
target of constitutional violence.

When Tyler states that the assumption that legitimacy enhances compliance has traditionally been accepted by lawyers and social scientists, but is
supported by no convincing data, he omits to say that legitimacy is the only
way to differentiate legal violence and plain violence. However, Tyler goes
on to say that:

> Legitimacy is a particularly important normative factor, for it is believed to
> be the key to the success of legal authorities. If authorities have legitimacy
> they can function effectively; if they lack it, it is difficult and perhaps
> impossible for them to regulate public behavior. As a result, those interested
> in understanding how to maintain the social system have been concerned
> with identifying the conditions that promote legitimacy ... people obey the
> law if they believe it is legitimate, not because they fear punishment.
> Lawmakers and law enforcers would do much better to make legal systems
> worthy of respect than try to instill fear of punishment.[9]

At this point it is important to note the 'power of conviction' that
professes legal violence in its many forms, and the intimate relationship

between violence and law. The general link between law and violence and the ways that law manages to work its lethal will, to impose pain and death while remaining aloof and unstained by the deeds themselves, is still an unexplored and hardly noticed mystery in the life of the law.[10] As Sarat and Kearns affirm, violence, as a fact and a metaphor, is integral to the constitution of modern law, and that law is a creature of both literal violence, and imaginings and threats of force, disorder and pain.[11] In the absence of such images and threats there is no law.[12]

Law's violent constitution does not end with the establishment of a legal order, but once established, law is maintained through force; it is maintained as an apparatus of violence that disorders, disrupts and re-positions pre-existing relations and practices all in the name of an allegedly superior order. That order demonstrates its 'superiority' in ferocious displays of force, and in subjugating, colonising, 'civilising' acts of violence.[13] Chapter 5, below, discusses constitutional examples of these different types of legal violence, for example, literal or textual violence, when a constitutional text juridifies and legitimates violence against the 'others', those qualified as 'outlaws'. There is a full submission to a superior reason, to a single and official *raison d'être*. But I contend that democratic legitimacy must play some role in order to enforce the law, in order to apply legal violence when it appears as inevitable.

Legal positivism solves the question of legal legitimacy and why the people obey the law in different ways. Some of the most important scholars of this doctrine simply assume that legality implies legitimacy and, therefore, we must obey the law because it is always legitimate. Raz analysed legitimate authority and also the obligation to obey the law. He considered that the law claims our allegiance and obedience, and every legal system claims authority.[14] This author pointed out that the paradoxical nature of authority can assume different forms, but all of them concern the alleged incompatibility of authority with reason and autonomy. Then the author, studying the nature of authority, claimed that such arguments do not challenge *de facto* authority, but rather the possibility of legitimate, justified *de jure* authority.[15] An application of Raz's definition of legitimate authority to the constitutional sphere will be more or less that the constitution must contain a justified effective authority. Raz continued by linking legitimacy to consent and this effective authority should be preserved or obeyed (because it is legitimate).[16] Raz considered that there is an important difference between the use of brute force to get one's way and the same done with a claim of right. Only the latter can qualify as an effective or *de facto* authority, and therefore we need to analyse the notion of non-relativised authority.[17]

Following this argumentation, the use of force with a claim of right is justified because of the legitimacy of the right. But legality and legitimacy are two different notions. Therefore, when public institutions are enforcing a law and that law is not endorsed by the people, the enforcement is simply violence. In these cases, law and constitutions are obeyed because of the fear of legal, but not legitimate, violence.

Raz considered that a rule that is not legally valid is not a legal rule at all. A valid law is a law, an invalid law is not.[18] Can a valid legal rule be illegitimate? In the answer to this question lies my main concern, postulated by Raz. How can we speak about legal validity without a link to 'we the people?' I agree with Raz when he affirms that there is no obligation to obey the law; there is no absolute or conclusive obligation to obey the law, but also there is not a *prima facie* obligation to obey it.[19] The author also claims that one should not expect a good law to give rise to an obligation to obey it; the obligation to obey the law implies that the reason to do that which is required by law is the very fact that it is so required.[20] Then Raz states that this should be part of the reason to obey.

On 28 June 1935, the Ministry of Justice of the Third Reich revised Paragraph 175 of the criminal code. The revisions provided a legal basis for extending Nazi persecution of homosexuals. Ministry officials expanded the category of 'criminally indecent activities between men' to include any act that could be construed as homosexual.[21] Then to respect 'decent activities between men' would be a *legal* and *valid* goal (in positivist terms) and may be understood at least as a part of the reason to obey Paragraph 175. Therefore, it would seem that the codification process is essentially the only way to assure some guarantees to achieve a legitimate reason to obey the law, to claim legitimate authority regardless of the final content of the norm. We can find less dramatic examples to stress the necessity of an extra-legal factor in order to consider a goal as valid and legal. Assuredly, this criticism is addressed to the doctrinal school of positivism.

Raz finally states:

> Most people have good prudential reasons to obey the law most of the time. There is the risk of incurring legal sanctions, criminal or other, which are unwelcome to most people most of the time, and there are numerous other 'social sanctions' which, though affecting different people in different ways and to different degrees, affect most people to a considerable extent. Furthermore, all those reasons are of the right kind. They are reasons to do that which the law requires because it requires it; hence they are unlike many moral reasons which are reasons to do that which the law requires for grounds not dependent on the fact that the law requires them.[22]

These prudential reasons to obey the law (Raz) are violence, threat and force. Once law is enforceable, people do not challenge its allegiance and over time law becomes consolidated and strengthened by other public institutions and practices. The normalisation process culminates. Raz does not pay particular attention to the non-moral 'prudential reasons' to obey the law, avoiding the possibility of an in-depth analysis of the violent character of law. As a conclusion of this point we can mention Derrida's work; quoting Montaigne, he states: 'that laws keep up their good standing not because they are just, but because they are laws: that is the mystical foundation of their authority, they have no other ... One obeys (laws) not because they are just but because they have authority.'[23]

Another very well-known theory to answer the question of why the people obey the law is Hart's 'habit of obedience'.[24] Hart presents his theory in relation to sovereignty. His first concern is the idea of a habit of obedience, which is all that is required on the part of those to whom the sovereign's laws apply.[25] He inquires whether such a habit is sufficient to account for two salient features of most legal systems: the continuity of the authority to make law possessed by a succession of different legislators, and the position occupied by the sovereign above the law, who created law for others and so imposes legal duties or 'limitations'.[26]

Hart notes the similarity between social rules and habits:

> in both cases the behavior in question must be general, though not necessarily invariable. But though there is this similarity there are three salient differences. First, for the group to have a habit it is enough that their behavior in fact converges. Deviation from the regular course need not be a matter for any form of criticism ... and pressure differs with different types of rule ... The second difference between habit and social norm is that where there are such rules, not only is such criticism in fact made, but deviation from the standard is generally accepted as a good reason for making it. Criticism for deviation is regarded as legitimate or justified in this sense, as are demands for compliance with the standards when deviation is threatened. The third feature is related to the internal aspects of rules. When a habit is general in a social group, this generality is merely a fact about the observable behavior of most of the group.[27]

With this differentiation Hart confronts 'legal habit' and 'social habit' and, therefore, the pressure of the legal system is different from that of the social one.

As Hart recognises that the sovereign is often onerous, and the temptation to disobey and the risk of punishment are considerable, it is hardly to be supposed that obedience, though generally rendered as such, is a 'habit' in the full or most usual sense of the word.[28] This risk or threat of punishment is one of the legal forms of violence discussed in this chapter. Raz's 'prudential forms' and Hart's 'risk of punishment' are in fact closely related conceptions and different ways to designate legal threats and tools to normalise patterns of obedience. There is a gradual affection of violence. It is this violence that generates obedience, the habit and the unity required by the sovereign, at least in the first instance. Constitutive rules that determine who the legal officials are and what procedures must be followed in creating new legal rules, 'are not commands habitually obeyed, nor can they be expressed as habits of obedience to persons'.[29] I agree with Raz and Hart when they define the theory as coercive orders where law affects human conduct in a non-optional or obligatory sense. The implementation of this requirement (obligation) determines the violent character of the law on a very initial and conceptual level.

Despite these different theories, it is very complicated to answer the question of why people obey the law with a single answer. Violence, coercion and appearance of legitimacy seem to play a determinant role in people's attitude. But when a law is not democratically legitimate we cannot claim obedience.

Violence as a Feature of Law

Before analysing legal-constitutional violence it is necessary to emphasise that there is a doctrinal sector that denies the existence of such violence. Some of these *deniers* are also well-known legal positivist scholars, who consider that once the violence is polished and rationalised legally, there is no coercion, threat or physical punishment equivalent to violence. Thus, they consider that legal 'legitimate' violence is not violence at all. For this doctrine legality always presupposes legitimacy and therefore, *per se*, legitimate violence is not violence. A good example of this doctrine is the work of Bobbio, who analysed three arguments to eliminate coercion as a characteristic feature of the concept of law, and to give a definition of law that does not depend on the idea of coercion.[30] These arguments are: (a) the general spontaneous observance of rules; (b) the existence in every legal system of rules without sanctions; and (c) the infinite regress (a legal rule is legal because it is sanctioned, the rule of the sanction which makes it legal must also be sanctioned, etc.).[31]

Despite Bobbio, I consider that law without violence is impossible. In this regard, Sarat states:

> Law depends on violence and uses it as a counterpunch to the allegedly more lethal and destructive violence situated just beyond law's boundaries. But the violence on which law depends always threatens the values for which law stands. Some of this violence is done directly by legal officials, some by citizens acting under a dispensation granted by law, and some by persons whose violent acts subsequently will be deemed acceptable ... Moreover, by equating the conditions of legal legitimacy with the masking [of law's

interpretive violence], much of jurisprudence promotes righteous indifference and, as a result, allows law's violence to continue unabated. Violence thus may be said to be integral to law in three senses: it provides the occasion and method for founding legal orders, it gives law (as a regulator of force and coercion) a reason for being, and it provides a means through which law acts.[32]

Law is not only maintained through violence, but is on some occasions created through violence, a source-founding violence. As Chapter 5 will demonstrate, violence, coercion and threat do not cease because they have legal coverage, but it is more reprehensible because it is law that determines who and what is considered outlawed, marginal and non-rationalised.

Violence has always been intimately related to law since its earliest origins; violence and law are intrinsic. Cover provides an excellent definition of jurisgenesis in Judaism's oldest rabbinic traditions. His analysis points out other examples of legal theology, and how authority was translated from the Hebrew word *Torah* and adopted in the Septuagint, the Greek Scriptures and post-scriptural writings as *nomos*, and then as the English phrase, 'the Law'.[33]

This violent connotation of law was also consubstantial in Athens. As Cohen contends, standard accounts of the history of legal institutions in Athens typically follow an evolutionary model: from an inherently unstable situation characterised by powerful aristocratic kinship groups, self-help and weak central institutions emerges a civic legal order capable of regulating the cycles of feud and violence to which the previous instability had inevitably given rise.[34] Legal stability was afforded by violence.

In literature, the moment in the institutional history of Athens at which this new legal order established itself is captured in Aeschylus' *Oresteia*, with its depiction of the foundation of the first Athenian homicide court, the Areopagus.[35] This dramatic foundational event represents the historical process by which the emerging polis wrested for itself the authority to enforce a final and binding resolution of disputes among its citizens.[36] With the introduction of the draconian homicide law in the last quarter of the seventh century, homicide, 'hitherto a source of blood feuds and vendettas, became a matter for resolution in a court of law'.[37] Cohen explains the role which enmity, revenge, envy and honour played in the appeals which Athenian litigants made to the values of the mass courts of untrained citizen-judges.[38] The author continues by stating that: 'In the defendant's strategy we find the argument that ... insults, rivalries, revenges, and violence are characteristic activities of certain kinds of men, and that such violence is simply a normal part of enmity and rivalry.'[39]

The symbiosis of law–violence is consolidated in Rome. This is important because it is in Rome that the basic foundations of the concept of law are established. Lintott summarises the relationship between violence and the law in Republican Rome in two main aspects: first, the acceptance and even prescription of self-help by law; and, second, the assumption by the law of the procedural character of self-help. Both things occurred in Rome and are significant for the Roman attitude towards violence, the first for obvious reasons, and the second because the formalisation of self-help in processes like *legis actio per manus iniectionem* and *vindicatio* show the intimate connection between *vis* (violence) and *ius* (law) that existed in the foundations of Roman law.[40] The author goes on to state that *vis* was a neutral concept, nearer to our 'force' than 'violence', so there was no difficulty in applying it to both illegal violence and legal self-help.[41] Important evidence on the relationship between law and violence is provided by Cicero's main argument on liberty to resist violence.[42]

The facts that Roman law incorporated and enforced law with violence, and that *vis* was consubstantial with the concept of law, are important because since then this symbiosis has not spread but goes deeper. The Romans did not regard political violence as mere primitive barbarism. Violence had always played a considerable part in settling private disputes, where it had been ritualised into legal process, but also remained in its natural form.[43] This ritualisation has remained intact until the present day, with the result that law cannot be understood without its violent character. Legal violence is not plain but legitimate violence.

In the late Republic, violence was used to force measures through an assembly, to influence the outcome of an election or trial, and to intimidate or even kill political opponents. Although a number of constitutional means were devised to check it and nullify its effects, these were not proof against persistent violence on a large scale.[44]

The Romans of the Republic seem genuinely to have considered it an essential constituent of *libertas* that a man should be allowed to use force in his personal interest, to secure what he believed to be his due. Consequently, the public Republican institutions did not even doubt the legitimacy of an extreme legal and constitutional violence. As Lintott concludes, the (Roman) constitution was unequalled in controlling violence. At the same time, the constitutional use of violence was encouraged, both by tradition and principle, and politicians applied these without foreseeing the consequences.[45]

The violence of the Roman Republic and its legal bond increased throughout the Middle Ages. In this regard the Holy Inquisition and its official and 'legal' coverage can be quoted as an example. Following this historical path of violence and law, Bartlett's analysis of enmity in medieval European legal systems argues that, as emerging national states were able to forbid the waging of private wars within their territories, private conflicts had to be fought primarily through litigation rather than violence.[46] The author continues by stating that:

this process should not be imagined as the self-unfolding of ideals of justice, but rather as an often bloody struggle for power among political elites in which ordinary citizens were, as often as not, hapless victims caught between king and seigneurs. Further, royal justice sought to displace local systems of mediation and adjudication which were often far more effective in resolving disputes. Indeed, royal justice often 'exacerbated disputes between individuals when local arbitration might have achieved successful reconciliation'.[47]

In this period, local communities might see little difference between the actions of royal officials who looted, raped and killed, and marauding seigneurs, unruly neighbours or common bandits.[48] The distinction between public and private violence was a rhetorical weapon of the monarchy as it entered, one contestant among many, an arena of conflicting powers and authorities.[49] This rhetorical weapon has changed from monarchy to oligarchy and official state dogma.

As Foucault remarks, 'Humanity does not gradually progress from combat to combat until it arrives at universal reciprocity, where the rule of law finally replaces warfare; humanity installs each of its violences in a system of rules and thus proceeds from domination to domination.'[50] Foucault defines the evolution of the relationship between violence and law through the analysis of the legal power to punish and the phenomenon of normalisation. The author centres his analysis on the most evident example of legal violence, criminal law, introducing a correlative history of the modern soul and of a new power to judge; a genealogy of the present scientific–legal complex from which the power to punish derives its bases, justifications and rules, from which it extends its effects and by which it masks its exorbitant singularity.[51] The work of Foucault is linked with the issue of this book not only because it focuses on legal criminal violence, but also because it introduces several examples of the cruelty of the sovereign in the eighteenth century (the century in which modern concepts of constitutionality arose). The work is also interesting because it shows how violence is constantly adapted in new eras.

In the eighteenth century the very excess of violence employed in institutions, such as public execution and torture, is one of the elements of its glory: the fact that the guilty man should moan and cry out under the blows is not a shameful side-effect, it is the very ceremonial of justice being expressed in all its force.[52] Torture was a strict judicial game and the public execution was to be understood not only as a judicial, but also as a political ritual. It belonged, even in minor cases, to the ceremonies by which power was manifested.[53] Foucault shows the link between the right to punish and the role of the sovereign, in this sense, to conceive this power as a consequence of the sovereign's right to declare war on its enemies.[54]

Punishment is enforced nowadays on the internal enemies that attack the constitution, the device of the dominating identity, class or stratum of the state, which is ultimately the state itself. Chapter 5, below, shows how the state uses constitutions as a device to normalise all non-official identities, by inflicting legal and political violence. This is the consequence of the new sovereign, the constitution. Therefore, there are two different spheres for inflicting the dose of required normalisation on the outlaw: the first, is basically dominated by the criminal code and judicial interpretation, and the second, is ruled by the constitutional-political apparatus.

Foucault then affirms that the Enlightenment was soon to condemn public torture and execution as an 'atrocity', a term that was often used to describe it, but without any critical intention, by jurist themselves. Furthermore, the atrocity of a crime was also the violence of the challenge flung at the sovereign; it was that which would move him to make a reply whose function was to go further than this atrocity, to master it, to overcome it by an excess that annulled it.[55]

Foucault continues, expounding that at the time of the Enlightenment it was not as a theme of positive knowledge that man was opposed to the barbarity of public executions, but as a legal limit: the legitimate frontier of the power to punish. Not that which must be reached in order to alter him, but that which must be left intact in order to respect him.[56] In the late eighteenth century there was a legal punitive reform. Crimes seemed to lose their violence, while punishments, reciprocally, lost some of their intensity, but at the cost of greater intervention. The new strategy was not to punish less, but to punish better; to punish with more universality and necessity; to insert the power to punish more deeply into the social body.[57] All this 'spirit' of violence had important influences on the new emerging revolutionary constitutions.

Bates remarks that the eighteenth century is usually looked to as the theoretical source for modern concepts of constitutionality, those political and legal forms that limit conflict. Yet the eighteenth century was also a period of almost constant war, within Europe and in the new global spaces of colonial rule. Surprisingly few commentators have established what connections there are between the violence of war and the elaboration of new ideas about constitutional limitation.[58] Bates goes on to contend that (in the eighteenth century) the civil forms of violence paralleled in intensity the great religious and political upheavals of the sixteenth and seventeenth centuries. In addition, all of these civil forms of violence were also developed in the Latin American emancipation processes. The founding constitutions of the new countries in Latin America – Uruguay and Ecuador in 1830, Chile in 1833 and Argentina in 1853 – were affected by legal violence in two main aspects: (1) these constitutions were the result of a war and a revolution against the European metropolis; and (2) Enlightenment and Jacobin French violence, the legal coverage of which had great influence on the founding fathers of Latin America. In this regard, in the larger spaces of conflict, the European practice of limited war broke down entirely, as states sought to annihilate their enemies or violently transform them into an image of themselves. Indeed, civil war, particularly in revolutionary France, mirrored and perhaps even exceeded the unrestrained violence of this inter-state warfare.[59] As a sort of rationalisation, the Enlightenment ideal, as a source, helped to fuel the totalising violence of the revolutionary period.[60]

To the Enlightenment's violence must be added the 'spectres of the Jacobin Terror', as Duverger states that recourse to violence was more serious and more frequent than before 1789, during a century in which France suffered the bloodiest repression and revolution in Western Europe.[61] The official Terror intended for the repression of internal enemies reigned throughout 1793 and 1794, and terror was widely used during the nine-teenth century.[62] Jacobin constitutionalism makes the use of violence one of its main resources to enforce unity. The Terror was 'legally legitimised' with the Ventôse Decrees of year II, which defined the adversary to the Revolution.[63] The seed of the Terror was still alive and linked to law, and it was exported around the world in the eighteenth century with the French constitutionalist pattern.

After the First World War, jurists (whatever their political tendencies) had to reconceptualise the foundations of state authority as the new state structures confronted social and economic crises that threatened the state from within, as these crises entered the domain of representational parlia-mentary politics, and the plural institutions of the new administrative state had to confront crises directly.[64] As we will see in the examples of Chile and Turkey analysed in Chapter 5, the lack of consensus and legitimacy of the French Third Republic are reproduced identically in these cases, where the only way to achieve legitimacy was through legal violence. French national sovereignty instead of popular sovereignty is reproduced as an attempt to normalise, juridify and objectivise non-official identities or outlaw nationa-lities. In the afore-mentioned examples, as in 1870s France, the classic notion of reasons of state was reconfigured as a juridical concept, in a new constitution that juridified the new state, and in the ideal of order and tranquillity in the nation conceived as a whole. This sacred political unity was enforced with all the state's powers and denied any unofficial identity, thereafter described as outlawed. The executive power of the state ought to be considered (legally and politically) the genuine representative of unity. If the legislative assembly produced the laws, the fundamental law of the unitary nation could be defended only by the singular authority of the executive.[65]

Recent history has shown us that reasons of state are too powerful and unique, too totalitarian, and have been enforced by all public authorities and their ramifications. The ideal of the *Union Sacrée* was exported to other statuses with plural identities and its enforcement is the main 'question d'état'. Not only was the external enemy characterised as an alien and a morally inferior race, as Jeismann stated, but so too was the 'internal enemy', which was assimilated or voided by the constitutional reason enforcers. For the jurist, the legitimation of the state itself was linked to the conceptualisation of political unity, which rested on the Constitution. In this respect, the French conception of national sovereignty is the main example of this sort of violent constitutional assimilation. The French Third Republic[66] was grounded in a constitutional foundation, and it is important to remember that the new French state was contested from the very moment of its accidental birth: 'there was never any foundational consensus, even on the mythological plane'.[67] From the start it was recognised that republican legitimacy grounded in legality would be successful only if the spirit of law was inculcated in the citizenry itself. Considering that both the parliamentary production of statute law and the republican constitution itself were zones of intense contestation, jurists could not locate authority in the neutral sphere of legality.[68]

All this accumulation of violent practices covered by 'legality' and 'constitutionality' over the centuries, and the normalisation of the coercive character of law has implications for our current understanding of law. The state becomes central in the process of jurisgenesis only because an act of commitment is a central aspect of legal meaning, and violence is one extremely powerful measure and test of commitment.[69] Law does not merely curtail violence; it also inflicts pain and death.[70] War, which passes for the archetypal and original violence in pursuit of natural ends, is now in fact a piece of violence that serves to found law.[71]

Legal violence acts in different ways, in different spheres. The next section differentiates between the creation, interpretation and finally enforcement of legal meaning. This characterisation is based on the different planes on which violence acts. But all three approaches are forms of legal violence.

In conclusion, law and violence have been always related, to the point that violence can be considered as a defining element of law, and not only a way to enforce or apply legal concepts.

LEGAL VIOLENCE: INTERPRETATION AND ENFORCEMENT OF LEGAL MEANING

Legal Meaning

The various violent practices expounded in the previous section fit into Cover's categorisation of *nomos*, a normative universe.[72] This normative universe is a world of vision and commitment, of shared values and shared aspirations, rather than opposed interests. The task of law is to participate in that *nomos*, and to support the generation of this normative vision and the life of commitment; the task of law is to tolerate, respect and encourage normative diversity, even when that diversity generates opposition to the rules and prescriptions of law itself.[73] This *nomos* or normative universe is defined by the constitution.

Cover states that law is a resource in signification that enables us to submit, rejoice, struggle, pervert, mock, disgrace, humiliate or dignify.[74] We construct meaning in our normative world by using the irony of jurisdiction, the comedy of manners that is *malum prohibitum*, the surreal epistemology of due process.[75] Cover concludes that there is a radical dichotomy between the social organisation of law as power and the organisation of law as meaning.[76] This dichotomy is manifested in folk and underground cultures in even the most authoritarian societies. The uncontrolled character of meaning exercises a destabilising influence upon power.[77] Meaning is always greater than power can accommodate, and where the law resorts to power, it acknowledges the limits of meaning. Law includes not only a *corpus juris*, but also a language and a mythos – narratives in which the corpus is located, and narratives that 'establish paradigms for behavior' and describe 'a repertoire of moves – a lexicon of normative action'.[78] On the one hand, state law participates in the generation of normative meaning; on the other hand, state law plays in the domain of social control and uses violence to enforce just one (namely, its own) conception of order.[79]

In this context, the legal order of the United States is analysed in terms of a conflict between the generation of a multiplicity of legal meaning (juris-generation) and the maintenance of legal order (juris-pathology). In this way, the representation of violence takes place in the symbolic order of law, morals and politics.[80] Cover's differentiation determines the scope in which violence (founding or preserving) interacts.

Depending on the concrete situation we face one sort of violence or the other. Thus, it seems logical to consider that the Supreme Court applies a preserving violence, especially in Anglo-Saxon systems that do not consider the constitutional courts as negative legislators (Kelsen). This dichotomy may be associated with Derrida's and Benjamin's definition of two types of violence related to law: 'founding violence', that is, that which institutes and positions law (law-making violence); and 'preserving violence', which conserves, maintains, confirms and ensures the permanence and enforceability of law.

As Cover affirms in the domain of legal meaning, it is force and violence that are problematic, the processes through which meaning is created in contexts less clearly marked by force than are the state's decrees.[81] And again, the supreme law in our systems establishing this meaning is the constitution. If, as Cover states, legal meaning is always force and violence, the only way to mediate with this legal trend is to establish legitimate elements, and probably the best guarantee to dismiss the violent element is to avoid the exclusivity that allows a single unit (the state) to establish the concrete legal meaning and enforce its decision.

Analysing anti-slavery constitutionalism, Cover affirms that the Constitution permitted the states to create and perpetuate slavery as part of their municipal law. The Constitution guaranteed certain national protections for slavery where it did exist, and imposed upon citizens of free states the obligation to cooperate in the corrupt national bargain to aid and perpetuate slavery. The renunciation of constitutional obligation was an expressive act that created a boundary defining fidelity to the implications of perfectionist beliefs.[82] This is a magnificent example of constitutional violence. As we will see in Chapter 5, these violent patterns have evolved, but they persist. Slavery, capital punishment, non-recognition and social and economic exclusion are old and new ways to sentence the outlaw.

The conclusion drawn by Cover is that coercion is necessary for the maintenance of minimum conditions for the creation of legal meaning in autonomous interpretative communities.[83] This coercion is only one form of the relationship between law and violence, albeit a very important one because it affects the meaning and essence of law, its conceptual core. Coercion is normally claimed when one has been forced by another to act, or refrain from acting, against one's will. Coercive pressure can overcome one's will and make a particular course of action unreasonably costly.[84] Hegel affirms that force or coercion is, in its very conception, directly self-destructive because it is an expression of a will which annuls the expression or determinate existence of a will. Hence, force or coercion, taken abstractly, is wrong. Coercion is exhibited in the world of reality by the fact that coercion is annulled by coercion; it is thus shown to be not only right under certain conditions, but necessary, that is, as a second act of coercion which is the annulment of one that has preceded.[85]

In the normative universe legal meaning is created by simultaneous engagement and disengagement, identification and objectification.[86] Creating legal meaning, however, requires not only the movement of dedication and commitment, but also the objectification of that to which one is committed.[87] The community posits a law, external to itself, that it is committed to obeying and that it does obey in dedication to its understanding of that law. Objectification is crucial to the language games that can be played with the law and to the meanings that can be created out of it.[88] Cover's objectification is another way to express Weber's rationalisation or Foucault's normalisation. Law's violence is hardly separable from the rule of law itself,

from the deadening normality of bureaucratic abstractions and routine interpretative acts that claim for law a position beyond positioning and universality made plausible only by the systematic privileging of some voices and
silencing of others.[89] Consequently, the very fact of juridification is related
to violence. Interpretative violence, physical force and enforcement are other
manifestations of legal violence.

As Sarat and Kearns state, any theory of law must locate violence at the
centre of its concerns. It must examine law's devices for transforming and
concealing its violence, for covering its tracks and for turning lifeless words
into bloody acts of violence.[90] According to these authors the concept of
violence permits an evaluative critique only in the sphere of law and justice
or that of moral relations.[91]

There is no natural or physical violence; we can speak figuratively of
violence with regard to an earthquake or even to a physical ailment, but we
know that these are not cases of *Gewalt* (violence) able to give rise to a
judgment, before some instrument of justice.[92]

One must first recognise meaning in a violence that is not an accident
arriving from outside the law. That which threatens law already belongs to
it, to the right to law (*au droit au droit*), to the origin of law.[93] On some
occasions we can conceive the homogeneity of law and violence, violence as
the exercise of *droit* and *droit* as the exercise of violence.[94] In these situations
Cover's literature is extremely enlightening. However, Derrida considers
that violence does not consist essentially in exerting power or a brutal force
to obtain this or that result, but in threatening or destroying an order.[95] This
Derridian order can be related to Cover's Amish, Baptist or anti-slavery
nomos. Derrida continues, contending correctly that:

> What States fear (the State being law in the greatest force) is not so much
> crime, even on the grand scale of the Mafia or heavy drug traffic, as long as
> they transgress the law with an eye toward particular benefits, however impor-
> tant they may be. The State is afraid of fundamental, founding violence,
> that is, violence able to justify, to legitimate or to transform the relations of
> law, and so to present itself as having a right to law.[96]

The state's fear is psychotic and equates any challenge with the only valid
legality.

Lysander Spooner, a 'pure constitutionalist', was also aware of
constitutional violence. Spooner placed the relationship between law and
violence not on the symbolic level, but in a more empirical world:

> It is true that law may, in many cases, depends upon force as the means of
> its practical efficiency. But are law and force therefore identical in their
> essence? According to this definition ... a command to do injustice, is as

much law, as a command to do justice. All that is necessary, according to this definition, to make the command a law, is that it issue from a will that is supported by physical force sufficient to coerce obedience. Then, if mere will and power are sufficient, of themselves, to establish law – legitimate law – such law as judicial tribunals are morally bound, or even have a moral right to enforce – then it follows that wherever will and power are united, and continue united until they are successful in the accomplishment of any particular object, to which they are directed, they constitute the only legitimate law of that case, and judicial tribunals can take cognizance of no other.[97]

Spooner also presupposes legitimacy in legality. Because of this presumption, Spooner's statement does not set a clear differentiation between legitimate and illegitimate violence, but infers that legal violence simply does not exist. Slavery is, and has always been, unconstitutional, and it not only violates human rights.

Spooner defined law not only under his positivistic perspective but also under a utilitarian one. Law is not science, and therefore the author needed to conclude his statement by adding an extra-positivistic argument to condemn slavery. This positivistic argument was based in a sort of meta-constitution that will represent the spirit and main principles of the text.[98]

It would seem that Spooner analysed the relationship between law and violence from a different sphere from that of Cover, Derrida or Foucault, but if we really pay attention to the basis of the definition, we appreciate that Spooner highlighted the notion of power and law. As we have seen before, Foucault highlighted the evolution of the role of the sovereign in inflicting punishment. Then Foucault, in a very Hegelian way, introduced a new notion into this relationship: knowledge. Power and knowledge go together in order to impose a full normalisation. Foucault stated correctly that power produces knowledge, that power and knowledge imply one another; that there is no power without the correlative constitution of a field of knowledge.[99] This sort of full and total violence is not the main object of this book, but no legitimate constitutionalism is a positive expression of this rational dictatorship and a ground to exclude outlaws and non-'constitutional' identities of the system.

Interpretation

Torture was a strict judicial game.[100]

Kelsen's thesis on legal interpretation can be understood in two different ways: first, every act of applying law is an act of creating law in a formal sense, establishing as it does the source of a valid legal norm. Second, every act of applying law is an act of creating law in a material sense, too, introducing as it does new content into the law.[101] In other words, interpretation is an act of law creation, a way to configure meaning.

This section focuses on the first type of power attributed to magistrates in the application of law. Only the yet-to-come (*avenir*) will produce intelligibility or interpretability of this law. This readability will then be as little neutral as it is non-violent; one can say that the order of intelligibility depends in its turn on the established order that it serves to interpret.[102]

As Cover states:

> Legal interpretation takes place in a field of pain and death ... 'Interpretation' suggests a social construction of an interpersonal reality through language. But pain and death have quite other implications. Indeed, pain and death destroy the world that 'interpretation' calls up ... The deliberate infliction of pain in order to destroy the victim's normative world and capacity to create shared realities we call torture.[103]

With this statement Cover shows how legal violence affects individuals' daily lives; violence goes from a more general level to a strictly individual sphere. Interpretation is the way in which violence is applied and concretised; it is the way to individualise violence. It may seem that Cover focuses his work on interpretation because he is an American scholar, and in common law systems the power of a judge to interpret appears more extensive. However, totalising and violent phenomena in the interpretation sphere also extends into the Continental legal systems, because interpretation is an indispensable phenomenon related to law.

Cover uses martyrdom as a starting place to understand the nature of legal interpretation in contemporary American law, and therefore links US constitutional history with the act of rebellion.[104] The act was, in form, an essay in constitutional interpretation affirming the right of political independence from Great Britain.[105] In this sense, the model followed by constitutions around the world, and especially the constitutions of Latin America, were also affected by a violent act. As Cover goes on to state, and as we see below, revolutionary constitutional understandings are commonly staked in blood. In them, the violence of the law takes its most blatant form. However, the relationship between legal interpretation and the infliction of pain remains operative even in the most routine of legal acts.[106] The interpretation or conversations that are the preconditions for violent incarceration are themselves implements of violence.[107]

Cover continues:

> The violence of judges and officials of a posited constitutional order is generally understood to be implicit in the practice of law and government. Violence is so intrinsic to this activity, so taken for granted, that it need not

be mentioned. For instance, read the Constitution. Nowhere does it state, as a general principle, the obvious – that the government thereby ordained and established has the power to practice violence over its people ... It is, of course, also directly implicit in many of the specific powers granted to the general government or to some specified branch or official of it. E.g., U.S. Const. art. 1, § 8, cl. 1 ('Power to lay and collect Taxes ... and provide for the common Defence'); id., cl. 6 ('To provide for the Punishment of counterfeiting') ...[108]

Then Cover clearly defines that interpretation is a practical activity, a form of practical wisdom, to impose meaning on the institution and to reconstruct it in the light of that meaning. However, interpretation is within a system designed to generate violence, because legal interpretation is as a practice incomplete without violence and because it depends upon the social practice of violence for its efficacy.[109]

Violence is finally what legitimates interpretation, because without violence interpretation has no efficacy, and without efficacy there is no legitimacy. Legal interpretation can never be 'free'; it can never be the function of an understanding of the text or word alone. Nor can it be a simple function of what the interpreter conceives to be merely a reading of the 'social text'.[110] Legal interpretation occurs in the context of a state monopoly of legitimate violence, the violent activity of an organisation of people.[111] Common law scholars and jurisprudents have given excellent accounts of how judicial interpretation in general, and the Supreme Court in particular, have interpreted law and constitution undemocratically and violently. But this is not an exclusive feature of common law systems; in Continental systems constitutional courts have reproduced the same phenomenon.

Enforcement

As Derrida remarked, 'Applicability, "enforceability", is not an exterior or secondary possibility that may or may not be added as a supplement to law',[112] as the very term expresses in English, 'en*force*ment' is a clear recourse to force.

Derrida, in an excellent exercise, semantically analyses the term enforcement: 'to enforce law' or 'enforceability of the law or contract'. Force is essentially implied in the very concept of *justice as law*. The word enforceability reminds us that there is not a law that does not imply in itself, *a priori* in the analytic structure of its concept, the possibility of being 'enforced', applied by force.[113] There are, to be sure, laws that are not enforced, but there is no law without enforceability, and no applicability or enforceability of the law without force, whether this force be direct or indirect, physical or symbolic, exterior or interior, brutal or subtly discursive and hermeneutic, coercive or regulative, and so forth.[114] There is no law without force;

enforceability is not an exterior or secondary possibility. Force is mainly involved in the concept of justice as law, in justice that becomes law.[115] Pascal said: 'It is right that what is just should be followed; it is necessary that what is strongest should be followed.'[116]

Then Derrida, analysing this statement with regard to the force of law, states:

> The beginning of this fragment is already extraordinary, at least in the rigor of its rhetoric. It says that what is just must be followed (followed by consequence, followed by effect, applied, enforced) and that what is strongest must also be followed (by consequence, effect and so on). In other words, the common axiom is that the just and the strongest ... is 'just' in one case, 'necessary' in the other: 'It is just that what is just be followed [in other words, the concept or idea of the just, in the sense of justice, implies analytically and *a priori* that the just be followed, enforced, and it is just – also in the sense of "justesse" to think this way], it is necessary that what is strongest be enforced'.[117]

Not only is the meaning of law violent, as Bobbio and Cover have shown, but so is the legality that presumes legitimacy.

As I have remarked before in the conceptual configuration of legal violence, the violence that in the Middle Ages was legitimised by a divine order transferred the source of legitimacy from God to reason in the modern era. The theoretical constitutional construction characterised by violence has continued and justified its practices to build up a single valid reason. Consequently, to the legal violence defined by Cover, Sarat, and others, particular historical factors must be added to qualify the violent character of constitutional constructions. Revolutionary US and French constitutionalism, which have influenced the rest of the world's legal systems, have been conditioned from birth by extreme violence, and this clearly conditioned the core of constitutionalism.

Notes

1. A. Sarat and T. R. Kearns, *Law's Violence*, Ann Arbor, MI: University Michigan Press, 1993, p. 5.
2. P. W. Kahn, *Sacred Violence, Torture, Terror and Sovereignty*, Ann Arbor, MI: University of Michigan Press, 2008, p. 98.
3. J. Derrida, *Rogues: Two Essays on Reason*, Stanford, CA: Stanford University Press, 2005, p. 86.
4. L. Kramer, *The People Themselves: Popular Constitutionalism and Judicial Review*, Oxford: Oxford University Press, 2004, p. 243.
5. A. Sarat and T. R. Kearns, *Law's Violence*, Ann Arbor, MI: University of Michigan Press, 1993, p. 10.

6. *Encyclopedia of Social Sciences* as quoted in A. W. Lintott, *Violence in Republican Rome*, Oxford: Oxford University Press, 1968.

7. J. Derrida, 'Force of law: the mystical foundation of authority', *Cardozo Law Review*, 11, 1990, 925.

8. T. R. Tyler, *Why the People Obey the Law*, Princeton, NJ: Princeton University Press, 2006, p. 21.

9. *Ibid.*, p. 57.

10. A. Sarat and T. R. Kearns, 'A journey through forgetting: toward a jurisprudence of violence', in A. Sarat and T. R. Kearns (eds), *The Fate of Law*, Ann Arbor, MI: University Michigan Press, 1991, p. 211.

11. A. Sarat and T. R. Kearns, *Law's Violence*, Ann Arbor, MI: University Michigan Press, 1993, p. 1.

12. *Ibid.*, p. 1.

13. *Ibid.*, p. 3.

14. J. Raz, *The Authority of Law: Essays on Law and Morality*, Oxford: Oxford University Press, 1979, Preface.

15. *Ibid.*, p. 4.

16. *Ibid.*, p. 8.

17. *Ibid.*, p. 8.

18. *Ibid.*, p. 9.

19. *Ibid.*, p. 233.

20. *Ibid.*, p. 234.

21. See the United States Holocaust Memorial Museum, Persecution of Homosexuals in the Third Reich, available at: http://www.ushmm.org/wlc/en/article.php?ModuleId=10005261, accessed 25 April 2012.

22. J. Raz, *The Authority of Law: Essays on Law and Morality*, Oxford: Oxford University Press, 1979, p. 243.

23. J. Derrida, 'Force of law: the mystical foundation of authority', *Cardozo Law Review*, 11, 1990, 939.

24. H. L. A. Hart, *The Concept of Law*, Oxford: Clarendon Press, 1986.

25. *Ibid.*, p. 50.

26. *Ibid.*, p. 50.

27. *Ibid.*, p. 55.

28. *Ibid.*, p. 50.

29. *Stanford Encyclopedia of Philosophy*, available at: http://plato.stanford.edu/entries/austin-john, accessed 25 April 2012.

30. N. Bobbio, 'Law and force', *Monist*, 49(3), 1965, 321.

31. *Ibid.*, p. 324.

32. A. Sarat (ed.), *Law, Violence, and the Possibility of Justice*, Princeton, NJ: Princeton University Press, 2001, p. 3.

33. R. Cover, 'Nomos and narrative', *Harvard Law Review*, 97, 1983, 4–10.

34. D. Cohen, *Law, Violence and Community in Classical Athens*, Cambridge: Cambridge University Press, 1995, p. 3.

35. *Ibid.*, p. 3.

36. *Ibid.*, p. 3.
37. *Ibid.*, p. 16.
38. *Ibid.*, p. 87.
39. *Ibid.*, p. 138.
40. A. W. Lintott, *Violence in Republican Rome*, Oxford: Oxford University Press, 1968, p. 22.
41. *Ibid.*, p. 23.
42. Cicero, *The Orations of Marcus Tullius Cicero*, vol. 2, London: G. Bell, 1913–21.
43. A. W. Lintott, *Violence in Republican Rome*, Oxford: Oxford University Press, 1968, p. 175.
44. *Ibid.*, p. 204.
45. *Ibid.*, p. 208.
46. D. Cohen, *Law, Violence and Community in Classical Athens*, Cambridge: Cambridge University Press, 1995, p. 17.
47. *Ibid.*, p. 17.
48. *Ibid.*, p. 17.
49. *Ibid.*, p. 17.
50. M. Foucault, *Discipline and Punish: The Birth of the Prison*, London: Penguin, 1977.
51. *Ibid.*, p. 23.
52. *Ibid.*, p. 34.
53. *Ibid.*, p. 47.
54. *Ibid.*, p. 48.
55. *Ibid.*, p. 56.
56. *Ibid.*, p. 74.
57. *Ibid.*, p. 75.
58. D. Bates, 'Constitutional violence', *Journal of Law and Society*, 34(1), 2007, 14–30.
59. *Ibid.*, p. 15.
60. D. Bates, 'Political unity and the spirit of law: juridical concept of the state in the late Third Republic', *French Historical Studies*, 28(1), 2005, 69–101.
61. M. Duverger, *Le système politique français*, Paris: Thémis Science Politique, Presses universitaires de France, 1996, p. 55.
62. *Ibid.*, p. 56.
63. A. Mestre and P. Guttinger, *Constitutionnalisme jacobin et constitutionnalisme soviétique*, Paris: Presses universitaires de France, 1971, p. 66.
64. D. Bates, 'Political unity and the spirit of law: juridical concept of the state in the late Third Republic', *French Historical Studies*, 28(1), 2005, 69–101.
65. D. Barthélemy, *Critique textuelle de l'Ancien Testament*, 50/4, Fribourg: Academic Press Fribourg/Éditions Saint-Paul, 2005, p. 74.

66. The French Third Republic followed the defeat of Louis-Napoleon in the Franco-Prussian War in 1870, and lasted until the creation of the Vichy regime after the invasion of France by the German Third Reich in 1940.

67. D. Bates, 'Political unity and the spirit of law: juridical concept of the state in the late Third Republic', *French Historical Studies*, 28(1), 2005, 71.

68. *Ibid.*, p. 71.

69. R. Cover, 'Nomos and narrative', *Harvard Law Review*, 97, 1983, 11.

70. A. Sarat and T. R. Kearns, 'A journey through forgetting: toward a jurisprudence of violence", in A. Sarat and T. R. Kearns (eds), *The Fate of Law*, Ann Arbor, MI: University Michigan Press, 1991.

71. J. Derrida, 'Force of law: the mystical foundation of authority', *Cardozo Law Review*, 11, 1990, 999.

72. R. Cover, 'Nomos and narrative', *Harvard Law Review*, 97, 1983, 11.

73. A. Sarat (ed.), *Law, Violence, and the Possibility of Justice*, Princeton, NJ: Princeton University Press, 2001, p. 55.

74. R. Cover, 'Nomos and narrative', *Harvard Law Review*, 97, 1983, 11.

75. *Ibid.*, p. 9.

76. *Ibid.*, p. 18.

77. *Ibid.*, p. 18.

78. A. Sarat (ed.), *Law, Violence, and the Possibility of Justice*, Princeton, NJ: Princeton University Press, 2001, p. 56.

79. *Ibid.*, p. 57.

80. S. McVeigh, P. Rush and A. Young, 'A judgment dwelling in law: violence and the relations of legal thought', in A. Sarat (ed.), *Law, Violence, and the Possibility of Justice*, Princeton, NJ: Princeton University Press, 2001, p. 101.

81. R. Cover, 'Nomos and narrative', *Harvard Law Review*, 97, 1983, 25.

82. *Ibid.*, p. 36.

83. *Ibid.*, p. 44.

84. E. N. Yankah, 'The force of law: the role of coercion in legal norms', *University of Richmond Law Review*, 2007–8, 1218.

85. G. W. F. Hegel, *Philosophy of Right*, Oxford: Clarendon Press, 1942, p. 36.

86. *Ibid.*, p. 44.

87. *Ibid.*, p. 45.

88. *Ibid.*, p. 45.

89. A. Sarat and T. R. Kearns, 'A journey through forgetting: toward a jurisprudence of violence', in A. Sarat and T. R. Kearns (eds.), *The Fate of Law*, Ann Arbor, MI: University Michigan Press, 1991, p. 209.

90. *Ibid.*, p. 212.

91. J. Derrida, 'Force of law: the mystical foundation of authority', *Cardozo Law Review*, 11, 1990, 983.

92. *Ibid.*, p. 983.

93. *Ibid.*, p. 983.

94. *Ibid.*, p. 989.

95. *Ibid.*, p. 989.
96. *Ibid.*, p. 989.
97. *Ibid.*, p. 989.
98. See L. Spooner, 'A defence for fugitive slaves, against the Acts of Congress of February 12, 1793, and September 18, 1850', Boston, Bela Marsh, 25; Cornhill, 'The illegality of the trial of John W. Webster', 1850, 'A plan for the abolition of slavery', 'Address of the free constitutionalists', 'Letter to Charles Summer', available at: http://lysanderspooner.org/node/4, accessed 25 April 2012.
99. M. Foucault, *Discipline and Punish: The Birth of the Prison*, London: Penguin, 1977, p. 27.
100. *Ibid.*, p. 40.
101. E. Bulygin, 'Sentenza giudiziaria e creazione di diritto', *Revista Internazionale di Filosofia del Diritto*, 44, 1967, 200.
102. *Ibid.*, p. 200.
103. R. Cover, 'Violence and the world', *Yale Law Journal*, 95, 1995, 1601–29.
104. *Ibid.*, p. 1604.
105. *Ibid.*, p. 1604.
106. *Ibid.*, p. 1608.
107. *Ibid.*, p. 1611.
108. *Ibid.*, p. 1611.
109. *Ibid.*, pp. 1618–19.
110. *Ibid.*, p. 1613.
111. M. Constable, 'The silence of law: justice in Cover's "Field of pain and death"', in A. Sarat (ed.), *Law, Violence, and the Possibility of Justice*, Princeton, NJ: Princeton University Press, 2001.
112. J. Derrida, 'Force of law: the mystical foundation of authority', *Cardozo Law Review*, 11, 1990, 983.
113. *Ibid.*, p. 925.
114. *Ibid.*, p. 927.
115. *Ibid.*, p. 927.
116. *Ibid.*, p. 935.
117. *Ibid.*, p. 935.

5

Comparing Constitutional Violence

MAINTAINING AND FOUNDATIONAL CONSTITUTIONAL VIOLENCE

Doctrinae quidem verae esse possunt; sed auctoritas, non veritas, facit legem.[1]

This chapter is an empirical demonstration of current constitutional violence and how symbolic and theoretical constitutional violence affects people. It examines comparative constitutional violence and legal realism, and it shows why constitutional violence is important and looks at the theory and the practice.

The chapter begins with an example of American constitutional violence based on the application of the death penalty in Puerto Rico: in contravention of the articles of the Puerto Rican Constitution; the expressed will of the people; the declared position of Puerto Rico's elected politicians (governor, senate and municipalities); and, finally, in contravention of international human rights conventions. American constitutional violence is inflicted on Puerto Rico in two different ways: first, through the application of an extradition clause in the American constitution (inter-state rendition clause), which provides for the extradition of a criminal back to the state where he or she has committed a crime; and, second, through the enforcement of capital punishment on Puerto Rican soil, in contravention of the will of the people of Puerto Rico and the constitution of the Commonwealth of Puerto Rico. In both examples the American constitution is violently enforced.

French constitutional violence is also analysed in two interrelated cases; the first deals with the constitutional accommodation of the debate between 'national sovereignty' and 'popular sovereignty' and its consequences for the entire French legal system. This example reveals how French constitutional violence produces violent homogenisation through constitutional legitimacy. The second example is strict case law and shows how the state apparatus has interpreted and enforced national identity in everyday issues.

Turkish and Chilean constitutional violence are then analysed and shown to be clearly affected by the French understanding of constitutionalism and ethno-nationalism. The example of Turkish constitutional violence is divided into two parts: the first is based on the military tutelage of political institutions, constitutions and state democracy. The military played, and still play, a fundamental role in Turkish political and constitutional history, and this control has taken place without any democratic legitimacy and, furthermore, with extremely violent enforcement against political dissidents and ethnic minorities. The second example is based on the constitutional accommodation and enforcement of extreme ethnic nationalism.

In the case of Chilean constitutional violence, the analysis is based primarily on the role that Chilean constitutionalism has developed in relation to the indigenous peoples. The Constitution as a founding act replaced the sovereign, created a new state and people, and forced different minorities to assimilate into the new nation. The alternative to assimilation was extermination. The role of constitutionalism in Chile meant the juridification of a new political order. In other words, constitutionalism in Chile gave legal coverage for genocide. The Chilean example can be applied analogously to other South American constitutional systems, for example, Argentina, Uruguay, Colombia or Brazil. Lately some states have sought to address the role of Native Americans in their constitutional texts (Bolivia and Ecuador).

The last example analysed in this chapter is how Spanish constitutional violence may influence democracy. After a period of transition from a military Fascist dictatorship to a constitutional monarchy, the Spanish Constitution of 1978 seemed to juridify democracy, yet some shadows and legacies of the military past remained because the transition did not break totally with the past.

From a general theoretical perspective this chapter explores two types of constitutional violence. In the first of these, the so-called 'foundational violence', the constitution is more a symbol than a simple law. The constitution is understood as a founding act, creating a new identity, a new state, a new political order against the political, ethnic or racial reality that it faces. A clear example of this sort of violence was the South African constitutional bills before 1996. The new empire is founded and represented by the new document and its theological effect.

The foundational act meant the violent imposition of a new reality, of a new enlightenment, on the 'savages' or the 'colonised people', and the constitution gave legal 'legitimacy' to the enforcers of the new order. In this sense, the constitution represented not only the creation of a new political entity, but an oppressive tool. In our law schools and constitutional courts we tend to regard the constitution as a covenant, as the expression of legal and political agreement between different subnational, social or political realities and actors, but if the 'other' is excluded from the founding pact, becoming an outlaw, the constitution becomes a tool of oppression at the service of the new nation against the excluded.

A sort of deconstruction of this foundational violence is impossible, because two hundred years after the independence of Mexico, Chile, Colombia, Paraguay and Venezuela some of the ethnic and cultural minorities have been completely exterminated, and deconstruction would also imply a re-foundation of the state, not only a new constituent process, but also the birth of a new country.

A different typology of constitutional violent enforcement is 'maintaining violence', where the constitution represents the power of the 'metropolis' as it violently enforces its sovereignty in contravention of human rights and international law. The main difference from 'foundational violence' is that the state does not (specifically) use the constitution in order to create a new state to challenge other identities, as the state already existed before the constitution. In 'maintaining violence' the state uses the constitution as a new tool to expand its rationalisation. The constitution is understood more as an act of legislation. The American, French and Spanish cases are examples of this 'maintaining violence', while the Chilean and Turkish examples are considered 'foundational violence'. 'Maintaining violence' acts both internally and externally. Thus, the use of the state apparatus and the constitutional structure to deny fundamental rights to African Americans before the Civil Rights Act of 1964 and the civil rights movement is a good example of 'maintaining violence'.

The different topics discussed in this chapter (the death penalty in America, the identity phenomenon and national sovereignty in France, the birth of Turkey, settlement at the expense of the indigenous peoples of Chile, and the Spanish transition to democracy) have been analysed by various authors in several disciplines (political science, history and law). But none have focused on the role played by the constitution and its violent enforcement during these events, and how a constitutional text legitimises acts that contravene the main declarations of human rights. This self-attributed legitimacy generates an obvious collision between constitutional and human rights legitimacies. This chapter examines this phenomenon in each case from the perspective of comparative law in order to arrive at valid conclusions about the violent character of constitutions around the world.

This violent character in many cases normalises and legitimises such behaviour, and in this respect Continental and common law systems vary little.

Some of the examples analysed focus on the so-called meta-judicial concepts found in political and programmatic constitutional articles, as defined by Schmitt, and the effect of a positive constitution on decisive political decisions (i.e., Article 2 of the French Constitution of 1958), as well as the strict juridical consequences of constitutional violence (case law).

US CONSTITUTIONAL VIOLENCE: A CONSTITUTIONAL PARADOX

Constitutions are matched to values in order to justify and legitimise their violent implementation. There are many ways to instrumentalise legal documents. In each case the constitution juridifies a different value: 'civilisation', 'rationalisation', 'national unity', 'official culture', etc. As an example, the violent imposition of the American Constitution on the Native American nations was legitimised for reasons of 'civilisation'. The American Constitution juridified this rationality against a people considered to be illiterate 'savages'.

An example of American constitutional violence is also found in the application of the death penalty in Puerto Rico. Capital punishment is enforced on the island in contravention of the articles of the Puerto Rican Constitution, in defiance of the popular will, and in contravention of the US–Puerto Rico compact agreement (Public Law 600).

The death penalty has been one of the most discussed topics in American legal doctrine. The constitutionality or legality of the death penalty has engaged the attention of the courts and legislatures in the United States and elsewhere for several decades, and these debates have been intense.[2] The death penalty is the highest level of violence that the state can exercise; and the point of interest in this chapter lies in the violent enforcement of a constitutional clause. Cover's work is quite thoughtful and precise on the death penalty and its links with legal violence.[3] In 1972, in *Furman v. Georgia*,[4] the federal Supreme Court declared the unconstitutionality of forty statutes relating to the death penalty and suspended its application throughout the nation. In 1976, the same court in *Gregg v. Georgia*,[5] reinstated the death penalty in the federal jurisdiction and left state governments to decide whether or not to apply it in their jurisdictions. In 1994, Congress passed the Violent Crime Control and Law Enforcement Act,[6] which expanded the application of the death penalty to sixty new crimes. In 2002, in *Atkins v. Virginia*,[7] the Supreme Court limited the death penalty by determining that it cannot be applied to criminals who have some form of mental retardation; and in *Roper v. Simmons*,[8] the court ruled that standards of decency have evolved so that executing minors is 'cruel and unusual punishment', and so prohibited by the Eighth Amendment.[9]

The constitutionality of the death penalty is a matter that remains disputed in the United States, but continues to be applied in most states.[10] American constitutional violence is embodied in the application of the death penalty against the provisions of human rights treaties and declarations. In this sense, American jurisdiction has become a threat to progress in human rights internally and abroad.

In due process clauses, the Constitution itself recognises the death penalty in saying that a person may be deprived of life as long as the government acts with due process of law.[11]

The American constitutional violence that is inflicted on Puerto Rico is divided into two examples. In the first example, we look at how this violence is applied through the enforcement of Article 4, Section 2, Clause 2 (the inter-state rendition clause) of the American Constitution, which provides for the extradition of criminals to the state where they committed a crime. A second example, *Puerto Rico v. Branstad*,[12] looks at the enforcement of capital punishment on Puerto Rican soil.

An analysis of the American constitutional case begins with *Soering v. United Kingdom*[13] in the European Court of Human Rights. While this is a case of public international law, it is closely related to the first example of American constitutional violence. The implementation of capital punishment based on constitutional legitimacy is constitutional violence. It represents an even greater level of violence if the death penalty is applied in contravention of the provisions of a subnational constitution, in contravention of the text of international treaties and conventions and customary international law, and in contravention of the will of the people of Puerto Rico. Puerto Rican constitutional guarantees and the bill of rights cannot be disregarded as they represent the most important juridical expression of the Puerto Rican people and also the juridification of human rights. In this respect, there is a conflict between human rights as established in a subnational (according to the federal level) constitutional juridification and an American constitutional clause.

In 1989, both the European Court of Human Rights (ECtHR) and the US Supreme Court decided important cases about the constitutionality of the death penalty. The ECtHR found a violation of the European Convention on Human Rights to arise from extraditing a defendant, 18 years old at the time of offence, to the United States to face the death penalty.[14] In *Soering v. United Kingdom*,[15] extradition to face the death penalty in the United States was challenged by the European Court under Article 3 of the European Convention on Human Rights, which provides: 'No one shall be subjected to torture or to inhuman or degrading treatment or punishment.'

The case was brought before the court on 25 January 1989 by the European Commission of Human Rights, then by the British government on 30 January 1989, and then by the West German government on 3 February 1989. The applicant, Mr Jens Soering, was born on 1 August 1966 and is a German national. He was detained in prison in England pending extradition to the United States to face charges of murder in the Commonwealth of Virginia.[16] The homicides in question were committed in Bedford County, Virginia, in March 1985. The victims, William Reginald Haysom (aged 72) and Nancy Astor Haysom (aged 53), were the parents of the applicant's girlfriend, Elizabeth Haysom, who is a Canadian national. At the time, the applicant and Elizabeth Haysom, aged 18 and 20, respectively, were students at the University of Virginia. They both disappeared from Virginia in October 1985, but were arrested in England in April 1986 in connection with cheque fraud.[17]

Soering confessed to the murders to British police officers, recounting the couple's efforts to overcome her parent's opposition to their relationship and the subsequent murders. Haysom was extradited to the United States, where she pleaded guilty as an accessory to the murder of her parents, and was sentenced to ninety years in prison. Soering was indicted in Virginia for capital murder and extradition was sought.[18] The British Embassy in Washington sought to obtain assurances that if Soering were surrendered to the United States and convicted, the death penalty would not be carried out, or, if it were not possible on constitutional grounds for the United States to provide such assurances, that the United States agree to recommend to the appropriate state authorities that the death penalty not be imposed or carried out.[19] The British argued that Article 4 of the extradition treaty between the United Kingdom and the United States applied.

There is no provision in the Extradition Acts relating to the death penalty, but Article IV of the United Kingdom–United States Treaty provides:

> If the offence for which extradition is requested is punishable by death under the relevant law of the requesting Party, but the relevant law of the requested Party does not provide for the death penalty in a similar case, extradition may be refused unless the requesting Party gives assurances satisfactory to the requested Party that the death penalty will not be carried out.

Lord Justice Lloyd (Divisional Court) considered that 'the assurance leaves something to be desired':

> Article IV of the Treaty contemplates an assurance that the death penalty will not be carried out. That must presumably mean an assurance by or on behalf of the Executive Branch of Government, which in this case would be the Governor of the Commonwealth of Virginia. The certificate sworn by Mr Updike, far from being an assurance on behalf of the Executive, is nothing more than an undertaking to make representations on behalf of the United Kingdom to the judge. I cannot believe that this is what was intended when the Treaty was signed. But I can understand that there may well be difficulties in obtaining more by way of assurance in view of the federal nature of the United States Constitution.[20]

Relations between the United Kingdom and the United States on matters concerning extradition are conducted by and with the federal and not the state authorities. However, with respect to offences against state laws the federal authorities have no legally binding power to provide, in an appropriate extradition case, assurances that the death penalty will not be imposed or carried out. In such cases this power rests with the state. If a state decides to make a promise in relation to the death penalty, the US government has the power to give an assurance to the extraditing government that the state's promise will be honoured. This fact is relevant, because Puerto Rico has abolished the death penalty at the state level. An analogous application of this clause and customary international law would allow Puerto Rico to ask for a guarantee whenever the other state does not make a promise. Thus, the first question that arises is whether equal treatment among American citizens is possible where state laws regulate capital punishment unevenly. This differing treatment is more relevant when the legislative solution depends on a strict dichotomy, the admission or the abolition of the death penalty. Uniform application cannot rely on a restrictive interpretation, especially when the issue affects human rights (*in dubio pro reo*).

According to evidence from the Virginia authorities, Virginia's capital sentencing procedure, and notably the provision on post-sentencing reports, would allow the sentencing judge to consider a representation to be made on behalf of the British government pursuant to the assurance given by the attorney for Bedford County.[21] The role reserved for the federal level is not only derived from the fact that this was a case of international extradition.[22]

After further attempts to secure a discretionary refusal of extradition failed in the United Kingdom, Soering filed an application in the European Court of Human Rights. The European Court noted that there was a serious likelihood that he would be sentenced to death if extradited to the United States. Soering maintained that in the circumstances and, in particular, having regard to the 'death row phenomenon', he would thereby be subjected to inhuman and degrading treatment and punishment contrary to Article 3 of the Convention.[23] The court said that the 'death row phenomenon' consisted of 'a combination of circumstances to which the applicant would be exposed if, after having been extradited to Virginia to face a capital murder charge, he were sentenced to death'.[24]

Another important decision is *Roger Judge* v. *Canada*,[25] of the UN Human Rights Committee (UNHRC). On 15 April 1987, Mr Judge was convicted on two counts of first-degree murder and possession of an instrument of crime by the Court of Common Pleas of Philadelphia in Pennsylvania. On 12 June 1987, he was sentenced to death by the electric chair. He escaped from prison on 14 June 1987 and fled to Canada. Mr Judge was deported from Canada in 1998 and returned to death row in Pennsylvania. Did Canada violate the International Covenant on Civil and Political Rights (ICCPR) by failing to seek assurances that the death penalty would not be carried out? The state party referred to Article 6, Paragraph 1, which declares that every human being has the right to life and guarantees that no one shall be arbitrarily deprived of his or her life. It submits that with respect to the imposition of the death penalty, Article 6, Paragraph 2, specifically permits its application in those countries that have not abolished it, but requires that it be imposed in a manner that respects the conditions outlined in Article 6. Also according to this party, Article 6 does not explicitly refer to situations in which someone is extradited or removed to another state where that person is subject to the imposition of the death penalty.

However, the state party noted that the Committee held that:

> if a State party takes a decision relating to a person within its jurisdiction and the necessary and foreseeable consequence is that that person's rights under the Covenant will be violated in another jurisdiction, the State party itself may be in violation of the Covenant.

The Committee thus found that Article 6 applies to the situation in which a state party seeks to extradite or remove an individual to a state where he or she faces the death penalty. The state party also considered that Article 6 allows state parties to extradite or remove an individual to a state where they face the death penalty as long as the conditions respecting the imposition of the death penalty in Article 6 are met. The state party argued that the Committee, in that case, did not seem to question whether the imposition of the death penalty in the United States met the conditions prescribed in Article 6.[26] Mr Judge responded to the request for information by the Committee on 24 January 2003 and commented on the state party's submission. He submitted that by relying on the decision in *Kindler v. Canada*,[27] in its argument that in matters of extradition or removal, the Covenant is not necessarily breached by an abolitionist state where assurances that the death penalty should not be carried out are not requested, the state party misconstrued not only the facts of *Kindler* but the effect of the Committee's decision therein.

Mr Judge argued that *Kindler* dealt with extradition as opposed to deportation. He recalled the Committee's statement that there would have been a violation of the Covenant 'if the decision to extradite without assurances would have been taken arbitrarily or summarily'. However, since the Minister of Justice considered Mr Kindler's arguments prior to ordering his surrender without assurances, the Committee could not find that the decision was made 'arbitrarily or summarily'. Mr Judge's case concerned deportation, which lacked any legal process under which the deportee might request assurances that the death penalty not be carried out.[28] The UNHRC unanimously found that Canada had breached its obligations under Article 6(1) of the ICCPR by deporting Mr Judge 'without ensuring that the death penalty would not be carried out'. In considering Canada's obligations, as a state party which had abolished the death penalty, when removing persons to another country where they are under sentence of death, the Committee recalled its previous jurisprudence in *Kindler v. Canada*, that it did not consider that the deportation of a person from a country that has abolished the death penalty to a country where he or she is under sentence of death amounts *per se* to a violation of Article 6 of the Covenant.

The Committee's rationale in this decision was based on an interpretation of Article 6, Paragraphs 1 and 2, which does not prohibit the imposition of the death penalty for the most serious crimes. It considered that as Canada itself had not imposed the death penalty, but had extradited Mr Judge to the United States to face capital punishment, the extradition itself would not amount to a violation by Canada unless there was a real risk that Mr Judge's rights under the Covenant would be violated in the United States. On the issue of assurances, the Committee found that the terms of Article 6 did not necessarily require Canada to refuse to extradite or to seek assurances, but that such a request should at least be considered by the removing state.[29] Canada was also found to be in breach of Articles 6 and 2(3) of the ICCPR for arbitrarily deciding to deport Mr Judge 'to a state where he is under sentence of death without affording him the opportunity to avail himself of an available appeal'. In consequence, the UNHRC determined that Mr Judge was entitled to an effective remedy, which would include Canada 'making such representations as are possible to the receiving state to prevent the carrying out of the death penalty'.

Finally, Canada was found to be under an obligation to provide the UNHRC, within ninety days, with 'information about the measures taken to give effect to its views'. The Human Rights Committee unanimously determined:

> For countries that have abolished the death penalty, there is an obligation not to expose a person to the real risk of its application. Thus, they may not remove, either by deportation or extradition, individuals from their jurisdiction if it may be reasonably anticipated that they will be sentenced to death, without ensuring that the death sentence will not be carried out.[30]

This decision marked a major departure from the Committee's prior jurisprudence. Just a decade earlier, the UNHRC had held in *Kindler v. Canada* that the deportation of a person from a country which has abolished the death penalty to a country where he or she is under sentence of death does not amount *per se* to a violation of Article 6 of the Covenant:

'Every human being has the inherent right to life. This right shall be protected by law. No one shall be arbitrarily deprived of his life.'

Besides the discussed jurisprudence and the ICCPR decision, it is important to quote the following public international law doctrine to demonstrate American isolationism on this issue:

a   the *Second Optional Protocol to the International Covenant on Civil and Political Rights, aiming at the abolition of the death penalty*, adopted by the UN General Assembly in 1989, is of worldwide scope. It provides for the total abolition of the death penalty, but allows state parties to retain the death penalty in time of war if they make a reservation to that effect at the time of ratifying or acceding to the protocol. Any state which is a party to the International Covenant on Civil and Political Rights can become a party to the protocol;

b   the *Protocol to the American Convention on Human Rights to Abolish the Death Penalty*, adopted by the General Assembly of the Organization of American States in 1990, provides for the total abolition of the death penalty, but allows state parties to retain the death penalty in wartime if they make a reservation to that effect at the time of ratifying or acceding to the protocol. Any state party to the American Convention on Human Rights can become a party to the protocol;

c   *Protocol No. 6 to the European Convention for the Protection of Human Rights and Fundamental Freedoms [European Convention on Human Rights] concerning the abolition of the death penalty*, adopted by the Council of Europe in 1982, provides for the abolition of the death penalty in peacetime; state parties may retain the death penalty for crimes 'in time of war or of imminent threat of war'. Any state party to the European Convention on Human Rights can become a party to the protocol;

d   *Protocol No. 13 to the Convention for the Protection of Human Rights and Fundamental Freedoms [European Convention on Human Rights] concerning the abolition of the death penalty in all circumstances*, adopted by the Council of Europe in 2002, provides for the abolition of the death penalty in all circumstances, including time of war or imminent threat of war. Any state party to the European Convention on Human Rights can become a party to the protocol.[31]

In the United States the doctrine of specialty binds the jurisdictional authority of a trial court. Where an assurance has been provided as a condition of surrender under an extradition treaty, that assurance acts as a jurisdictional bar against prosecution on any charge other than the one specified in the surrender, and only on the agreed-upon terms and conditions.[32] Most US courts of appeal have consistently and stringently upheld these requirements.[33] Courts should accord deferential consideration to the limitations imposed by an extraditing nation in an effort to protect US citizens in prosecutions abroad. Moreover, in evaluating the exact limitations set by the extraditing nation, courts should not elevate legalistic formalism over substance. To do otherwise would strip comity of its meaning.[34] In the unlikely event that a state court allowed the breach of a formal extradition assurance against the imposition of the death penalty, it is virtually certain that the federal appellate courts would reverse and remand with instructions to apply the assurance to the letter. Furthermore, the US government possesses the legal power to enforce specialty requirements. First, the government could (and very possibly would) file a letter brief with the trial court or an amicus brief supporting the defendant's habeas application, demonstrating that the breach of an extradition assurance is both unlawful and clearly not in the national interest. Second, if that action failed to persuade state authorities, the federal government has a long-recognised right to obtain an injunction in the federal courts to halt the ongoing violation of a domestically enforceable treaty by local or state authorities.[35] Since strict, good-faith compliance with extradition assurances is essential for securing the return of future suspects from abolitionist nations, the United States has a vested interest in opposing any breach of a binding assurance provided against the imposition of the death penalty. It is also important for counsel to understand that formal and explicit assurances must be obtained *prior to* the extradition of the defendant to the United States whenever possible. Recent case law clearly indicates that the sending state has no right to insist on retrospective assurances following the surrender, and that all assurances must be explicitly agreed to by the United States in advance.[36] This data shows that a citizen of an abolitionist state, including an incorporated or unincorporated territory of the United States, may be extradited to another state to be executed. It seemed that death penalty regulation and enforcement in the United States was limited to state level and that the federal government agreed with its implementation as a painful consequence of a federal system, where some state constitutions institutionalise this sort of punishment and others do not. It is now necessary to discuss the peculiar political and juridical relationship existing between the United States and the Commonwealth of Puerto Rico.

Puerto Rico has a special political status in its relations with America and this introduces more variables into the equation of extradition. However, American constitutional violence remains unattenuated in a territory where its own constitution and public opinion oppose capital punishment. The enforcement of the death penalty is an instrument to implement other interests in Puerto Rico. The fact that there are human lives at stake dramatises the political use of the American constitution.

After two years of military government, in 1900 the American Congress adopted the first statutory law to organise the territory of Puerto Rico, known as the Foraker Act. This law established a new government consisting of a governor and an executive council, appointed by the president of the United States; a house of representatives, consisting of a chamber of deputies; a judicial system with a supreme court; a US district court; and a non-voting resident commissioner in Congress. The president of the United States continued to appoint the members of the Puerto Rico Supreme Court. The US Congress reserved the power to nullify laws passed by the Puerto Rican legislature.[37]

The American Supreme Court began to elucidate crucial constitutional issues raised by the acquisition of new overseas territories in May 1901. These decisions, called the *Insular Cases*, remain transcendent because they contain the basic parameters that define the power the federal Congress can exert on US dependent territories, such as Puerto Rico and the US Virgin Islands.[38] These judicial decisions created a new constitutional theory, according to which the American constitutional map would have to distinguish between states and territories, but also among types of territories (incorporated and unincorporated). The unincorporated territories were defined by the US Supreme Court as territories that *belong to* but are not part of the United States. The US Supreme Court concluded that Puerto Rico was in the group of unincorporated territories.[39] By virtue of the territorial clause of the unincorporated territories, the US Congress has plenary powers.

The plenary powers theory was used throughout the nineteenth century to define the contours of the powers exercised by Congress in relation to Native American tribes (a striking example can be seen in *United States* v. *Kagama*,[40] where the Supreme Court found that Congress had complete authority over all Native American affairs) and the regulation of issues related to immigration. The assignment of a plenary power to one body divests all other bodies of the right to exercise that power. The court clarified that plenary powers are not synonymous with absolute powers, and left the eventual and gradual evolution of case law to determine the content of those rights. By using plenary powers, Congress could legislate in the territories in a way that would not be possible in the states because of the division of powers stipulated in the American Constitution. This power could be exercised to benefit or discriminate against territories and populations.[41]

In the exercise of its plenary powers, in 1917 Congress passed a second statutory act for Puerto Rico, the Jones–Shafroth Act or Jones Act. This act was sponsored by Representative William Atkinson Jones and conferred US citizenship on Puerto Ricans. In 1950, the United States government passed

Public Law 600, authorising Puerto Rico to draft its own constitution the following year. Under this act a referendum was called and approval for drafting a constitution was given. A constitutional assembly met to draft the constitution between 1951 and 1952. The framers had to follow only two basic requirements established under Public Law 600. The first condition was that the document must establish a republican form of government for the island. The second was the inclusion of a bill of rights. The constitution was subsequently approved by a popular referendum and ratified by the US Congress. Under this constitution, Puerto Rico is a state that is freely associated with the United States.

Public Law 600 only authorised the adoption of a new constitution for internal governance. Puerto Rico remained under the American Constitution and federal laws. The law itself left in force important provisions of the statutory acts of 1900 and 1917.[42] The limits of the autonomy recognised for the Commonwealth of Puerto Rico have been questioned in some decisions by the US Supreme Court – which has interpreted the territorial clause (Article IV, Section 3-2) of the US Constitution as still controlling Puerto Rico.[43] At the time, the framers of the commonwealth constitution drafted a provision prohibiting capital punishment – the death penalty had already been abolished in Puerto Rico in 1929 – but the framers wished to make it abundantly clear that capital punishment would not exist under commonwealth status. In so doing, they were acting in accordance with the people of Puerto Rico's clear cultural, moral and religious convictions against the death penalty.[44] The constitution of Puerto Rico in relation to the death penalty leaves no doubt about the abolition of capital punishment in its jurisdiction. The preamble states that the democratic system is fundamental to the life of the Puerto Rican community: 'We understand that the democratic system of government is one in which the will of the people is the source of public power, the political order is subordinate to the rights of man, and the free participation of the citizen in collective decisions is assured.'

It is also important to quote the first section of Article 1, which affirms that:

> The Commonwealth of Puerto Rico is hereby constituted. Its political power emanates from the people of Puerto Rico and shall be exercised in accordance with their will, within the terms of the compact agreed upon between the people of Puerto Rico and the United States of America.

This article is of core importance because it defines the people of Puerto Rico as a separate entity from the people of the United States and not part of it. Therefore, the people of Puerto Rico 'agreed' with the US Congress. Perhaps the most interesting sovereignty and federalism questions arise in Puerto Rico. Puerto Rico is not a state, but it does constitute one of the ninety-four federal districts of the United States. Because of Puerto Rico's commonwealth relationship with the United States, Congress effectively had to approve its constitution when accepting the relationship. Thus, it can be argued that Congress effectively has two policies in Puerto Rico: prohibition of capital punishment in the constitutional document, while providing applicable death penalties in the 1988 and 1994 federal statutes.[45]

According to these two constitutional precepts, democracy (the popular will of the people of Puerto Rico) is particularly significant when defining issues that affect the people of Puerto Rico. Article II, Section 7 clearly affirms that the right to life, liberty and the enjoyment of property is recognised as a fundamental right of man, and that the death penalty shall not exist. The Section 10 of the same article states that the right of the people to be secure in their persons, houses, papers and effects against unreasonable searches and seizures shall not be violated. Section 19 states that the foregoing enumeration of rights shall not be construed restrictively, nor does it contemplate the exclusion of other rights not specifically mentioned which belong to the people in a democracy. The power of the legislative assembly to enact laws for the protection of the life, health and general welfare of the people shall likewise not be construed restrictively. All these constitutional articles and principles are routinely violated by American federal institutions based on a partial reading of the territorial clause and disregarding the (shared) sovereignty of the people of Puerto Rico – as Article 1, Section 1 of the Constitution recognises. The enforcement of the death penalty in Puerto Rico is against the concept of democracy (the *demos* being the people of Puerto Rico). Despite high crime rates,[46] opposition to the death penalty is widespread throughout all social classes in Puerto Rican society. Except for religion and gender, no other demographic variable is significantly related to opinion on capital punishment in Puerto Rico; this means that Puerto Ricans of different incomes, ages and education groups have similar levels of opposition.[47] Cámara-Fuertes *et al.* noted that of those who gave a valid answer to the question: 'Do you favour or oppose the death penalty?' (eliminating 'I do not know' and 'it depends' responses), 73 per cent stated that they opposed the death penalty, while 27 per cent favoured it.[48] Other expressions of the rejection of the death penalty by Puerto Rican public representatives support the conclusions of this empirical exercise. In this respect, Resolution 52 of the Senate of the Commonwealth of Puerto Rico of 13 January 2009, and Resolution 2 of the government of the municipality of Utuado are clear examples of popular opposition to the imposition of the death penalty. One of the probable explanations for the uniform opposition to the death penalty in Puerto Rico is precisely the phenomenon of elite-driven opinion. Capital punishment was abolished in many industrialised democracies against prevailing public opinion. Cámara-Fuertes *et al.* addressed important issues regarding fairness in judging death penalty cases in Puerto Rico. First, given the general opposition to the death penalty among the general public, how fair is it for the federal government to continue to seek this punishment in Puerto Rico?[49] The death penalty is prohibited explicitly by the Puerto Rican Constitution, which was approved by the Puerto Rican people and ratified by the American Congress and President Truman.[50] More importantly than what the Constitution states, however, is the fact that opposition to capital punishment is widespread throughout Puerto Rican society.

Second, capital punishment is applicable in Puerto Rico only in federal cases. This raises the issue of language. All procedures in federal courts are conducted in English, and juries selected in a possible death penalty case on the island have to be competent in English. The problem is that the main language spoken in Puerto Rico is Spanish and only a minority of the population is bilingual. This creates doubts about the fairness of a trial in a federal court with this possible penalty.[51]

The first case law that exemplifies American constitutional violence in Puerto Rico is *United States of America* v. *Hector Oscar Acosta Martínez & Joel Rivera Alejandro*,[52] in which the enforcement of the death penalty was attempted on Puerto Rican soil. On 24 January 2000, the US Attorney General authorised the US Attorney for the district of Puerto Rico to seek the death penalty against defendants in the event of conviction. Thereafter, the government filed its notice of intent to seek the death penalty. Though not necessarily in this order, the defendants' main arguments in challenging the applicability of the federal death penalty in Puerto Rico were:

1   that because the constitution of the Commonwealth of Puerto Rico expressly prohibits capital punishment, the federal death penalty is 'locally inapplicable' within the meaning of Section 9 of the Puerto Rican Federal Relations Act, 48 USC § 734;

2   that as part of the bilateral agreement governing the federal government's relations with Puerto Rico, the commonwealth constitution (even if considered a federal statute) may not be unilaterally altered by Congress; and

3   that applying the federal death penalty to citizens of Puerto Rico, without their consent, and in view of their lack of representation in the enactment of federal law, is unfair.[53]

The defendants' first argument is clarified by a literal reading of the Puerto Rican Constitution as reproduced in the preceding paragraphs of this section. The defendants' second argument is in part premised on the theory that the constitution of the Commonwealth of Puerto Rico is a statute of

Congress. This theory has been repeatedly rejected by the First Circuit Court of Appeals.[54]

In this way, in voting to approve the Constitution, the people of Puerto Rico had a reasonable expectation that the death penalty would not be applicable. With respect to the third argument, it must said that Puerto Rico's status changed from that of a mere territory to the unique status of a commonwealth. The federal government's relations with Puerto Rico changed from being bound merely by the territorial clause, and the rights of the people of Puerto Rico as United States citizens, to being bound by the US and Puerto Rican constitutions, Public Law 600, the Puerto Rican Federal Relations Act, and the rights of the people of Puerto Rico as American citizens.[55] Thereafter, the authority exercised by the federal government emanated from the compact entered into between the people of Puerto Rico and the Congress of the United States.[56] As stated by the *Quiñones* court:

> In 1952, Puerto Rico ceased being a territory of the United States subject to the plenary powers of Congress as provided in the Federal Constitution. The authority exercised by the federal government emanated thereafter from the compact itself. Under the compact between the people of Puerto Rico and the United States, Congress cannot amend the Puerto Rico Constitution unilaterally, and the government of Puerto Rico is no longer a federal government agency exercising delegated power.[57]

Accordingly, the main question to answer is whether the US Attorney General can authorise the US Attorney for the district of Puerto Rico to seek the death penalty. The question may have different answers (political reasons, juridical control and the exercise of sovereignty), but none of them can justify a violent enforcement of the American constitutional system.

The second case under analysis, *Puerto Rico v. Juan Martínez Cruz*,[58] confirms the violent enforcement of the law. It is important to note that violence is not only represented by the enforcement of the death penalty, but also by the behaviour of the US Attorney General and the US Attorney for the district of Puerto Rico in authorising actions that were illegal (according to the Puerto Rican Constitution and human rights treaties) and undemocratic (in contradiction of the will of the people of Puerto Rico). In *Puerto Rico v. Juan Martínez Cruz* the Supreme Court of Puerto Rico decided whether the governor of the Commonwealth of Puerto Rico had a mandatory duty to grant a request for extradition made by the governor of Pennsylvania. On 3 June 2002, the governor of Pennsylvania required from the state governor of the Commonwealth of Puerto Rico the extradition of Juan Martínez Cruz. It was alleged that Mr Martínez Cruz was wanted for trial on charges of murder and other felonies. On 17 June 2002, the request for extradition was initiated according to the *Ley Uniforme de Extradición Criminal*, Law 4 of 24 May 1960, LPRA § 1881 *et seq.* (Puerto Rican Uniform Criminal Extradition Act) and its federal counterpart, 18 USC § 3182. The defendant announced that he would not agree to be extradited with the possibility of being sentenced to the death penalty in Pennsylvania. The public ministry, meanwhile, argued that this was not a case which concerned the death penalty and the Constitution of Puerto Rico, but rather that the case was determined by the extradition clause of the US Constitution, Article IV, Section 2 and the provisions of *Puerto Rico v. Branstad*.[59] Certainly, the inter-state rendition clause does not differentiate between states that apply the death penalty and abolitionists. Through this litigation strategy, the public ministry distinguished between the main process, its possible penalty (speculation), the question of extradition, and the enforcement of a constitutional duty. The Court of First Instance considered that: first, the extradition clause of the US Constitution does not apply to Puerto Rico; and, second, federal extradition law 'does not establish guidelines regarding the controversy of the case', leaving to the states the authority to legislate on this matter. Third, the Uniform Extradition Act must be interpreted according to the mandate of the constitution of the Commonwealth of Puerto Rico, which prohibits the death penalty. The court concluded that the extradition of Mr Martínez Cruz could be implemented only to the extent that there were assurances that Pennsylvania would not seek the death penalty. In the absence of such guarantees, there could be no extradition. In consequence, the court interpreted the constitutional clause respecting state law and made an analogy of international legislation and customary international law regulating extradition where assurances were sought if the death penalty could be applied. The refusal could be interpreted as an act of sovereignty of the Commonwealth of Puerto Rico and the application of international law on extradition instead of constitutional provisions. In the eyes of the Attorney General this was an unpatriotic act that had little to do with the death penalty. The Attorney General appealed the decision. On 17 October 2005, the intermediate court confirmed the first instance decision. The Attorney General continued with the strategy of Washington and appealed to the Supreme Court of Puerto Rico and the case was decided on 5 May 2006.

The Supreme Court of Puerto Rico considered that the extradition clause is not self-enforceable and requires federal and state legislation to be implemented. The court stated that the Extradition Act of 1793 was passed with this goal. Federal law states:

> Whenever the executive authority of any State or Territory demands any person as a fugitive from justice, of the executive authority of any State, District, or Territory to which such person has fled, and produces a copy of

an indictment found or an affidavit made before a magistrate of any State or Territory, charging the person demanded with having committed treason, felony, or other crime, certified as authentic by the governor or chief magistrate of the State or Territory from whence the person so charged has fled, the executive authority of the State, District, or Territory to which such person has fled shall on demand of the executive authority of the State from which he fled, be delivered up, to be removed to the State having jurisdiction of the crime.

The Extradition Clause is generally implemented by State laws, making it the duty of the governor to deliver the fugitive to the demanding State. Even though it has been said that the extradition process is one of comity, the Extradition Clause articulates, in mandatory language, the concepts of full faith and credit needed to foster national unity and facilitates the smooth functioning of the criminal justice system. Thus, extradition of fugitives from one State to another is not dependent on 'mere' comity or on contract.[60]

The Puerto Rico Supreme Court went on to state that federal law does not occupy the field in this area, so that states, territories and the Commonwealth of Puerto Rico can use their own procedural law, as indeed they have done. Even when states, territories and the Commonwealth can legislate, the truth (always according to the Puerto Rican Supreme Court) is that the legislative process cannot be more onerous than that provided in federal law or in the provisions of the American Constitution. In other words, states are free to effect extradition under less stringent requirements, but are not permitted to make extradition any more difficult. Therefore, the Supreme Court of Puerto Rico considered that the request of a guarantee (in congruence with state law) makes extradition more difficult. The extradition clause seeks to prevent a state from becoming a sanctuary for criminals seeking to evade criminal laws, and also tries to avoid the Balkanisation of the administration of the criminal justice system among the jurisdictions that coexist in the United States. While a simple declaration by the requesting state would allow the smooth implementation of the constitutional extradition clause and the respect of the constitution of the Commonwealth of Puerto Rico, the request of a guarantee does not interfere with the main goals of the extradition clause. The non-imposition of the death penalty does not mean legal impunity and avoidance of the consequences of criminal acts. The death penalty is a punishment among others in criminal law; its abolition does not mean the abolition of criminal punishment. What really provokes a Balkanisation in a decentralised judicial system is a disregard for differences, even at the cost of contravening a constitution and defying the will of the people. A more onerous interpretation does not mean a *reformatio in peius* as reached by a contrary interpretation of the Puerto Rican Constitution. Was the Puerto Rican constitutional disposition taken into account at some point by the Supreme Court of the Commonwealth? Or did the shadow of the American constitution darken the vision of the judges?

The first time that the US Supreme Court interpreted the extradition clause was in *Kentucky v. Dennison*,[61] stating:

> Looking, therefore, to the words of the Constitution – to the obvious policy and necessity of this provision to preserve harmony between States, and order and law within their respective borders ... – the conclusion is irresistible, that this compact, engrafted in the Constitution, included, and was intended to include, every offence made punishable by the law of the State in which it was committed, and that it gives the right to the executive authority of the State to demand the fugitive from the executive authority of the State in which he is found; that the right given to 'demand' implies that it is an absolute right; and it follows that there must be a correlative obligation to deliver, without any reference to the character of the crime charged, or to the policy or laws of the State to which the fugitive has fled ... The act does not provide any means to compel the execution of this duty, nor inflict any punishment for neglect or refusal on the part of the executive of the State; nor is there any clause or provision in the Constitution which arms the government of the United States with this power. Indeed, such a power would place every State under the control and dominion of the general government, even in the administration of its internal concerns and reserved rights. And we think it clear that the federal government, under the Constitution, has no power to impose on a State officer, as such, any duty whatever, and compel him to perform it.[62]

The US Supreme Court in *Puerto Rico v. Branstad* overturned the decision in *Dennison, ante*, which prevented the federal government from compelling a state governor, through *mandamus*, to surrender to the complaining state authorities a fugitive from justice who had sought refuge in the asylum state. However, the Supreme Court left intact the general rule of *Dennison* that the obligations imposed by federal law for extradition are mandatory, stating: 'We reaffirm the conclusion that the commands of the Extradition Clause are mandatory, and afford no discretion to the executive officers or courts of the asylum State.'[63] Harmonisation between states cannot require homogenisation and the violation of state law, especially if such a law is in the Constitution. The American constitutional clause aims at judicial harmonisation in order to provide some certainty to the legal system. This principle of jurisprudence requires a concord with respect to the diversity that a federal and decentralised system necessarily implies. But by applying the constitutional clause of extradition, as the Supreme Court of Puerto Rico and the Attorney General did in this case, a *de facto* power was endowed on the federal government to impose a duty without considering other important aspects, such as democracy and customary international law, while at the same time disregarding the Puerto Rican Constitution.

The next issue quoted by the Supreme Court of Puerto Rico to justify extradition was the *Ley Uniforme de Extradición Criminal de Puerto Rico* and the Uniform Extradition Act of 1936 of the National Conference of Commissioners on Uniform State Law. According to the Supreme Court of Puerto Rico, in the case under analysis the Puerto Rican Uniform Extradition Act sought to bring viability to the mandate of the extradition clause of the American Constitution. The law mandates that its provisions must be interpreted in a consistent manner with other jurisdictions that have adopted the uniform law, 34 LPRA § 1881b. Surprisingly, the Supreme Court of Puerto Rico did not mention the necessity of adapting the application of pre-constitutional dispositions to the Puerto Rican constitutional text. According to the point of view stated by the Supreme Court, the federal level was the exclusive valid reference for the legal development and application of the Puerto Rican Uniform Extradition Act. Following the magistrate's juridical logic, Article 1, Section 1 of the Puerto Rican Constitution, which states that the Commonwealth of Puerto Rico is hereby constituted and its political power emanates from the people and shall be exercised in accordance with their will, as well as the terms of the compact agreed between the people of Puerto Rico and the United States, were not applicable to this case. Since the law had not been amended or substituted after the Constitution was approved in Puerto Rico and ratified by the US Congress, it seemed that its application must respect the new juridical reality of Puerto Rico. If the Puerto Rican Uniform Extradition Act were to be currently passed it would also have to respect the Puerto Rico constitutional mandate. Therefore, the Puerto Rican Supreme Court also had the duty to deny any unconstitutional act. In this sense, the governor met his legal obligation at both the federal and state levels by requesting the guarantee of non-execution of the death penalty.

Another argument used by the Puerto Rican Supreme Court to authorise extradition was the inappropriateness of speculation about the possible result of the process. In this instance the Supreme Court was mixing different realities. It was not speculation about a possible decision, but the un-enforceability of a specific punishment. The Supreme Court obviated the difference between the main regular criminal process and its execution. There was no intromission or speculation regarding the regular process. The Supreme Court sentence violently imposed the American Constitution in contravention of the Puerto Rican one – and against the will of the people of Puerto Rico and customary international law. In order to avoid the enforcement of the death penalty, on 27 June 2007, the Secretary of Justice of the Commonwealth of Puerto Rico presented in the name of the governor

(Aníbal Acevedo Vilá, 2004–8) to the Subcommittee on the Constitution and the Committee of the Judiciary of the United States Senate a testimony concerning the federal death penalty. In this testimony, the head of the government of Puerto Rico affirmed that the Commonwealth repudiates death as a form of punishment by the federal government.[64]

Acevedo considered that the quest for a uniform public policy at the federal level was outweighed by significant political, social and cultural differences, as well as by the problems and risks associated with the pursuit of death penalties in jurisdictions that are opposed to that form of punishment. This argument is very interesting because it demonstrates that uniformity, a main objective set by the extradition clause of the American Constitution and the Extradition Act of 1793, is enhanced by respecting the state constitution and the people's will instead of a partial interpretation of the American Constitution. The testimony of Governor Acevedo held that the imposition of the federal death penalty in Puerto Rico is not supported by the special and extraordinary political relationship with the United States. The people of Puerto Rico had not consented to the imposition of the federal death penalty.[65]

Through the testimony, the governor demanded that the American Congress, in coordination with the Commonwealth authorities, restore the balance, mutual respect and comity that the people of Puerto Rico envisaged as a fundamental part of their relationship with the United States. Puerto Rico, he argued, is entitled to such consideration because of the long-standing prohibition of the death penalty, which is deeply rooted in its social, political, economic, moral, cultural and religious values and traditions, and the extraordinary political process from which it evolved. The governor urged Congress to consider and pass legislation which would definitively eliminate the possibility of the death penalty being imposed in Puerto Rico.

The governor stated that, at the very least, the people of Puerto Rico deserved the measure of respect that would motivate Congress to impose severe statutory limitations on the exercise of discretion by federal authorities when determining whether or not to seek the death penalty in Puerto Rico.[66] However, Congress did not address the governor's request and continues to perpetuate a constitutionally violent status quo.

By way of conclusion, it is interesting to note the constitutional paradox that is revealed by this case. Although the American Constitution is imposed by force, the Puerto Rican one remains as a guarantee against the death penalty. Another issue is the transcendence given to the Puerto Rican Constitution at the federal level, especially when it is compared with any clause of the American one.

The action of the federal power and the Supreme Court of Puerto Rico in this case exemplifies that constitutional violence is present not only in relation to the enforcement of the death penalty, but also in the way the 'sovereign' uses the constitution to impose an official rationalisation. The use of the constitution in this example generates frustration among the people of Puerto Rico, and this frustration is a manner of generating and consolidating behaviour patterns and controlling possible future acts against the 'sovereign'. The above example takes place in a constitutional democracy that is probably the best in the world and which incorporates more guarantees than any other national system. The following examples demonstrate that constitutional violence is not a phenomenon peculiar to the United States. The violent use of the constitution by the sovereign is a risk found in any legal system inherited from jus-positivism. Nevertheless, there are various tools to mitigate constitutional violence. A possible solution to violence by the sovereign is the application of public international law dispositions. In the cases reported these dispositions include: the International Covenant on Civil and Political Rights; the Second Optional Protocol to the ICCPR, aiming at the abolition of the death penalty; the American Convention on Human Rights; and the Protocol to the American Convention on Human Rights.

FRENCH CONSTITUTIONAL VIOLENCE: LIBERTÉ, EGALITÉ, FRATERNITÉ, UNIFORMITÉ

The second example of constitutional violence is based on French constitutionalism. The Revolution of 1789 and the first constitution of 3 September 1791 proclaimed a national sovereignty, and this was later changed in the Jacobin constitution of 1793 to popular sovereignty. French constitutional history shows that both contradictory definitions have been used to base sovereignty. Lately, in the constitutions of 1946 and 1958, an eclectic solution with little legal or political sense has been constitutionalised. The debate on national sovereignty indicates how the central power of Paris understands pluralism. Both examples demonstrate that the French Constitution has been used to formalise centralism, unity and uniformity. A single official culture has been imposed through the constitution and state apparatus (in Althusser's sense)[67] and in contravention of human rights.

The French nation had the coverage of constitutional rationality and the presumption of representing the universal values of the Enlightenment to expand its empire to minorities. This extreme centralism has biased the French Republic since its foundation and it has proved an example for other constitutional systems (Chilean and Turkish, for example) to homogenise or directly exclude intra-border cultures.

This section analyses two interrelated cases: the first deals with the constitutional accommodation of the debate between 'national sovereignty' and 'popular sovereignty', and its consequences for the French legal system.

This case reveals how French constitutional violence produced a violent homo-genisation through constitutional legitimacy. The second example is strict case law that reveals how the state apparatus has interpreted and enforced national identity in everyday aspects. This second example of French constitutional violence is a consequence of the first example. Both examples can be considered as 'maintaining violence' because the French Constitution has been used to control the 'threat' generated by various realities to the official and constitutional identity. While our analysis focuses on the constitutional law of the Fifth Republic (1958 Constitution), a historical introduction is necessary to understand the past and present importance of the constitutional conceptualisation of national sovereignty. I consider that French constitutional history started in 1789. Other authors might suggest that the French constitutional tradition can be more critically tied to the events and legal conflations leading to the *Lois fondamentales du royaume* (fundamental laws of the kingdom), which introduced the idea of self-limitation of power.[68]

From 1789 to 1875, nine constitutions were adopted and two projects were discussed without being approved.[69] The Vichy regime under the Nazi occupation drafted the *Loi de révision constitutionelle* of 10 July 1940. After the occupation, France had two more constitutions, the constitution of the Fourth Republic (27 October 1946) and the current constitutional text of the Fifth Republic (4 October 1958). A total of eleven constitutions that corro-borate the violent political instability mentioned in the preceding chapter.[70]

The constitutional statement of 'national sovereignty' has its origins in Article 3 of the Declaration of the Rights of Man and of the Citizen, 1789, which stated that:

> the principle of all sovereignty resides essentially in the nation. No individual may exercise authority that does not proceed directly from the nation (or the laws of that nation). Nation and state are different realities, except in France. In the formulation of national sovereignty, the nation is the holder of the sovereignty; it is endowed with free will exercised by its representatives.[71]

The main idea is that power belongs to the nation and not to an individual (king) or group of individuals.[72]

This theory seems to overcome some of the fears and troubles (monarchy, oligarchy) defined in Chapter 2, above. However, problems arise with the unifying and homogenising interpretation given to the term nation, which excludes any sort of discordance and minority. In other words, national identity in France aims to be mono-nuclear. Article 1 of the Constitution of 1791 codified national sovereignty and stated that sovereignty is indivisible, inalienable and imprescriptible. Sovereignty belongs to the nation; no group of people, nor any individual, may assume the exercise of this sovereignty. The nation elects representatives – who do not own sovereignty, but exercise it through the representation of the nation.[73] The main purpose of the constituent assembly of the Constitution of 1791 was to limit voting rights and prevent the overturning of the liberal bourgeoisie by the popular masses.[74] Two years later, the Jacobin and Revolutionary Constitution of 1793 introduced a major change by proclaiming popular rather than national sovereignty.

Under this new formulation every citizen owns a piece of sovereignty and all decisions must come from the citizens.[75] If supreme power belongs to a crowd, each member has a portion equal to the rest. As each citizen cannot exercise his portion of sovereignty alone he must elect representatives to act on his behalf.[76] This does not preclude that every citizen has a natural right to participate in each election (which implies universal suffrage). The right to vote is inalienable for each member of society. Only citizens hold sovereignty, and neither deputies nor the government may take over the tenure.[77]

In French constitutional history, the notions of popular and national sovereignty have been applied in various constitutions. The principle of popular sovereignty has been declared twice: in 1793 and the Constitution of Year III. Currently, the debate is limited to a formal question and the constituent assembly of 1946 was unable to decide between the two interpretations and chose the formulation: 'National sovereignty belongs to the French people', and this text can be read in the constitutions of 1946 and 1958. This definition of commitment solves nothing between two incompatible theories and the formulation of 1946 is ambiguous and unreal.[78] Delegates or representatives do not express the will of the people or the nation, but the will of a majority.[79]

In France, the old Athenian conception of *demos* has been limited to the term nation and these are totally different notions. A nation is a group of people who share culture, ethnicity or language. France has never been a mono-national state; there are other ἔθνη – *ethne* – who have been assimilated or rationalised through constitutional violence. When the Constitution established national unity as the basis of French democracy, unity was not limited to social classes, as the Constitution of 1794 intended, or to national territorial unity (1946–58). Enforcement of national unity involves legal and political acts that have restricted the fundamental rights of the people. In France, the state creates a nation and not the opposite. We will see that the state has been created by exterminating other nations and cultures.

The unity of the French people was preserved in the constitutional decision *statut de la Corse* of 9 May 1991. In this case the *Conseil Constitutionnel* clearly stated that the Constitution only recognises the French people, composed of all French citizens, without distinctions of origin, race or religion. The same conclusion was quoted by the French Constitutional Council on 15 June 1999, in relation to the European Charter for Regional or Minority Languages. The principle of the unity of the French people is a constitutional value.[80] Ardant states that because of the non-recognition of the rights of racial and religious minorities France has refused communitarism, unlike other countries.[81] It is not simply a question of communitarism, as the state obsession with unity and uniformity is a clear legacy of Jacobin constitutionalism that survives today. Jacobin constitutionalism has many similarities with Soviet constitutionalism and its centralised dictatorship.[82] Thus, the roots of Jacobin uniformity appear in the origins of French constitutional history and remain there today. Jacobins and Soviets had an identical goal, namely, the unity of society.[83] For both systems, the division of society is only an accident, since its origins and vocation lead to uniformity.[84] Although unity appeared to refer to social classes, in both France and the Soviet Union unity was extended to cultural and identity issues.[85]

The current French Constitution no longer makes reference to national sovereignty, but takes an eclectic form of two antagonistic conceptions. Both theories have always coincided in that French democracy is based on the unity of the people or the nation.

However unity and democracy can be opposed concepts. Unity may be a legitimate principle of the state and a constitutional aim, but democracy cannot depend on it. Democracy is something else. The independence of Algeria is a clear example of this impossible link and also a case of extreme constitutional violence, which ended on 5 July 1962, when the Évian Accords proclaimed the independence of Algeria. When the people of Guinea (1958), Algeria (1962), Comoros (1975) and Djibouti (1977) became independent, Article 1 of the current French Constitution – 'France shall be an indivisible, secular, democratic and social republic' – was copied and applied.

French democracy also depended on national unity, and the Algerians were considered as part of an indivisible French Republic. In consequence, Article 1 is legal, but invalid, as democracy in France does not depend on the principle of unity. The people of Algeria, by exercising a human right and resisting a process of ethnic cleansing initiated in 1945, were opposed to the French Constitution, but not to democracy and human rights. The military and political enforcement of Article 1 of the Constitution of 1958 contravenes the preamble of the Vienna Convention on the Law of Treaties and the Vienna Convention on Succession of States in respect of Treaties of 1978, which prohibit the threat or use of force and requires universal respect for, and observance of, human rights and fundamental freedoms. In this respect the former French prime minister, Michel Rocard,[86] provides evidence that the French identity is built on the destruction and absolute negation of other identities.[87]

A second case that may serve as an example of the interpretation of national unity as uniformity, in contravention of the fundamental rights of French minorities, is the enforcement of Article 2 of the Constitution of 1958, which states that the language of the Republic is French. This means that the only official language of the Republic is French, and it is also a constitutive element of national identity. Public authorities are required to use only the official language. The French language enjoys a monopoly in the relationship between citizens and public services.[88] Therefore, any other language in use in French territory is not considered official and is automatically excluded from the national identity: as a result Dutch, Basque, Occitan, Franco-Provençal, Corsican, Breton, Alsatian and Catalan are not French languages. According to the French constitutional identity, an individual cannot be both French and Basque. These languages cannot enjoy specific rights without being deemed to threaten the indivisibility of the Republic, equality under the law and the unity of the French nation.[89] In other words, the principle of the unity of the French people seems to be the best way to preserve aspects of indivisibility, amid the transformations of national and international society.[90]

In 1998, a public official in the city of Perpignan prevented a citizen from officially changing the name 'Marti' to 'Martí', and argued that in France it is impossible to register names with letters that are not French.[91] Any name can be registered in France – providing that only French characters are used. In the case under study, the rejection focused on the field of legality and identity. An appeal was made to the *Procureur de la République* (public prosecutor), who has the power to require rectification by the civil registry administration.[92] The public prosecutor ruled that there was no reason to allow the correction of a name, noting that the letter 'í' with an accent is not a character in the French alphabet. In 2001, a court in Perpignan refused to change the registry entry because acts of civil status must be written in French – the only language of the Republic according to Article 2 of the Constitution. The court of appeal of Perpignan also quoted Article 21 of Law 118 of 2 Thermidor year II (20 July 1794): 'public events must be written in French in the territory of the Republic', which necessarily requires the use of the Latin alphabet.[93] The public officer's centralist and uniformist schizophrenia created various implausible arguments, such as equating the Latin alphabet with French spelling and a 'lingua franca'.

The letter 'í' is accepted in other Latin languages and is, therefore, a Latin character. The court of appeal's reasoning is based on a rule from the period of the Jacobin Terror. This is a good example of how the state uses all its resources, regardless of their origin or current legitimacy, to implement constitutional violence. As Baylac states, the French public administration cannot accept a diacritic symbol if it is not in French, because its use would undermine the essence of the state.[94] Later in 2001, the second court of appeal of Montpellier confirmed the rejection. The public prosecutor added that the French Constitutional Council ruled unconstitutional the preamble of the European Charter for Regional or Minority Languages (CETS 148) adopted in 1992, because it recognises the right to use a regional or minority language in private and public life.[95]

According to the French Constitutional Council, the use of French is compulsory for the public administration and other languages cannot be used; and, moreover, there is no right to use another language in dealings with the administration. In 2004, the last instance of appeal in France, the Court of Cassation in Paris, confirmed the refusal of the appeal. The process finally reached the European Court of Human Rights in 2007. The key relevance is the issue of how the state apparatus enforces the French Constitution in contravention of human rights. The declaration of unconstitutionality of the preamble to the European Charter for Regional or Minority Languages has other effects. Thus, the preamble of the European treaty states that the right to use a regional or minority language in private and public life is an *inalienable* right in accordance with the principles embodied in the United Nations International Covenant on Civil and Political Rights, and according to the spirit of the Council of Europe Convention for the Protection of Human Rights and Fundamental Freedoms. Therefore, the declaration of unconstitutionality by the French Constitutional Council of the preamble and the denial of the right to use a regional or minority language in private and public life contravenes human rights and fundamental freedoms. Therefore, the declaration of unconstitutionality contradicts all of these public international legal doctrines. Other fundamental rights were also violated in the case, analysed by various public officials in the name of the French Constitution. The use of the term '*inalienable*' means that it is a personal freedom that cannot be taken away – and the meaning is the same in the Latin alphabet.

The rejection of a change of name registration also violates Article 8.1 of the European Convention on Human Rights: everyone has the right to respect for his or her private and family life, home and correspondence. Public authority interference is also barred by Article 8.2 of the same convention:

> there shall be no interference by a public authority with the exercise of this right except such as is in accordance with the law and is necessary in a democratic society in the interests of national security, public safety, for the economic well-being of the country, for the prevention of disorder or crime, for the protection of health or morals, or for the protection of the rights and freedoms of others.

Finally, constitutional enforcement contravenes Article 14:

the enjoyment of the rights and freedoms set forth in this convention shall be secured without discrimination on any grounds such as sex, race, colour, language, religion, political or other opinion, national or social origin, association with a national minority, property, birth or other status.

Constitutional violence meant, as the public prosecutor stated as an argument, that France did not ratify Article 27 of the International Covenant on Civil and Political Rights, which states that in those states in which ethnic, religious or linguistic minorities exist, persons belonging to such minorities shall not be denied the right, together with the other members of their group, to enjoy their own culture, to profess and practice their own religion or to use their own language. The same applied to Article 30 of the Convention on the Rights of the Child: in those states in which ethnic, religious or linguistic minorities or persons of indigenous origin exist, a child belonging to such a minority or who is indigenous shall not be denied the right, together with other members of his or her group, to enjoy his or her own culture, to profess and practice his or her own religion or to use his or her own language.

As also happened in the American constitutional case analysed, the French Constitution and its interpretation and enforcement contravenes human rights treaties and conventions. A non-ratification of an international treaty establishing human rights is a negligence of the state's obligations towards its citizens, the international community and human rights. It is also a way to excuse, but not to legitimise, violence that is allowed by the constitution. The non-ratification of these articles demonstrates a contradiction and the refusal *a contrario sensu* to recognise other *ethne* in France.

French constitutionalism has been a model for other constitutional systems. Its influence is very clear in the cases of Chile and Turkey discussed below. In both constitutional systems, the French pattern is applied in issues such as homogenising national sovereignty, and providing a centralised state that denies any link between territory and subnational identities. In a case similar to the analysed French case, in August 2002 the Turkish government placed severe restrictions on the use of Kurdish, prohibiting the language in education and broadcast media.[96] In March 2006, Turkey allowed private television channels to begin programming in Kurdish. However, the Turkish government said that they must avoid showing children's cartoons or educational programmes that teach the Kurdish language.[97] In Chile, the official language is Spanish (although it is not recognised as such in the Constitution) and there is no recognition of Mapuche. Both cases are examples of 'foundational violence'. As in France, the constitutional systems in Turkey and Chile are affected by violent revolutionary processes.

TURKISH CONSTITUTIONAL VIOLENCE: MEŞRUTIYET

The example of Turkish constitutional violence is divided into two different phenomena: the first is based on the military tutelage of political institutions, constitutions and state democracy. The military play a fundamental role in Turkish political and constitutional history. Military control has occurred without any democratic legitimacy and with the use of violence against dissidents and minorities. The second example is based on the constitutional accommodation and enforcement of extreme ethnic nationalism.

The preamble and Articles 2 and 3.1 of the current Turkish Constitution are the best expression of this ethnic nationalism. Both examples are interdependent on each other. The military has tried to achieve legitimacy through ethnic nationalist policies and the Constitution. In order to analyse the Turkish constitutional system it is necessary to analyse the thought and work of Mustafa Kemal Atatürk – the 'founding father' of Turkey.

For more than two hundred years the model of European modernity has been perceived in societies such as Turkey and Iran as the exclusive model for adopting modernisation. To become modern was to have a strong, centralised state, following the model of post-Napoleonic France, and an industrial society.[98] Kemal wanted a republic, intensely, almost physically. Like the French radicals, Kemal was dedicated to the veneration of the republican ideal.[99]

Republic! A term once taboo, it translates into Turkish (*cumhuriyet*) as an eternal regime and is linked to the supreme reference – the French Revolution.[100] The *cumhuriyet* or republican regime has its roots not in Mustafa Kemal, but in the Ottoman reform process of the nineteenth century. Initiated by Sultan Mahmud II (1808–1839), the Ottoman reforms were basically aimed at the centralisation and modernisation of the state apparatus.[101] However, Kemal revived and redefined the term, and expanded it to include the idea that Turkey should be a republic. Those who employed the term *cumhuriyet* in their political discourse were mostly referring to the notion of democracy, rather than a particular form of government. The word itself eventually acquired so subversive a connotation that it was rarely used in political vocabulary. Well-advised people preferred words such as *meşrutiyet* (constitutional regime).[102] In the context of these reforms, a constitutional movement emerged that achieved the proclamation of an Ottoman Constitution in 1876.

Based on the sovereignty of God and its legal order defined by religious law, this first Ottoman Constitution had a strong religious connotation. The absolute authority of the sultan was at least formally grounded in religious legitimacy and the Ottoman parliament was only an advisory body.[103] In Europe the process of modernisation was associated with the gradual development and expansion of critical reason, together with the gradual enhancement of individual autonomy and the emergence of civil society. However, in Ottoman Turkey and Iran the reverse was true. Modernisation was embraced by an intelligentsia made up of bureaucrats and military officers, who identified their own interests with those of the state.[104] The emerging commercial and industrial bourgeoisie was composed overwhelmingly of members of non-Muslim minorities, who enjoyed foreign protection and were increasingly seen as alien and eventually as a threat to the survival of the state.[105] This elitist role survives today. Victory in the 1922 War of Independence immensely strengthened Mustafa Kemal's position. He became the *Halâskar Gazi* (Saviour and Conqueror) and was determined to use this situation to consolidate his position in the post-war era. Kemal started to consolidate his political position even before the War of Independence formally ended with the signing and ratification of the Treaty of Lausanne (24 July 1923).[106]

The Constitution of 1921 was the fundamental law of Turkey from 1921 to 1924. On 29 October 1923, the Republic of Turkey was proclaimed by means of a constitutional amendment, and Gazi Mustafa Kemal was elected president. Immediately after the opening of the new parliamentary year on 1 March, the caliphate was abolished and all the members of the Ottoman dynasty were ordered out of the country. After extensive discussions, a new republican constitution was adopted in April 1924. This replaced the Ottoman Constitution of 1876, which had been modified in 1909 and again in January 1921 when the first assembly adopted the 'Law of Fundamental Organization'. This was a *de facto* constitution of the resistance movement and enabled it to function for all practical purposes as a republic within the legal framework of the Ottoman Empire.[107]

The issue of minorities was already discussed in the Treaty of Lausanne. Although the problem of minorities was less difficult than it had once been, Turkey was obliged to protect such minorities as remained in her territory as an obligation she voluntarily assumed under the national pact, under the Treaty of Lausanne and under her new constitution.[108] In this respect, with the recognition of the independence of the new Turkey, the issue of Kurdistan and the limits of the Soviet Republic of Armenia were 'solved' in the eyes of the international community; the only disappointment for the Turks was Mosul (Iraq).[109] In consequence, the imposition of respect for minorities imposed by the Treaty of Lausanne concerned the Greek minority in Smyrna. By an interchange of population agreement of January 1923, about 100,000 Greeks remaining in Turkey were deported to Greece and about 400,000 Turks remaining in Macedonia and Thrace were deported by Greece to Turkey during 1924.[110]

The Constitution of 1924 sought to provide Turkey with a representative and democratic government. All the sovereign powers of the nation – executive and legislative – are vested in the unicameral Grand National Assembly. The Assembly was elected by all male citizens aged 18 and above. The members of the Council of Executive Commissioners (the Cabinet) were chosen from the membership of the Assembly and were individually and collectively responsible to the Assembly. A bill of rights defined those liberties which were the prerogative of all Turkish citizens, regardless of race or religion. The permanency of the Republic was secured by the provision that no amendment may be made that seeks to alter the form of government. An interesting section of the Constitution dealt with the powers and privileges of the president of the Republic. Fear had been expressed that the great personal prestige of Mustafa Kemal Pasha, combined with his leadership of the Popular Party and his constitutional prerogatives, might lead to the gradual transformation of the Republic into a virtual military dictatorship.[111]

Clear influences of French constitutionalism include Article 3: 'Sovereignty belongs without restriction to the nation', and Article 4: 'The Grand National Assembly of Turkey is the sole lawful representative of the nation, and exercises sovereignty in the name of the nation'.[112] National sovereignty was Kemal's source of legitimacy and a way to homogenise other minorities. Kurdish rebellions continued in the new state after the Constitution was approved. The rebellions were seen as a threat to the new republic and Kurds were victims of new laws and 'mandatory' violence.[113]

The second important aspect of the Constitution of 1924 is the institutionalisation, legitimisation and recognition of military control. This role reserved by the 'immortal leader and the unrivalled hero'[114] determined the understanding of Turkish constitutionalism and the excessive role given to the Turkish army. The famous reforms of Atatürk in the 1920s and 1930s (the adoption of European family law, clock and calendar, measures and weights, clothing and alphabet, as well as the suppression of religious orders and shrines) had all been proposed long before he came to power.[115]

These measures were carried out to secularise, Westernise and 'enlighten' Turkey. The example of the most important dictatorship in the Mediterranean, Fascist Italy, was important to the Turkish leadership, and the manner in which Mussolini seemed to forge national unity impressed many in Turkey.[116] There were many similarities between the Italian Fascist regime and the Kemalist regime: extreme nationalism, with its attendant development of a legitimising historical mythology and racist rhetoric, and the emphasis on national unity and solidarity with a denial of class conflicts.[117] The Constitution remained in force until a coup d'état in 27 May 1960, and was then replaced by the Constitution of 1961. Kemalism had been enforced for thirty-six years.

The second constitution, of 1961, was drafted under the supervision of the National Unity Committee (NUC), a heterogeneous group of army officers that ruled the country during the interim period after the military coup.[118]

This new constitution reflected the democratic shortcomings of the previous constitution, in particular, the all-powerful position of the majority group in parliament, which was an instrument for the authoritarian rule of Atatürk and his successor İnönü. The former principle of unified power was replaced by a system of checks and balances to prevent the majority group in the Assembly from having an almost free hand. Furthermore, the new constitution contained a full bill of civil liberties, with Article 2 declaring the Turkish Republic to be a national, democratic, secular and social state based on human rights.[119] Yet this military-guided top-down 'democratisation' did not provide what its instigators sought: political stability. On the contrary, the new constitution became the legal background for the Second Republic's slide into social conflict and a series of political crises leading to two further military interventions (1971 and 1980).[120] In 1980, a new military coup introduced the current Turkish Constitution. As far the reconstruction of political life was concerned, the military more or less followed the procedures of 1960–1961.[121] The military leadership followed a *fait accompli* process that gave legitimacy to the military commander in power. Again, the military considered that the Turkish people were unable to decide on certain issues and so democratically 'corrected' the political situation themselves. This perceived popular incapacity required the military to make 'enlightened' interventions. The reproduction of the coup d'état as a *modus operandi* was intended to create some normality in the military control of political and democratic life. The coup was subsequently legitimised with the democratic approval of a new constitution. But these were actually two distinct acts. The referendum approved the constitutional content, but not the usurpation of the popular will. The military tutelage over civilian politics was regarded as normal, and the Constitution was a way to achieve a retroactive legitimacy. The constitutional role given to military tutelage and the use of force does not legitimise the *de facto* coup d'état supported by the military. This is a clear example of constitutional violence, or at least a violent use of constitutional legitimacy. The Turkish armed forces had intervened in democracy three times before 12 September 1980, but each coup was short-lived and the military had returned to their barracks.[122]

When in September 1980 the Turkish armed forces overthrew their democratic government, claiming that anarchy, terror, separatism and economic crisis had crippled Turkish society, they imposed a form of state terror. Some authors claimed that the military intervention in September 1980 was supported by the Turkish public and significant numbers of the political and economic elites.[123] The military's intervention was seen as a bitter pill that had to be swallowed for stability.[124] This conclusion was a way to normalise and justify a militarily violent 'constitutional founding'. No mention was made of opposition in Kurdistan (because the above-mentioned authors also diluted the Kurdish and Armenian minorities in the Turkish nation),[125] or the lack of guarantees for the opposition to the coup: some 43,000 people were arrested under 'suspicion' of being terrorists and there were 282 political killings.[126] The death penalty and arrests were enforced by an interim government without any sort of legitimacy. Many of the arguments expressed to justify the military coup d'état (supposed popular support, economic accomplishments, terrorism, support for America and NATO) coincide with the arguments used to defend the military coups in Chile in 1973 and Argentina in 1976. However, as a result of these military 'enlightenments', the Chilean and Argentinian military 'tutors' were prosecuted and convicted for crimes against humanity. Violence in this example involves two realities: first, the evident violent use of constitutional legitimacy to justify a military coup d'état; and' second, the 'normalisation' of these acts in Turkish society.

The new constitution was subjected to a referendum on 7 November 1982. Approval or rejection was linked directly to the figure of General Evren, because a temporary article of the Constitution (during the transition from military to civilian rule) stipulated that he would automatically become president for a seven-year term if the Constitution was adopted.[127] The obvious democratic deficiencies led to a military leadership taking power as of 1991. The current constitution was amended on 17 May 1987, and in 1995, 2001 and 2007.[128] On 12 September 2010, Turkish voters approved in a popular referendum a heavily debated package of constitutional amendments with a particular focus on the judicial institutions. The amendments made decisive changes regarding Turkey's Constitutional Court and its Supreme Board of Prosecutors and Judges. In addition, the new constitution paved the way for the trial of military personnel by civilian courts for all issues that are not internal military affairs. In terms of civil liberties, the amendments improved the protection of the family, women, the disabled and children, as well as liberalising rules regarding public employees and trade unions. Moreover, for the first time in Turkish history, an ombudsman was to be appointed by parliament. The campaign that preceded the referendum, however, turned into a vicious battle between the government, political parties, the military and the juridical establishment.

Even a cursory reading of the constitutional text reveals the aim of reviving the figure and political work of Kemal Atatürk; it reproduces mimetically some of the failures of the Constitution of 1924. Here we find the second example of constitutional violence. The preamble of the constitutional text is a mission statement:

> In line with the concept of nationalism and the reforms and principles introduced by the founder of the Republic of Turkey, Atatürk, the immortal leader and the unrivalled hero, this Constitution, which affirms the eternal existence of the Turkish nation and motherland and the indivisible unity of the Turkish state ...

The metaphysical claim ('eternal existence') is not just a romantic aspiration. Like France, Turkey claims to be a mono-nuclear nation; there is no recognition of diversity or minorities and these are simply ignored. The preamble follows with another important consequence of the influence of France on Atatürk:

> The understanding of the absolute supremacy of the will of the nation and of the fact that sovereignty is vested fully and unconditionally in the Turkish nation ... The recognition that no protection shall be accorded to an activity contrary to Turkish national interests, the principle of the indivisibility of the existence of Turkey with its state and territory ... The recognition that all Turkish citizens are united in national honour and pride, in national joy and grief, in their rights and duties regarding national existence, in blessings and in burdens, and in every manifestation of national life ...

In Turkey there is not only national sovereignty, but also a 'national life', 'national honour and pride' and 'national joy and grief': an antiquated declaration that is reminiscent of fascist nationalism. National sovereignty is also mentioned in Article 3: 'The Turkish state, with its territory and nation, is an indivisible entity. Its language is Turkish.' The enforcement of this article is a reproduction of the French constitutional example.

Turkish ethnic nationalism is clearly accommodated in a constitution that promotes a single official ethnicity at the expense of other groups. Turkish constitutional nationalism is a repressive official nationalism based on constitutional 'reason', assimilationist policies and military enforcement. Therefore, the Turkish Constitution, while attempting to appear democratic, allows for the violation of the human rights of the minorities that live in Turkey. The Kurdish population of 15 million comprises 20 per cent of the population in Turkey.[129] The people of Kurdistan speak one of the few surviving original languages of the Mesopotamian people. The Republic of Turkey has denied the existence of the Kurds and their language, culture, ethnicity and traditions with a constitutional text that contravenes human rights conventions. As mentioned in the case of French constitutional violence, the human rights of minorities are explicitly set out in the Universal Declaration of Human Rights, the international covenants, the Convention on the Elimination of All Forms of Racial Discrimination, the Convention on the Rights of the Child, the Declaration on the Rights of Persons Belonging to National or Ethnic, Religious and Linguistic Minorities and other widely adhered to human rights treaties and declarations. In Turkey, there is the compulsory application of Articles 1, 2, 7 and 23 of the Universal Declaration of Human Rights; Articles 2, 7 and 13 of the International Covenant on Economic, Social and Cultural Rights; Articles 3 and 5 of the Convention against Discrimination in Education; and Articles 2, 17, 28, 29 and 30 of the Convention on the Rights of the Child. Turkey is a member of the European Court of Human Rights. A literal interpretation of the Constitution demonstrates the need for the recognition of the Kurds in Turkey. In this respect, the case of Mrs Leyla Zana, Mr Hatip Dicle, Mr Orhan Doğan and Mr Selim Sadak is an excellent example of how human rights are denied. In 1994 Leyla Zana and others were sentenced to fifteen years' imprisonment for their political activities in support of the fundamental rights of the Kurdish people. Leyla Zana was well known in Turkey as the country's first ever Kurdish woman to be elected to the Turkish parliament. Leyla Zana's parliamentary immunity was eventually lifted. Based on her actions at the inauguration and her subsequent speeches and writings in defence of Kurdish rights, a Turkish court initiated proceedings against her in September 1994 for treason.[130] In its judgment of 17 July 2001, the European Court of Human Rights in Strasbourg noted the lack of independence and impartiality of the State Security Court in Ankara, as well as breaches of the rights of the defence and the presence in court of military judges. This judgment prompted the Turkish authorities to hold a new trial of Leyla Zana and others.[131]

The text adopted by the European Parliament condemns the decision by the State Security Court in Ankara, and also condemns the breaches of the rights of defence that occurred during the new trial of Leyla Zana and others. These breaches included the presence of the state prosecutor in all the rooms where the judges were required to take decisions concerning the accused, the failure to acknowledge the right of the accused to be released in accordance with the ECtHR judgment of 17 July 2001, and the inability of the defence to check the veracity of the accusations made by the state prosecutor. In June 2004, the Turkish Supreme Court ordered the release of Leyla Zana after ten years' imprisonment for speaking Kurdish in the Turkish parliament.[132]

International humanitarian law and international litigation can be effective in redressing internal (national) denial of fundamental rights. Although not envisioned within the Convention's text, the power to recommend measures of redress for human rights violations has emerged in the jurisprudence of the ECtHR since 19 January 2000.[133] The decisions in *Gençel v. Turkey* (53431/99) and *Öcalan v. Turkey* (46221/99) are good examples of how the ECtHR has redressed human rights violations legitimised by the Turkish Constitution.

In *Gençel v. Turkey*, a specialised tribunal known as the State Security

Court convicted the applicants of being members of or having aided and abetted illegal armed organisations. They were given prison sentences. The bench of this court included military judges, who submitted to military obedience and the chain of command. The ECtHR found that the composition of the bench was unsatisfactory and that a civilian who was required to answer criminal charges before a State Security Court that included a military judge on its bench had a legitimate reason to fear that the court would not be independent and impartial. It unanimously found that there had been a violation of Article 6, Section 1 of the Convention in each of these fourteen cases.[134] Therefore, the court recommended that the applicant be granted a new trial before a court that met the requirements of Article 6 of the Convention, specifically the requirement that the applicant be given a fair trial.[135]

The second case, *Öcalan v. Turkey*, concerns an application brought by a Turkish national, Abdullah Öcalan, then incarcerated in Imrali Prison (Bursa, Turkey). At the time of the events, the Turkish courts had issued seven warrants for Mr Öcalan's arrest and a wanted notice (Red Notice) had been circulated by Interpol. He was accused of founding an armed gang in order to destroy the integrity of the Turkish state and of instigating terrorist acts resulting in loss of life. This case also concerned the presence of military judges on the bench and the Grand Chamber reached a similar conclusion.

After these recommendations and the many other disputes that the Turkish government lost at the European level, the government introduced a bill in the national parliament to reform the State Security Court system. As a result of this legislation, the use of military judgments to produce results in specific cases eventually resulted in a much broader effect, namely, a reform of the national legal system.[136] This example shows that the disproportionate role of the military (a non-democratic body) in Turkey is seen as suspicious by Western countries and a contravention of human rights. The reform of the State Security Court, and consequently the legal system itself, can be understood as a constructive example that helped lead the way in removing the military from the constitutional sphere.

On 12 June 2011, the conservative party of Prime Minister Recep Tayyip Erdogan, AKP (Justice and Development), won the elections with 49.9 per cent of the votes and a total of 326 of the 550 seats in the Turkish Grand National Assembly – sufficient to form a government without partners (the control threshold being 276 seats). However, the AKP failed to obtain the 330 seats necessary to initiate a referendum on amending the Constitution. Under the current law, the Constitution can be changed by a majority of 367 deputies. If an initiative is supported by only 330 deputies, then the changes, or the proposed constitution, must be put to a referendum.

Erdogan's top priority in this election was to draft a new constitution and push for major changes that included a shift to a presidential system. The proposed amendments included articles that would allow collective bargaining rights for public sector workers and affirmative measures for women. The proposed reforms included amendments to the judicial system, curbs on the power of military courts and an article abolishing the immunity currently enjoyed by the leaders of the 1980 coup. Other measures would guarantee gender equality and introduce measures to protect children, the elderly and the disabled.

One of the proposed amendments increased the number of judges on Turkey's highest court from eleven to seventeen. It also granted parliament, which is controlled by Erdogan's party, the power to appoint several judges.[137]

In his victory speech delivered from the balcony of his party head-quarters in Ankara, Erdogan made a pledge to serve all Turks, regardless of ethnicity or religion. These reforms seem to reduce the democratic deficit of Turkey, and there is an excellent possibility that by including ethnic minorities in the constituent process a more plural and democratic Turkey can be achieved. As Erdogan remarked, the new constitution will have to reflect a different understanding of Kurdish citizenship and not continue to impose a totally secular and exclusive constitutional identity.[138]

CHILEAN CONSTITUTIONAL VIOLENCE: CIVILISING THE INDIANS

This section focuses on the case of foundational constitutional violence against indigenous individuals and nations in Chile. In countries where ethnic and cultural genocide was initiated during the Spanish colonisation and continued by the new post-colonial states, it seems impossible to achieve a plausible retroactive solution for the pre-Columbian nations. However, the consequence of genocide does not mean that current democracies are exempted from recognising, apologising and seeking solutions for that genocide.

I have analysed the case of Chilean constitutional violence, yet clear analogies can be drawn with other states on the continent because this phenomenon has been reproduced with more or less virulence throughout Latin America – where the profoundly democratic way of life of the thirteen British colonies did not exist.[139]

The analysis is based primarily on the role that Chilean constitutionalism developed in relation to the indigenous peoples. The constitution as a founding act replaced the sovereign, thereby creating a new state, a new people and enforcing the assimilation of the minorities into the new nation. The alternative to assimilation was extermination. The role of constitutionalism represented the juridification of this new political order. In this respect, the Constitution always offered coverage and legal legitimacy to the 'necessary' ethnic cleansing. In a classical study of genocide, Lemkin observes two main phases: the destruction of the organisational patterns of the oppressed group; and their replacement by those of the oppressor group.[140] This second event makes genocide a central issue in national and post-colonial experiences in Latin America.[141] Kaempfer explains that most prominent intellectuals and statesmen agreed on the incompatibility of the national project and indigenous populations.[142] As Sarmiento[143] stated, the Spanish in exterminating a 'savage' people whose territory they wished to occupy did just what all 'civilised' people have done. Sarmiento also considered that thanks to this injustice, America is now occupied by Caucasians ('the most perfect, smartest' and most productive race on earth'), rather than being abandoned to savages who were incapable of progress.[144] In other words, the most prominent intellectuals, with notable exceptions, provided the best arguments to justify the extermination of the Indians by nation-states. The best-known episodes of the extermination were the Pacification of Araucanía in Chile and the Desert Campaign in Argentina.[145]

As in the cases discussed earlier in this chapter, the extreme violence of the emancipation or founding process predetermined constitutional development and enforcement. In Latin America, we find the terrible paradox that the process of national independence was born of the indigenous resistance to Spanish colonialism.[146] Between 1811 and 1830, various attempts were made in Chile to regulate national coexistence as the Chilean War of Independence revealed that independence had far from unanimous support among Chileans – divided between loyalists and supporters of independence. This era has been regarded as a period of 'constitutional testing' or 'organisation of the Republic'.[147]

One approach for homogenising a divided people was the French method of national sovereignty. Article 3 of the constitutional project of Juan Egaña (1811) stated that sovereignty resides essentially in the nation and is exercised by representatives. The same formulation appears implicitly in the provisional constitution of 1818 and also in the first Chilean Constitution of 1822, which consecrates national sovereignty in Article 1. This prime constitutional doctrine is excellent evidence of how the founding fathers solved the problem of the indigenous peoples. In this regard, Article 47, Section 6 of this first constitutional text stated that among the powers of the Congress was that of civilising the Indians of the territory.[148] After three more constitutions in five years (1823, 1826 and 1828), the Constitution of 1833 was approved. With this text the state was organised in step with the needs of society and a period of major institutional stability began that lasted nearly a century. In the twentieth century, the 1925 Constitution enshrined a pure presidential system and gave the state an important role in economic and social development.[149]

Since the military occupation of Araucanía in 1861 the indigenous people have been systematically incorporated into the national state. This assimilation was done according to the homogenising and exclusory pattern of the nation-state.[150] It was performed with particular force and violence in the case of the Mapuche, after their defeat and the military occupation of their territory.[151] The 'Pacification of Araucanía' and the *Ley sobre la propiedad indígena* (Native Ownership Act) of 1866 established a substantial difference between the relations of the Mapuche with the Spanish crown and the new Chilean state. The first difference was that for the coloniser the Mapuche represented a valid negotiating partner, but for the Chileans they were an obstacle with a single solution: cultural and territorial annexation.[152] Certainly, the coloniser's recognition of the Mapuche as a valid negotiating partner came after the Disaster of Curalaba of 21 December 1589, in which the Spanish governor was killed by the Mapuches. The effects of this event quickly spread throughout the territory south of the Bio-Bio River and expelled the Spanish north of the river.[153] The importance of this event is that the Spanish crown recognised by royal decree the independence of the Mapuche, and the Bio-Bio River was the limit of two independent nations. With the independence of Chile this autonomy was ignored, with the Mapuche territory being arbitrarily integrated into the Republic of Chile.[154] The consequences of this conquest and the territorial and cultural reduction are still felt today.

The Constitution was an instrument to legitimate the second stage of a cultural genocide, to expand and consolidate the new constitutional nation and to force the assimilation of the 'uncivilised' (according to Article 47, Section 6 of the Constitution of 1822).

After sixty-five years without important constitutional changes, in July 1980, the council of state presented its recommendations to the president. The junta then hammered out the final text. Without any public education campaign or discussion the new constitution was ratified by 67 per cent of those voting in a plebiscite on 11 September 1980. Chileans and foreign residents over the age of eighteen had only to show their national identity card and could vote at any polling station. Blank ballots counted as 'yes'. Many deemed the vote to have been fraudulent. The constitution was made effective on 11 March 1981.[155]

The most controversial article was Transitional Provision 24, which eliminated due process of law by giving the president broad powers to curtail the rights of assembly and free speech and arrest, exile or banish into internal exile any citizen – with no rights of appeal except to the president himself.[156] According to the 1980 document, the cornerstone of the military regime's constitutional doctrine was the establishment of a permanent tutelary role for the armed forces.[157] The constitution was amended in 1989,

1991, 1997, 1999, 2000, 2003 and 2005.[158] The last amendment eliminated some of the remaining undemocratic articles. However, none of these reforms recognised the multinational character of the Chilean state, the indigenous peoples as nations, their right to self-determination or the genocide committed by the founding fathers.

Since the military occupation of Araucanía in 1861, the indigenous peoples have been systematically incorporated into the national state. This assimilation was done according to the homogenising and exclusory pattern of the nation-state.[159] It was enforced especially violently in the case of the Mapuche – after their defeat and the military occupation of their territory.[160] The 'Pacification of Araucanía' and the *Ley sobre la propiedad indígena* (Native Ownership Act) of 1866 established a substantial difference between the previous relations of the Mapuche with the Spanish crown and those with the new Chilean state. The first difference was that for the Spanish the Mapuche had represented a valid negotiating partner, but for the Chileans they were an obstacle to a single cultural and territorial annexation.[161]

Regarding the situation and constitutional accommodation of Native American nations in Chile, it is important to note that in 1972 the government of Salvador Allende passed the first law referring to the indigenous peoples of the country as a whole. Law 17729 of 15 September 1972 defined indigenous persons and lands and other important issues. The main goals set in the law were to stop the division of the land of the indigenous peoples (Article 14); to recover the indigenous lands (a term recognised lately by the United Nations) through a legal process of expropriation (Article 29–32); and to create an Institute for Indigenous Development (Article 34–52).[162] The application of this law was a step forward towards the recognition of the indigenous peoples by the state, but still intended their integration through Allende's *Socialismo a la Chilena*, which ultimately represented a new sort of assimilation. However, the military dictatorship put a violent end to the reform implemented by Frei and Allende over the previous ten years. Some 64.7 per cent of the expropriated land was returned to its former owners. The counter-reform process was marked by repression and violence; Mapuche leaders were shot and disappeared, while the expropriations were revoked.[163] On 22 March 1979, a new law was passed (*Decreto Ley* 2568), which modified the indigenous legislation. The dictatorship period was a regression in the situation and rights of the natives in Chile, since the exclusive goal of state policy was to eradicate the indigenous communities.[164] It may seem that Chile, Argentina and Peru would not have existed without the consolidation of genocide – but the work of Lastarria and others shows this not to be true.

The 1990s saw a transition to democracy that ended the seventeen-year dictatorship. Law 19253, which included the basis for implementing policies to protect indigenous lands (Article 39), was passed in 1993.[165] The new democratic regime seemed to open up the possibility that indigenous needs and demands could be heard by the new Chilean authorities without fear of state repression. The indigenous legislation was intended to represent this new scenario, but the original project sent to Congress suffered many changes; among these was the denial of a constitutional recognition of the indigenous population as a 'people' or a 'nation' by the Chilean state.[166] Article 1 of this law implemented an assimilationist national sovereignty; yet the state recognised the main Chilean indigenous groups: the Mapuche, Aymara, Rapa Nui or Easter Island, the Atacameña, Quechua, Collas and Diaguita in the north, and the Alacalufe Kawashkar and Yamana or Yagan communities. The law stated that the state values their existence as an essential part of the roots of the Chilean nation and its integrity and development, and that their customs and values should be respected.[167] This recognition as an essential part of the nation omits the possibility of singularity and therefore denies any sort of collective right as a people rather than a community.

Law 19253 is the basis for other regulations relating to the indigenous peoples, such as Law 20249 of 16 February 2008. On 19 October 2008, President Bachellet signed an act that aimed to achieve a constitutional recognition of the indigenous peoples by Congress. The president stated that she expected a constitutional recognition of the original indigenous peoples of Chile, and to produce a common base for dialogue that would make democracy deeper, more inclusive and more plural.[168] On 7 April 2009, the Chilean Senate approved the draft of a constitutional reform on the recognition of the indigenous peoples that recognises the multicultural nature of the Chilean nation; recognises local communities and indigenous organisations and their members; recognises the right to preserve, strengthen and develop their identity, culture, language, institutions and traditions; recognises the right to participate in economic, social, political and cultural development within the framework of the national legal order; and states that indigenous peoples may organise their lives according to their customs, while respecting the constitution and laws.[169] However, this constitutional amendment does not meet the requirements of international legislation, and Chile still does not recognise indigenous peoples as valid negotiating partners.

There are multiple international treaties and UN declarations, resolutions and working groups on indigenous peoples.[170] It is important to highlight the Indigenous and Tribal Populations Convention, 1957 (No. 107), of the International Labour Organisation. This convention was an initial attempt to codify the international obligations of states with respect to indigenous and tribal populations, and was the first international convention on the subject. It was adopted by the ILO at the request of the United Nations and ratified by twenty-seven countries.[171] However, it has an integrationist approach that reflects the development discourse of the time at which it was adopted. This approach began to be questioned during the 1970s, when the United Nations started to examine in more detail issues concerning indigenous and tribal peoples, and when indigenous peoples began to become more internationally visible. A committee of experts convened in 1986 by the governing body of the ILO concluded that 'the integrationist approach of the Convention was obsolete and that its application was detrimental in the modern world'. It was revised between 1988 and 1989 through the adoption of Convention No. 169. Following the adoption of this convention, the old convention, No. 107, is no longer open for ratification yet remains in force in eighteen countries (a number of which have significant indigenous populations), and is still a useful instrument as it covers many areas that are key for indigenous peoples.[172]

Chile ratified ILO Convention No. 169 on 15 September 2009.[173] The Convention states in its preamble that the basic idea of the agreement is to 'recognize the aspirations of these peoples to exercise control over their own institutions, ways of life and economic development and to maintain and develop their identities, languages and religions, within the framework of the States in which they live'. The Convention also recognises the indigenous peoples as 'peoples' and not as 'populations', and encourages 'recognition of, and respect for, ethnic and cultural diversity' instead of integration. In Article 13, Section 2, the Convention introduces the concept of indigenous territories, stating that the use of the term *lands* in Articles 15 and 16 shall include the concept of territories that cover the total environment of the areas which the peoples concerned occupy, or otherwise use. Article 14, Section 1 also confirms that the rights of ownership and possession of the peoples concerned over the lands which they traditionally occupy shall be recognised. Article 15, Section 1 establishes that the rights of the peoples concerned to the natural resources pertaining to their lands shall be specially safeguarded. These rights include the right of these peoples to participate in the use, management and conservation of these resources.[174] The Chilean legal system must be adapted to this internationally enforceable doctrine, and this will mean profound amendments to the Chilean consti- tutional text and a complete application of the articles. Chile has been using its legislation to ignore this mandatory convention. The committee of experts on the application of conventions in its 2008 Review Report (approved by the ILO in 2009) on the application of Convention No. 111 on Discrimination requested the government of Chile to provide information on the evolution of the constitutional amendment regarding indigenous peoples, including information on measures taken to ensure the participa- tion of indigenous peoples in the process.[175]

The Declaration on the Rights of Indigenous Peoples was one of the most negotiated resolutions in UN history and took twenty-two years to gain approval. The declaration is a type of bill of rights for indigenous peoples. Article 3 includes the right of self-determination ('Indigenous peoples have the right to self-determination. By virtue of that right they freely determine their political status and freely pursue their economic, social and cultural development'); Article 4 includes the right of autonomy ('Indigenous peoples, in exercising their right to self-determination, have the right to autonomy or self-government in matters relating to their internal and local affairs, as well as ways and means for financing their autonomous functions'); and Article 6 includes the right of nationality ('Every indigenous individual has the right to a nationality'). There is a clear contradiction between the Chilean legal pseudo-recognition and international mandatory legislation, as well as a clash of legitimacies between human rights and the Constitution of Chile (among others). Chile, according to the United Nations, is a multi-national state and this statement contradicts the Chilean constitutional system from its origins in 1811. The Chilean Constitution must be adapted to this mandatory international doctrine. The only valid constitutional mutual recognition would be that Chile recognises that the indigenous peoples (the Mapuche, Aymara, Rapa Nui or Easter Island, the Atacameña, Quechua, Collas and Diaguita in the north, and the Alacalufe Kawashkar and Yamana or Yagan communities) have the right to be considered nations and can exercise their right to self-determination. The recognition must be mutual, free and valid. Otherwise, the result will be a perpetuation of the effects of a second stage of genocide and the imposition of constitutional violence.

SPANISH CONSTITUTIONAL VIOLENCE: DEFENSA NACIONAL

The example of Spanish constitutional violence is a case of a violent positive constitution (Schmitt), and an article that constitutionalises the threatened use of force. The positivisation of a threat of force is *per se* violence and contravenes international legislation on human rights. Article 8, Section 1 of the Spanish Constitution of 1978 states that the armed forces (constituting the army, navy and air force) must guarantee the sovereignty and independence of Spain, defend its territorial integrity and maintain constitutional order. The constitutionalisation of the armed forces is uncommon in Western European legal systems.[176] It is difficult to understand the specific issue of the constitutional role of the Spanish military. Discussions were raised about whether or not a constitutionalisation of the armed forces was necessary – but not about the content of the article. One of the reasons for the constitutional position of the armed forces was an earlier Article 37 of a statutory law of 1967.[177] This pre-democratic law stated that the armed forces guarantee the unity and independence of the home-land, the integrity of its territories, national security and the defence of institutional order. The parallelism between the two articles is evident.[178] It is necessary to emphasise the non-democratic origins of this significant law. The Franco regime passed this law and observed that 'the Movement [the Spanish Fascist movement] must be the chief actor in the progress and growth of Spain'. General Franco considered this statutory law to be a basic law of the state that would take precedence and could be modified only by referendum.[179] The Constitution of the regime covered important aspects, such as the 'nation-state', national sovereignty, the head of state, the govern-ment of the nation, the National Council, justice and the armed forces. One doctrinal sector (Aguado Renedo and others) considers that the reform of Franco's legal-political system through channels provided by the system itself significantly illustrates the originality of the Spanish transition from an authoritarian to a democratic system.[180] However, the Fascist origin of Article 8, Section 1 is not an isolated incident in Spanish constitutionalism and organisation of the state.

The democratic Spanish state assumed and constitutionalised the pre-democratic rules that the old regime had imposed. The well-known Spanish transition never completely broke with its immediate past. For this reason, Spanish officers who committed crimes against humanity were never judged in Spain, and most judicial and military officials were not purged with the arrival of democracy.[181] On the specific issue of Article 8, Section 1, the influence of the Franco regime is clear. This article constitutionalises the notion of 'national defence', which replaced the old concept of war.[182] National defence under the second clause of Article 2 of the statutory law 6/1980 aimed to permanently ensure the unity, sovereignty and indepen-dence of Spain; as well as its territorial integrity and constitutional order. Therefore, Article 8, Section 1 and Article 2 of the statutory law are heirs of an impossible pretension. No law or constitution can assure a perpetual goal, while the simply meta-juridical declaration as a sort of principle is a manner of limiting or attempting to condition the will of the Spanish people.

The 'internal effects' of Article 8, Section 1 are also clearly linked with Article 2 of the Spanish Constitution, which states that the Constitution is based on the indissoluble unity of the Spanish nation as the common and indivisible homeland of all Spaniards. Thus, the internal projection is intended to prevent secession or fragmentation of the territory, thereby representing an internal aggression against territorial integrity that also challenges Article 2.[183] If, for example, there were an attempted democratic and non-violent secession of regions from the union, then the military could be understood to have the constitutional role of defending territorial integrity; instead of being controlled by civil institutions and subject to civil agreements (such as a negotiated dissolution). In other words, there is a dilemma conditioned by a constitutionally threatened requirement. The question is whether the Constitution would need to be changed to release the military from their mandated duty to protect territorial integrity, or if the military could simply be ordered to remain outside of political negotiations and respect political agreements. The answer to this question is unclear even when the constitutional system clearly submits the military power to civil institutions.

While the Spanish political system is not supervised by the military as in Turkey, the armed forces have played a role. The coup d'état of 1981 was closely related to the events of the Spanish transition to democracy and had legal and political effects, as well as subconsciously affecting the political climate. Another example would be the statements and declarations of senior military officers (Mena and others) during the process of amending the Statute of Autonomy of Catalonia.[184] On 4 December 2010 (*Real Decreto* 1673/2010) the Spanish government declared a 'state of emergency' because a strike by air traffic controllers had largely closed the country's air space. The Spanish armed forces took control of air traffic control towers.

This dilemma was also a key issue in Yugoslavia, where the military was a significant federal institution and initially attempted to forcibly maintain the territorial integrity of Yugoslavia. This produced a constitutional crisis. Eventually, the military was dissolved and individual units and officers realigned themselves along essentially ethnic or regional lines.

Regardless of the answer to the impasse, Article 8, Section 1 is a threat to use force, and therefore contravenes international human rights agreements. In this respect, Article 2, Section 4 of the Charter of Human Rights affirms that all members shall refrain in their international relations from the threat or use of force against the territorial integrity or political independence of any state, or in any other manner inconsistent with the purposes of the United Nations.

Article 8, Section 1 directly contravenes the following resolutions of the General Assembly of the United Nations:

Resolution 2160 (XXI) of 30 November 1966, on the strict observance of the prohibition of the threat or use of force in international relations, and of the rights of peoples to self-determination. The resolution is aimed at peoples subjected to colonial oppression, but it clearly affirms that states should strictly observe, in international relations, a prohibition of the threatened use of force.

Resolution 2625 (XXV) of 24 October 1970 on principles of international law concerning friendly relations and cooperation among states in accordance with the Charter of the United Nations. In this declaration states must refrain in international relations from the threat of the use of force and uphold equal rights and self-determination. The declaration also states that no consideration of whatever nature may be invoked to warrant resorting to the threat of the use of force in violation of the Charter. Neither acquisition of territory resulting from the threat of the use of force nor any occupation of territory resulting from the threat of the use of force in contravention of international law will be recognized as a legal acquisition or occupation.

The prohibition enunciated in Article 2(4) of the Charter is part of *jus cogens*, that is, it is accepted and recognised by the international community of states as a norm from which no derogation is permitted, and which can be modified only by a subsequent norm of general international law that has the same peremptory character. Hence, universal *jus cogens*, such as the prohibition embodied in Article 2(4), cannot be omitted at a regional level. Furthermore, the Charter's prohibition of the threat or use of armed force is binding on states both individually and as members of international organisations, such as NATO, as well as on those organisations themselves.[185]

Article 8, Section 1 of the Spanish Constitution also violates the provisions of Articles 51 and 52 of the Vienna Convention on the Law of Treaties of 1969; Articles 51 and 52 of the Vienna Convention on the Law of Treaties between States and International Organizations or between International Organizations of 1986; and the preamble of the Vienna Convention on Succession of States in respect of Treaties of 1978. Moreover, it is important to draw attention to Article 52 of the above-mentioned Vienna Convention, according to which 'a treaty is void if its conclusion has been procured by the threat or use of force in violation of the principles of international law embodied in the Charter of the United Nations', paramount among these principles being Article 2(4). The law of the UN Charter provides two exceptions from the prohibition expressed in Article 2(4) (the mechanism of the so-called 'enemy state' clauses (Articles 53 and 107) should be left aside as they are now unanimously considered obsolete). The first exception, embodied in Article 51 of the Charter, is available to states that find themselves the victims of aggression.[186] Aggression is violent and military in nature and opposed to a democratic and peaceful process of secession. An analogous application of these international treaties would declare void Article 8 of the Spanish Constitution.

Ballbé explains in a well-known work in Spain the evolution of militarism in Spain.[187] On 21 January 2011, I had the opportunity to talk to him about the origin of, and debates behind, Article 8 of the current Spanish Constitution. Ballbé, who participated in the constituent debates of 1978 assisting the drafter Solé Tura, argued that Article 8 was seen as a guarantee for the population, and the constitutionalisation of the army as a safeguard against a possible military coup d'état.

Certainly, the military action of Lieutenant Colonel Tejero in Congress and the military takeover of the city of Valencia by General Milans del Bosch is evidence of the Spanish political atmosphere in the early 1980s. Although the Spanish transition was not itself violent, it was surrounded by violence. At the time the transition was about to begin, violence, the threat of violence and the memory of violence were all very much present.[188]

But over the past thirty-three years the perception has changed and a victory in 1978 for the Constitution represents a challenge to democracy and human rights in 2011.[189] The solution may be a constitutional amendment; however, this idea has never been discussed or placed on the Spanish political agenda.

Notes

1. T. Hobbes, *The Leviathan*, Oxford: Oxford University Press, 2009.
2. V. C. Jackson and M. Tushnet, *Comparative Constitutional Law*, New York: Foundation Press, 2006, p. 155.
3. R. Cover, 'Violence and the world', *Yale Law Journal*, 95, 1995, 1601–29.
4. 408 US 238 1972.
5. 428 US 242 1976.
6. HR 3355, Pub. L. 103–322, 1994.
7. 536 US 304 2002.
8. 543 US 551 2005.
9. V. C. Jackson and M. Tushnet, *Comparative Constitutional Law*, New York: Foundation Press, 2006.
10. The death penalty is allowed in thirty-eight states and banned in the remaining twelve states of the United States.
11. J. K. Lieberman, *A Practical Companion to the Constitution: How the Supreme Court has Ruled on Issues from Abortion to Zoning*, Berkeley, CA: University of California Press, 1999, p. 137.
12. 483 US 219 1987.
13. 11 ECtHR, ser. A, 1989.
14. V. C. Jackson and M. Tushnet, *Comparative Constitutional Law*, New York: Foundation Press, 2006, p. 155.
15. Judgment, 7 July 1989, 161 ECtHR.
16. UNHCR, *Soering v. The United Kingdom*, available at: http://www.unhcr.org/cgi-bin/texis/vtx/refworld/rwmain?docid=3ae6b6fec, accessed 10 March 2011.
17. *Ibid.*
18. V. C. Jackson and M. Tushnet, *Comparative Constitutional Law*, New York: Foundation Press, 2006, p. 158.

19. *Ibid.*, p. 158.
20. UNHCR, *Soering* v. *United Kingdom,* available at: http://www.unhcr. org/cgi-bin/texis/vtx/refworld/rwmain?docid=3ae6b6fec, accessed 10 November 2010.
21. *Ibid.*
22. *Gregg* v. *Georgia,* 153 US 242 1976.
23. V. C. Jackson and M. Tushnet, *Comparative Constitutional Law,* New York: Foundation Press, 2006. p. 159.
24. *Ibid.*, p. 159.
25. CCPR/C/78/D/829/1998.
26. *Roger Judge* v. *Canada,* CCPR/C/78/D/829/1998, UNHRC.
27. *Kindler* v. *Canada (Minister of Justice)* [1991] 2 SCR 779, SCC, 26 September 1991, available at: http://www.unhcr.org/refworld/docid/ 3ae6b6ed0.html, accessed 12 November 2010.
28. *Roger Judge* v. *Canada,* CCPR/C/78/D/829/1998, UNHRC, available at: http://www.unhcr.org/refworld/country_HRC_CAN,4562d94e2,404887e f3,0.html, accessed 11 November 2010.
29. *Ibid.*
30. Available at: http://users.xplornet.com/~mwarren/return.htm, accessed 11 November 2010.
31. Source: Amnesty International.
32. See *United States* v. *Rauscher,* 119 US 407, 422 1886.
33. See *United States* v. *Andonian,* 29 F.3d 1432, 1435 (9th Cir.) 1994. Based on international comity, the principle of specialty generally requires a country seeking extradition to adhere to any limitations placed on prosecution by the surrendering country.
34. *United States* v. *Baez,* 349 F.3d 90, 93 (2nd Cir.) 2003.
35. *Sanitary Dist. of Chicago* v. *U S,* 266 US 405 1925.
36. See *Benitez* v. *Garcia,* 495 F.3d 640 (9th Cir.) 2007, available at: http:// users.xplornet.com/~mwarren/return.htm, accessed 12 November 2011.
37. J. J. Álvarez González, *Derecho constitucional de Puerto Rico y relaciones constitucionales con los Estados Unidos,* Bogotá: Temis, 2010, p. 8.
38. *Ibid.*, p. 9
39. *Ibid.*, p. 9.
40. 118 US 375 1886.
41. J. J. Álvarez González, *Derecho constitucional de Puerto Rico y relaciones constitucionales con los Estados Unidos,* Bogotá: Temis, 2010, p. 9.
42. *Ibid.*, p. 10.
43. Article IV, Section 3-2 of the US Constitution states: 'The Congress shall have power to dispose of and make all needful rules and regulations respecting the territory or other property belonging to the United States; and nothing in this Constitution shall be so construed as to prejudice any claims of the United States, or of any particular state.'

   In reference to the *Insular Cases,* the US Supreme Court considered that territories belonged to, but were not *part of* the United States. Therefore, under the territorial clause Congress had the power to determine which parts of the Constitution applied to the territories.

In 1980, the US Supreme Court ruled that Congress acts with respect to Puerto Rico under the territorial clause (*Harris* v. *Rosario*, 446 US 651). In *US* v. *Sanchez* mentioned above, the Court stated that Congress retains authority to determine the status of the territory in accordance with the territorial clause and the Treaty of Paris as it deems consistent with the national interest. It confirms that adoption of a local constitution in 1952 did not alter the status of Puerto Rico under the territorial clause. The US Supreme Court has also described the jurisdiction under the territorial clause as a 'temporary' condition regulated by Congress until the establishment of a local self-government. This was included in the decision on *Reid* v. *Covert*, 354 US 1 1957. Source: http://www.puerto ricousa.com/english/views.htm.

44. *Diario de Sesiones de la Asamblea Constituyente*, 1104–05, 1519, 2566, Equity Publishing, 1961. Source: Westlaw 106 F.Supp. 2d. 311.
45. R. K. Little, 'Federal death penalty: history and some thoughts about the Department of Justice's role', *Fordham Urban Law Journal*, 36, 1999, 347–57.
46. Puerto Rico is one of the jurisdictions of the United States with the highest levels of violent crime. In 1999, Puerto Rico had a crime rate of 14.6 murders per 100,000 citizens. Except for the District of Columbia, no other state had such a high rate. Source: Federal Bureau of Investigation, 2000.
47. L. R. Cámara-Fuertes, J. J. Colón-Morera and H. M. Martínez-Ramírez, 'The death penalty in Puerto Rico', *Centro Journal*, 18(11), 2006, 147–65.
48. *Ibid.*, p. 150.
49. *Ibid.*, p. 160.
50. *Ibid.*, p. 160.
51. *Ibid.*, p. 161.
52. *United States of America* v. *Hector Oscar Acosta Martínez & Joel Rivera Alejandro*, D. PR CR No. 99-044, SEC, Westlaw 106 F.Supp. 2d, 311.
53. *Ibid.*
54. See *United States* v. *Quiñones*, 758 F.2d 40, 42 (1st Cir.) 1985; *Figueroa* v. *People of Puerto Rico*, 232 F.2d 615, 620 (1st Cir.) 1956.
55. *Cordova & Simonpietri Ins. Agency, Inc.* v. *Chase Manhattan Bank, N.A.*, 649 F.2d 36, 41 (1st Cir.) 1981 (Breyer, J.). Source: Westlaw 106 F.Supp. 2d. 311.
56. See *Calero-Toledo*, 416 US at 672, 94 S.Ct. 2080 (noting that the Commonwealth 'is a political entity created by [Public Law 600] and with the consent of the people of Puerto Rico and joined with the United States of America under the terms of the compact') (citing *Mora* v. *Mejias*, 206 F.2d 377, 387 (1st Cir.) 1953; *Quiñones*, 758 F.2d at 42; *Cordova*, 649 F.2d at 40; *Caribtow Corp.* v. *Occupational Safety and*

Health Review Com'n, 493 F.2d 1064, 1065 (1st Cir.) 1974; *Dario Sanchez v. United States*, 256 F.2d 73, 74 (1st Cir.) 1958; *Moreno Rios*, 256 F.2d at 70; *Figueroa*, 232 F.2d at 617; *Mora*, 206 F.2d at 387, fn 13. In *Harris v. Rosario*, 446 US 651, 651–652, 100 S.Ct. 1929, 64 L.Ed. 2d 587 1980.

57. See *United States* v. *Quiñones*, 758 F.2d 40, 42 (1st Cir.) 1985.
58. 2006 TSPR 74–167 DPR.
59. 483 US 219 1987.
60. D. W. North, 'The obstruction of the extradition derailment', *Suffolk University Law Review*, 28, 2001, as quoted in *Puerto Rico* v. *Juan Martínez Cruz*, 2006 TSPR 74–167 DPR.
61. 65 US (24 How.) 66 1861.
62. As quoted in *Puerto Rico* v. *Juan Martínez Cruz*, 2006 TSPR 74–167 DPR.
63. *Ibid*.
64. Commonwealth of Puerto Rico, Department of Justice, Testimony of Aníbal Acevedo Vilá, Governor of the Commonwealth of Puerto Rico, 27 June 2007. Available at: http://www.justicia.gobierno.pr/rs_template/v2/divleg/download/Statement_for_Federal_Death_Penalty_Oversight_Hearing.pdf, accessed 10 December 2011.
65. *Ibid*.
66. *Ibid*.
67. L. Althusser, *Lenin and Philosophy and Other Essays*, London: New Left Books, 1977.
68. P. Ardant, *Institutions politiques et droit constitutionnel*, *libraire générale de droit et de jurisprudence*, Paris: E.J.A., 2007, p. 364.
69. The French constitutions from 1791 to 1875 were: 3 September 1791; 24 June 1793 (not applied); 5 Fructidor year III (22 August 1795); 22 Frimaire year VIII (15 December 1799); Charter of 4 June 1814; Charter of 14 August 1830; 4 November 1848; 14 January 1852; 21 May 1870 (not applied).
70. P. Ardant, *Institutions politiques et droit constitutionnel*, *libraire générale de droit et de jurisprudence*, Paris: E.J.A., 2007, p. 364.
71. *Ibid*., p. 161
72. *Ibid*., p. 161.
73. *Ibid*., p. 161.
74. M. Duverger, *Le système politique français*, Paris: Thémis Science Politique, Presses universitaires de France, 1996, p. 39.
75. D. G. Lavroff, *Le droit constitutionnel de la V république*, Paris: Dalloz, 1999, p. 25.
76. M. Duverger, *Le système politique français*, Paris: Thémis Science Politique, Presses universitaires de France, 1996, p. 193.
77. *Ibid*., p. 193.
78. P. Ardant, *Institutions politiques et droit constitutionnel*, *libraire générale de droit et de jurisprudence*, Paris: E.J.A., 2007, p. 163.
79. *Ibid*., p. 163.
80. *Ibid*., p. 427.

81. *Ibid.*, p. 427.
82. A. Mestre and P. Guttinger, *Constitutionnalisme jacobin et constitutionnalisme soviétique*, Paris: Presses universitaires de France, 1971, p. 10.
83. *Ibid.*, p. 12.
84. *Ibid.*, p. 13
85. *Ibid.*, p. 13.
86. See http://tempsreel.nouvelobs.com/opinions/20091102.OBS6600/l-identite-nationale-selon-rocard-un-debat-imbecile.html or http://www.lepoint.fr/actualites-politique/2009-11-20/identite-nationale-un-debat-inutile-et-dangereux-selon-rocard/917/0/397303.
87. J. M. Colombani, *Les infortunes de la république*, Paris: Grasset, 2000.
88. P. Ardant, *Institutions politiques et droit constitutionnel, libraire générale de droit et de jurisprudence*, Paris: E.J.A., 2007, p. 427.
89. Decision of the Conseil Constitutionnel, 9 May 1991, as quoted in Ardant, *Institutions politiques et droit constitutionnel*, p. 427.
90. *Ibid.*, p. 427.
91. A. Baylac-Ferrer, *Catalunya Nord, Societat i Identitat, reflexions, vivències i panorama català*, Canet: Trabucaire, 2009, p. 39.
92. *Ibid.*, p. 40.
93. *Ibid.*, p. 40.
94. *Ibid.*, p. 40.
95. See Decision No. 99-412 DC, 15 June 1999, Conseil Constitutionnel, which states that the European Charter for Regional or Minority Languages is unconstitutional and not the opposite.
96. Kurdish performers banned: Appeal from International PEN, see http://www.freemuse.org/sw6195.asp.
97. Available at: http://www.websters-online dictionary.org/definitions/Kurdish%20language?cx=partner-pub 0939450753529744%3Av0qd01-tdlq&cof=FORID%3A9&ie=UTF 8&q=Kurdish%20language&sa=Search#922, accessed 20 December 2011.
98. T. Atabaki and E. J. Zürcher, *Men of Order, Authoritarian Modernization under Atatürk and Reza Shah*, London: I. B. Tauris, 2004, p. 1.
99. A. Jevakhoff, *Kemal Atatürk, les chemins de l'Occident*, Paris: Tallandier, 1989, p. 324.
100. *Ibid.*, p. 324.
101. *Ibid.*, p. 46.
102. *Ibid.*, p. 47.
103. Available at: http://static.sdu.dk/mediafiles//8/3/2/%7B83271B78-3413-49C1-ADA7-5974AA35D283%7D1009%20DJ.pdf, accessed 11 December 2011.
104. T. Atabaki and E. J. Zürcher, *Men of Order, Authoritarian Modernization under Atatürk and Reza Shah*, London: I. B. Tauris, 2004, p. 47.
105. *Ibid.*, p. 2.

106. E. J. Zürcher, *Turkey: A Modern History*, London: I. B. Tauris, 2004, p. 167. The Treaty of Lausanne, 24 July 1923, was a peace treaty resulting from the Turkish War of Independence, which settled the Anatolian and East Thracian parts of the partitioning of the Ottoman Empire. The treaty also led to the international recognition of the sovereignty of the new Republic of Turkey as the successor state of the defunct Ottoman Empire. See http://wwi.lib.byu.edu/index.php/Treaty_of_Lausanne.

107. E. J. Zürcher, *Turkey: A Modern History*, London: I. B. Tauris, 2004, p. 168.

108. E. Mead Earle, 'The new constitution of Turkey', *Journal of Public and International Affairs*, 40(1), 1925, 73–100.

109. A. Jevakhoff, *Kemal Atatürk, les chemins de l'Occident*, Paris: Tallandier, 1989, p. 318.

110. E. Mead Earle, 'The new constitution of Turkey', *Journal of Public and International Affairs*, 40(1), 1925, 83.

111. *Ibid.*, p. 86.

112. *Ibid.*, p. 89.

113. A. Jevakhoff, *Kemal Atatürk, les chemins de l'Occident*, Paris: Tallandier, 1989, p. 345.

114. Preamble of the current constitution of Turkey.

115. T. Atabaki and E. J. Zürcher, *Men of Order, Authoritarian Modernization under Atatürk and Reza Shah*, London: I. B. Tauris, 2004, p. 9.

116. E. J. Zürcher, *Turkey: A Modern History*, London: I. B. Tauris, 2004, p. 186.

117. *Ibid.*, p. 186.

118. *Ibid.*, p. 186.

119. *Ibid.*, p. 186.

120. *Ibid.*, p. 187.

121. E. J. Zürcher, *Turkey: A Modern History*, London: I. B. Tauris, 2004, p. 280.

122. S. Aydin-Düzgit and Y. Gürsoy, 'International Influences on the Turkish Transition to Democracy in 1993', Working paper No. 87, Center on Democracy, Development, and the Rule of Law, Freeman Spogli Institute for International Studies, Stanford University, 2008.

123. *Ibid.*, p. 5.

124. *Ibid.*, p. 6.

125. Voting was made compulsory and only in the Kurdish southeast were relatively high percentages of 'no' votes recorded.

126. W. H. Hale, *Turkish Politics and the Military*, London: Routledge, 1994.

127. E. J. Zürcher, *Turkey: A Modern History*, London: I. B. Tauris, 2004, p. 281.

128. The last of these amendments was passed by a referendum on 21 October 2007.

129. CIA, *The World Factbook, Turkey*, 2010.

130. Available at: http://www.europarl.europa.eu/meetdocs/2004_2009/documents/ fd/nt_zana_/nt_zana_en.pdf, accessed 11 December 2011.

131. Text adopted by the European Parliament on 22 April 2004, P5-TA (2004) 0377. 0199/2004, available at: http://www.europarl.europa.eu/sides/get Doc.do?pubRef=//EP//TEXT+TA+20040422+ITEMS+DOC+XML+V 0//EN&language=EN#sdocta27, accessed 11 December 2011.

132. Available at: http://www.europarl.europa.eu/meetdocs/2004_2009/documents/fd/nt_zana_/nt_zana_en.pdf, accessed 11 December 2011.

133. D. Popovic, 'Prevailing of judicial activism over self-restraint in the jurisprudence of the European Court of Human Rights', *Creighton Law Review*, 42(361), 2009, 12, 396.

134. Netherlands Institute of Human Rights, Utrecht School of Law, available at: http://sim.law.uu.nl/SIM/CaseLaw/hof.nsf/d4d0dd240bfee7ec125684 90035df05/2148fa813b16510241256dc8005443b7?OpenDocument, accessed 6 January 2012.

135. D. Popovic, 'Prevailing of judicial activism over self-restraint in the jurisprudence of the European Court of Human Rights', *Creighton Law Review*, 42(396), 2009, 13.

136. *Ibid.*, p. 13.

137. Available at: http://articles.cnn.com/2010-09-12/world/turkey.referendum_ 1_amendments-reform-package-judiciary?_s=PM:WORLD, accessed 6 January 2012.

138. Available at: http://www.bbc.co.uk/news/mobile/world-europe-13744972.

139. A. Kaempfer, 'Lastarria, Bello y Sarmiento en 1844: genocidio, historiografía y proyecto nacional', *Revista Crítica Literaria Latinoamericana*, 63–4, 2006a, 9.

140. R. Lemkin, *Axis Rule in Occupied Europe*, Washington, DC: Carnegie Endowment for International Peace, 1944.

141. A. Kaempfer, 'Lastarria, Bello y Sarmiento en 1844: genocidio, historiografía y proyecto nacional', *Revista Crítica Literaria Latinoamericana*, 63–4, 2006a, 9–24.

142. *Ibid.*, p. 10.

143. Domingo Faustino Sarmiento (15 February 1811–11 September 1888), respected writer and political innovator, was an Argentine activist, writer, statesman and the seventh president of Argentina.
    Andrés de Jesús María y José Bello López (29 November 1781–15 October 1865) was a Venezuelan humanist, poet, lawmaker, philosopher, educator and philologist, whose political and literary works constitute an important part of Spanish American culture. Bello is featured on the old 2,000 Venezuelan bolívar and the 20,000 Chilean peso notes. There is also a decoration, the Venezuelan Order of Andrés Bello. Source: Wikipedia.

144. A. Kaempfer, 'Lastarria, Bello y Sarmiento en 1844: genocidio, historiografía y proyecto nacional', *Revista Crítica Literaria Latinoamericana*, 63–4, 2006a, 25.

145. A. Kaempfer, 'Lastarria, Bello y Sarmiento en 1844: genocidio, historio-grafía y proyecto nacional', *Revista Crítica Literaria Latinoamericana*, 63–4, 2006a, 9.

The Pacification of Araucanía was the term used by Chilean officials to refer to the military campaigns and acculturation of the autonomous Mapuche territories. The Desert Campaign was a military campaign directed by Julio Roca, which established Argentine dominance over Patagonia. On the indigenous extermination, see also A. Kaempfer, 'Alencar, Blest Gana y Galván: narrativas de exterminio y subalternidad', *Revista Chilena de literatura*, 69, 2006b, 89–106; D. F. Sarmiento, *Obras completas*, Buenos Aires: Luz del Día, 1948–56; B. O'Higgins, 'Proclama a los Araucanos (1818)', in J. L. Romero (ed.), *Pensamiento político de la emancipación (1790–1825)*, vol. II. Caracas: Ayacucho, 1997, pp. 200–2.

146. J. V. Lastarria, 'Investigaciones sobre la influencia social de la conquista y el sistema colonial de los españoles en Chile', as quoted in Kaempfer, 'Lastarria, Bello y Sarmiento en 1844: genocidio, historiografía y proyecto nacional', p. 9.

147. Biblioteca Nacional del Congreso de Chile, Historia Constitucional Chilena, available at: http://www.bcn.cl/ecivica/histcons, accessed 14 December 2011.

148. *Biblioteca de la Academia Nacional de la Historia*, 2, 1961, 401.

149. Biblioteca Nacional del Congreso de Chile, Historia Constitucional Chilena, available at: http://www.bcn.cl/ecivica/histcons, accessed 14 December 2011.

150. Institut de Drets Humans de Catalunya, *El pueblo mapuche*, Serie de conflictos olvidados, 2008.

151. A. Bello, *Etnicidad y ciudadanía en América Latina. La acción colectiva de los pueblos indígenas*, Santiago: Comisión Económica para América Latina y el Caribe (CEPAL), 2004.

152. *Ibid.*, p. 103.

153. *Ibid.*, p. 104.

154. Institut de Drets Humans de Catalunya, *El pueblo mapuche*, Serie de conflictos olvidados, 2008.

155. Available at: http://www.princeton.edu/~pcwcr/reports/chile1980.html, accessed 14 December 2011.

156. Available at: http://countrystudies.us/chile/87.htm, accessed 14 December 2011.

157. *Ibid.*

158. Available at: http://pdba.georgetown.edu/Constitutions/Chile/chile05.html, accessed 14 December 2011.

159. Institut de Drets Humans de Catalunya, *El pueblo mapuche*. Serie de conflictos olvidados, 2008, p. 101.

160. A. Bello, *Etnicidad y ciudadanía en América Latina. La acción colectiva*

de los pueblos indígenas, Santiago: Comisión Económica para América Latina y el Caribe (CEPAL), 2004.

161. *Ibid.*, p. 103.
162. Available at: http://biblioteca.serindigena.org/libros_digitales/derechos_indigenas/leyes/76.htm.
163. Comisión Nacional de Verdad y Reconciliación, as quoted in Institut de Drets Humans de Catalunya, *El pueblo mapuche*, Serie de conflictos olvidados, 2008, p. 109.
164. A. Bello, *Etnicidad y ciudadanía en América Latina. La acción colectiva de los pueblos indígenas*, Santiago: Comisión Económica para América Latina y el Caribe (CEPAL), 2004, p. 131.
165. Available at: http://biblioteca.serindigena.org/libros_digitales/derechos_indigenas/leyes/index1.htm, accessed 15 December 2011.
166. *Ibid.*, p. 115.
167. Law 19253, available at: http://www.leychile.cl/Navegar?idNorma= 30620, accessed 15 December 2011.
168. Institut de Drets Humans de Catalunya, *El pueblo mapuche*, Serie de conflictos olvidados, 2008, p. 98.
169. Available at: http://www.senado.cl/prontus_galeria_noticias/site/artic/ 20090409/pags/20090409150917.html, accessed 15 December 2011.
170. See Resolution 1995/30, Commission on Human Rights, A permanent forum for indigenous people in the United Nations system, UN Doc. E/CN4/1995/30, 1995; Resolution 1995/31, Report of the Working Group on Indigenous Populations of the Subcommission on Prevention of Discrimination and Protection of Minorities; Resolution 1995/32, Establishment of a working group of the Commission on Human Rights to prepare a draft declaration in accordance with Paragraph 5 of General Assembly Resolution 49/214 of 23 December 1994; C.H.R. Resolution 56/140 of 19 December 2001, International Decade of the World's Indigenous People; Resolution 63/161 of 18 December 2008, the General Assembly to facilitate the participation of representatives of indigenous peoples' organisations in the Expert Mechanism on the Rights of Indigenous Peoples established in accordance with Human Rights Council resolution 6/36 of 14 December 2007.
171. Available at: http://www.ilo.org/indigenous/Conventions/no107/lang--en/ index.htm.
172. *Ibid.*
173. Available at: http://www.ilo.org/ilolex/cgilex/pdconv.pl?host=status01 &textbase=iloeng&document=7647&chapter=19&query=C169%40ref &highlight=&querytype=bool, accessed 16 December 2011.
174. *Ibid.*
175. Available at: http://www.politicaspublicas.net/panel/reforma/ documentos/ 690-ceacr-chile-c111.html, accessed 16 December 2011.
176. C. Aguado Renedo, in M. E. Casas Baamonde and M. Rodríguez-Piñero

y Bravo Ferrer (eds), *Comentarios a la Constitución*, 3rd edn, Madrid: Fundación Wolters Kluwer, 2008; E. Alvárez Conde and V. Garrido Mayol (eds), *Comentarios a la Constitución Española*, Valencia: Tirant lo Blanch, 2004; F. Garrido Falla *et al. Comentarios a la Constitución*, Madrid: Civitas, 2001; O. Alzaga Villaamil *et al. Comentarios a la Constitución Española de 1978*, Madrid: Editorial Cortes Generales y Derecho Reunidas, 1999.

177. C. Aguado Renedo, in M. E. Casas Baamonde and M. Rodríguez-Piñero y Bravo Ferrer (eds), *Comentarios a la Constitución*, 3rd edn, Madrid: Fundación Wolters Kluwer, 2008, Art. 8.

178. *Ibid.*, p. 8.

179. G. S. Payne, *The Franco Regime 1936–1975*, Madison, WI: University of Wisconsin Press, 1987, p. 526.

180. C. Aguado Renedo, in M. E. Casas Baamonde and M. Rodríguez-Piñero y Bravo Ferrer (eds), *Comentarios a la Constitución*, 3rd edn, Madrid: Fundación Wolters Kluwer, 2008, Art. 8.

181. In this context, on 14 October 2008, Judge Baltasar Garzón affirmed his jurisdiction to judge the disappearance of 130,000 persons during the Franco regime. See http://news.bbc.co.uk/2/hi/8606910.stm and coup d'état on 23 February 1981.

182. O. Alzaga Villaamil *et al. Comentarios a la Constitución Española de 1978*, Madrid: Editorial Cortes Generales y Derecho Reunidas, 1999, Art. 8, available at: http://vlex.com/vid/articulo-8-fuerzas-armadas-330906, accessed 16 December 2011.

183. *Ibid.*

184. See editorial, *New York Times*, 24 January 2006, available at: http://www.nytimes.com/2006/01/24/opinion/24tue4.html?_r=1, accessed 17 December 2011.

185. B. Simma, 'NATO, the UN and the use of force: legal aspects', *European Journal of International Law*, 10, 1999, 1–22.

186. *Ibid.*, p. 20.

187. M. Ballbé Mallol, *Orden público y militarismo en la España constitucional*, Madrid: Alianza Editorial, 1983.

188. M. Rosenfeld, 'Constitution-making, identity building, and peaceful transition to democracy: theoretical reflections inspired by the Spanish example', *Cardozo Law Review*, 19(1891), 1998, 139.

189. Stanford University conference, 'New Agents in International Law', available at: https://www.stanford.edu/dept/DLCL/cgi-bin/web/events/conference-new-agents-international-law, accessed 20 December 2011.

Afterword

The first conclusion that I want to emphasise is the understanding of human rights as a democratic feature. As Chapter 3 concludes, democracy, as a system, cannot be limited to a simple election method cloistered within borders. Democracy must be interpreted and enforced with a human rights baseline.

The five examples of legal violence expounded in this book demonstrate that constitutional enforcement is violent because it is illegitimate. In this sense, state or constitutional illegitimate force is plain violence. My point is that we cannot assume the legitimacy of the state (Schmitt) or constitutional violence (Kelsen) based on theological theories. Twenty-first-century society needs to overcome political theology as a source of constitutional legitimacy.[1] Kantorowicz, Taubes, Brecht, Schmitt and Cover, too, defined the depth of theological influence in political and legal theory. This influence is clear in constitutions and constitutionalism.

It is important to note that violence may be considered legitimate and necessary, but not every sort of violence is acceptable. Regardless of where the violence originates, it must respect democracy and human rights in a broad sense. There is no contradiction between democracy and human rights, because the two issues are related in several ways. The interrelation is summarised in three connections.[2] International legal commitments are now increasingly made by governments that can be held accountable for their commitments by their own people.[3]

International human rights and democracy are not only connected, but they act symbiotically – they are mutually dependent. In other words, there is no democracy without human rights or human rights without democracy.

In this regard, Risse *et al.*'s theory of socialisation of human rights norms affirms that human rights norms have constitutive effects, because good human rights performance is a crucial identifier of a member of the community of liberal states. Human rights norms help to define a category of states as 'liberal democratic states'.[4] Risse *et al.* note that in some cases these liberal 'clubs' are quite specific: in the case of the European Union, for example, formal and informal rules and norms specify that only democratic states with good human rights records can join the club.[5] In the case of the Organization of American States, members declare 'the need to consolidate,

as part of the cultural identity of each nation in the Hemisphere, democratic structures and systems which encourage freedom and social justice,
safeguard human rights, and favor progress' (Managua Declaration of
1993).[6] Therefore, if, as Simmons states, international politics has become
more populist in nature, if not more democratic,[7] it is also factual that
democracy has become progressively more 'international', facing multiculturalism and globalisation (within the state's borders) and the new era of
the Internet that completely alters the nature of legal relations.[8] Thus, the
conclusion is a plea for the strengthening of the international dimension of
democratisation to reverse constitutional violence.

I agree with Risse *et al.*'s assertion that international factors are not the
only factors responsible for democratisation. Rather, international norms
and networks may provide key support for democratisation processes at
crucial stages, and they are necessary, though far from sufficient, conditions
for the most recent wave of democratisation.[9]

The link between democracy and human rights is captured in Article 21(3)
of the Universal Declaration of Human Rights, which states:

> the will of the people shall be the basis of the authority of government; this
> will shall be expressed in periodic and genuine elections which shall be by
> universal and equal suffrage and shall be held by secret vote or by equivalent
> free voting procedures.

Thus, the European Union believes that democracy and human rights are
universal values that should be vigorously promoted around the world.
Having come into force on 1 January 2007, the European Instrument for
Democracy and Human Rights (EIDHR) is the concrete expression of the
EU's intention to integrate the promotion of democracy and human rights
into all its external policies.[10]

The second link between international human rights and democracy is
not restricted to the essence of the concept of democracy, but includes the
growing support of human rights implementation and enforcement within
the state's own borders. Not only do human rights provide key support for
democratisation, as seen in the examples of constitutional violence, but
human rights and their implementation are legitimate democratically.
Simply put, the *demos* want human rights.

The democratic legitimacy of human rights is analogous to Simmons'
theory of costs versus benefits. Simmons considers that governments ratify
human rights for both sincere and strategic reasons. Governments calculate
the costs versus the benefits in the contexts of their values, region, national
institutions and time horizons.[11] Specialised doctrine has shown the growing
support of the citizenship for the implementation of human rights.[12]

The third link between international humanitarian law and democracy is the emergence of new agents in the sphere of public international law. These new players (NGOs, substate entities and individuals) in the international arena favour democracy and human rights. These agents broadly interpret human rights and challenge the state, the major disruptive agent of human rights.

These new agents in the international arena are modifying the logic of public international law by generating new interactions that are structured in terms of networks, and transactional networks are increasingly visible in international politics.[13] These interactions are what Risse *et al.* define as ;socialization' of human rights norms into domestic practices.[14] The authors state that even instrumental adoption of human rights norms, if it leads to domestic structural change such as re-democratisation, sets into motion a process of identity transformation, so that norms initially adopted for instrumental reasons are later maintained for reasons of belief and identity.[15] Therefore, using Risse *et al.*'s terms, these new agents are contributing to the strengthening of human rights.

Helen Stacy synthesises in three main arguments the critiques of the international human rights system. She states that critiques of international human rights fall into three categories.[16] The 'sovereignty critique' argues that the problems of international human rights lie in the international system itself. 'Sovereigntists' view any attempt at supplanting the role of government as doomed to failure.[17] They would simply leave law in the hands of the state to be decided along lines of national interest. The second main critique of international human rights arises out of the role of civil society under globalisation. 'Civil societists' argue that the real human rights actions in these days of globalisation do not spring from international and governmental institutions, but rather from newer, informal sources such as non-governmental advocacy groups. I do not see the contradiction between the implementation of human rights in public spheres and in new sources. On the contrary, they complement one another.

Third, 'multiculturalists' argue that any attempt to institutionalise international standards in a multicultural world is philosophically flawed and culturally divisive.[18] This argument seems to me the most dangerous of all. The starting point is not only an incorrect view of multiculturalism and tolerance. Ablation, inequality between men and women, racism, child exploitation, paedophilia and homophobic behaviour cannot be justified in any case, not even based on a misconception of multiculturalism.

All three critiques are clearly defined and responded to in the works of Stacy. She demonstrates that these critiques are incomplete and they divert the attention from the need to craft institutional responses to these tensions. These theories ultimately justify actions that are against human rights and the international dimension of democracy. In this respect, Stacy's 'sovereigntists' will consider legitimate the examples of constitutional violence expounded in this work. As Stacy affirms, the issue here is the meaning of state sovereignty – the assertion that governments are the supreme legal authority within their own borders, not subject to international rules or institutions beyond them.[19] This doctrine will agree with Schmitt's criticism of international law.[20] Applying this theory, China's 1989 Tiananmen Square massacre would be justified in terms of national interest or sovereignty. What national interest differs from democratic interest?

None of the criticisms that Stacy expounds can be a valid argument in the twenty-first century for decreasing the implementation and application of international humanitarian law. Especially if we understand that there is a mutual dependence between democracy and human rights.

When I wrote these words, democratic revolutions were occurring in Tunisia, Algeria, Jordan, Yemen and Egypt. The information regarding these revolutions was transmitted via social networks, mobile phones and other electronic technology tools; the data is not the subject of political censorship imposed by the sender or recipient state. The people participating in these demonstrations are placing international pressure on their domestic governments. This fact demonstrates the feasibility and viability of universal human rights and the effectiveness of international pressure. Contrary to the assertions of the 'sovereigntists', the state no longer has an exclusive monopoly on sovereignty in its territory. Citizens, substate authorities and the international community are now involved in the issue. These revolutions demonstrate not only a deep schism between the people and the state, but also the extent to which domestic and transnational advocacy networks are working together. The state's edge is exceeded by the people itself.

The current evolution of international humanitarian law makes necessary the inclusion of other agents, such as substate agents, associations and other collegial bodies participating as full actors. As doctrine has repeatedly shown, states are the largest disrupter of human rights. In this context, due to the recognition of these agents as subjects of human rights, and as full actors, the international scenario will be a way of challenging the major obstacle in the implementation of democracy and human rights. In other words, democracy and human rights enforcement cannot be limited to human beings *stricto sensu*.

The rights enshrined in the International Covenant on Economic, Social and Cultural Rights, and subsequent human rights instruments covering group rights (e.g., indigenous peoples, minorities, people with disabilities), are equally essential for democracy, as they ensure an equitable distribution of wealth, and equality and equity with respect to access to civil and political rights.[21]

A broad interpretation of human rights is necessary to protect minorities, identities and nations, for example, Native Americans, Kurds, etc. An analogous application of the criminal procedure principle of *in dubio pro reo*, in a sort of '*in dubio pro human rights*', will be useful in this respect. Therefore, the denial of *locus standi* to these agents by the European Court of Human Rights is counterproductive to a full implementation of human rights.

The point is not to ground democracy and human rights in the ontology of the human individual, but in a notion of real democratic collectivity, considering a human democratic collectivity as a community rooted in democracy and international human rights, which applies sovereignty, takes decisions and enforces democratically legitimated violence within the framework and limits of human rights. It seems to me that in these collectivities, it is more feasible to implement real democracy and respect for human rights. Human communities are not isolated from each other; they co-exist, from Rome, Buenos Aires to Tel Aviv or Islamabad,[22] to a minimum expression of the federal level, and also to the United Nations. Historical and modern experience shows that the state has not been able to become such a community.

If, as Habermas states, to be legitimate, laws, including basic rights, must either agree with human rights or issue from democratic will-formation,[23] the Constitution of Bosnia and Herzegovina is excellent proof that the international community understands this point and knows how to link human rights, democracy and constitutionalism. The preamble of the Bosnia and Herzegovina constitution states that the constitution is:

> based on respect for human dignity, liberty, and equality, dedicated to peace, justice, tolerance, and reconciliation, and convinced that democratic governmental institutions and fair procedures best produce peaceful relations within a pluralist society. The Constitution is guided by the Purposes and Principles of the Charter of the United Nations, committed to the sovereignty, territorial integrity, and political independence of Bosnia and Herzegovina in accordance with international law, determined to ensure full respect for international humanitarian law, and inspired by the Universal Declaration of Human Rights, the International Covenants on Civil and Political Rights and on Economic, Social and Cultural Rights, and the Declaration on the Rights of Persons Belonging to National or Ethnic, Religious and Linguistic Minorities, as well as other human rights instruments.[24]

This constitution defines its rights as 'human rights and fundamental freedoms' instead of as constitutional rights.[25]

As Habermas says, the essence of the constitution will not compete with the sovereignty of the people only if the constitution itself emerges from an inclusive process of opinion- and will-formation on the part of citizens.[26]

Further, constitutional legitimacy requires not only the recognition of human rights and democracy as supreme to the constitution itself, but also the placing of the human being, and not states, at the epicentre of international and domestic law.

Notes

1. E. H. Kantorowicz, *The King's Two Bodies, Study in Mediaeval Political Theology*, Princeton, NJ: Princeton University Press, 1997; A. Brecht, *Politische Theorie. Die Grundlagen des politisches Denkens im 20. Jahrhundert*, Tübingen: Deutsche Ausgabe, 1976; J. Taubes, *Religionstheorie und politische Theologie, vol. 1: Der Fürst dieser Welt, Carl Schmitt und die Folgen, vol. II: Gnosis und Politik, vol. III: Theokratie*, Paderborn: Wilhelm Fink Verlag/Ferdinand Schöningh, 1983.
2. B. A. Simmons, *Mobilizing for Human Rights: International Law in Domestic Politics*, Cambridge: Cambridge University Press, 2009, p. 25.
3. *Ibid.*, p. 26.
4. T. Risse, S. C., Ropp and K. Sikkink, *The Power of Human Rights: International Norms and Domestic Change*, Cambridge: Cambridge University Press, 1999; K. Sikkink, K. Sanjeev and R. James (eds), *Restructuring World Politics: Transnational Social Movements, Networks, and Norms*, Minneapolis, MN: University of Minnesota Press, 2002, p. 9.
5. *Ibid.*, p. 10.
6. V. P. Vaky and H. Muñoz, *The Future of the Organization of American States*, New York: Twentieth Century Fund Press, 1993.
7. *Ibid.*, p. 35.
8. M. Castells, *The Information Age: Economy, Society and Culture: Trilogy, vol. 1: The Rise of the Network Society*, 1996, *vol. 2: The Power of Identity*, 1997, *vol. 3: End of Millennium*, 1998, Oxford: Blackwell, 2nd edn 2000.
9. T. Risse, S. C. Ropp and K. Sikkink, *The Power of Human Rights: International Norms and Domestic Change*, Cambridge: Cambridge University Press, 1999, p. 38.
10. Available at: http://ec.europa.eu/europeaid/what/human-rights/index_en.htm, accessed 20 December 2011.
11. B. A. Simmons, *Mobilizing for Human Rights: International Law in Domestic Politics*, Cambridge: Cambridge University Press, 2009, p. 111.
12. H. M. Stacy, *Human Rights for the 21st Century: Sovereignty, Civil Society, Culture*, Stanford, CA: Stanford University Press, 2009, p. 8; see also K. Sikkink, K. Sanjeev and R. James (eds), *Restructuring World Politics: Transnational Social Movements, Networks, and Norms*, Minneapolis, MN: University of Minnesota Press, 2002.
13. M. E. Keck and K. Sikkink, *Activists beyond Borders*, Ithaca, NY: Cornell University Press, 1998, p. 1.

14. T. Risse, S. C. Ropp and K. Sikkink, *The Power of Human Rights: International Norms and Domestic Change*, Cambridge: Cambridge University Press, 1999, pp. 236–78.
15. M. E. Keck and K. Sikkink, *Activists beyond Borders*, Ithaca, NY: Cornell University Press, 1998, p. 10.
16. H. M. Stacy, *Human Rights for the 21st Century: Sovereignty, Civil Society, Culture*, Stanford, CA: Stanford University Press, 2009, p. 8
17. *Ibid.*, p. 5.
18. *Ibid.*, p. 8.
19. *Ibid.*, p. 10.
20. C. Schmitt, *Der Nomos der Erde im Völkerrecht des Jus Publicum Europeaum*, Berlin: Duncker und Humblot, 1979.
21. Available at: http://www.unis.unvienna.org/pdf/Democracy_Human_Rights_2008.pdf, accessed 22 December 2011.
22. *Ibid.*
23. J. Habermas, 'Constitutional democracy: a paradoxical union of contradictory principles?', *Political Theory*, 29(6), 2001, 767.
24. Constitution of Bosnia and Herzegovina of 1995, available at: http://www.servat.unibe.ch/icl/bk00000_.html, accessed 20 December 2011.
25. *Ibid.*, Art. 2.
26. J. Habermas, 'Constitutional democracy: a paradoxical union of contradictory principles?', *Political Theory*, 29(6), 2001, 771.

Bibliography

Abat i Ninet, A. (2009). 'Playing at being gods', *Philosophia Quarterly of Israel*, 38(1): 41–55.

Abat i Ninet, A. (2010). 'Demagogy and democratic loyalty instead of oligogy and constitutional patriotism', *Vienna Journal of International Constitutional Law*, 2(10): 641–62.

Abat i Ninet, A. and Monserrat Molas, J. (2008). 'Monism versus dualism in the current Spanish constitutional system', *International Review of Constitutionalism*, 8(1): 1–41.

Abat i Ninet, A. and Monserrat Molas, J. (2009). 'From popular sovereignty to constitutional sovereignty?' Workshop paper, AAPS, Texas A&M, 22–24 October 2009.

Ackerman, B. (1993). *We the People: Foundations*. Cambridge, MA: Belknap Press of Harvard University Press.

Ackerman, B. (1997). 'Temporal horizons of justice', *Journal of Philosophy*, 94(6): 299–317.

Ackerman, B. (2007). 'The living constitution', *Harvard Law Review*, 120: 1737–93.

Ackerman, B. (2011). *The Decline and Fall of the American Republic*. Cambridge, MA: Harvard University Press.

Ackerman, B. and Fishkin, J. S. (2004). *Deliberation Day*. New Haven, CT: Yale University Press.

Ackerman, B. and Katyal, N. (1995). 'Our unconventional founding', *University of Chicago Law Review*, 62: 475–573.

Ackerman, B. and Rosenkrantz, C. (1991). *Fundamentos y alcances del control judicial de constitucionalidad*. Madrid: Centro de Estudios Constitucionales, p. 15

Adler, M. D. (2006). 'Popular constitutionalism and the rule of recognition: whose practices ground US law?', *Northwestern University Law Review*, 100(2): 719–806.

Aguado Renedo, C. (2008). In M. E. Casas Baamonde and M. Rodríguez-Piñero y Bravo Ferrer (eds), *Comentarios a la Constitución*, 3rd edn Madrid: Fundación Wolters Kluwer.

Althusser, L. (1977). *Lenin and Philosophy and Other Essays*. London: New Left Books.

Alvárez Conde, E., and Garrido Mayol, V. (eds) (2004). *Comentarios a la Constitución Española*. Valencia: Tirant lo Blanch.

Álvarez González, J. J. (2010). *Derecho constitucional de Puerto Rico y relaciones constitucionales con los Estados Unidos*. Bogotá: Temis.

Alzaga Villaamil, O. *et al*. (1999). *Comentarios a la Constitución Española de 1978*. Madrid: Editorial Cortes Generales y Derecho Reunidas.

Amar, A. R. (1994a). 'The consent of the governed: constitutional amendment outside Article V', *Columbia Law Review*, 94: 457–508.

Amar, A. R. (1994b). 'The Constitution versus the court: Some thoughts on Hills on Amar', *Northwestern University Law Review*, 94: 205–210.

Amar, A. R. and Hirsch A. R. (1998). *For the People*. New York: Free Press.

Aquinas, St Thomas (1981). *Summa Theologica and Doctoris Angelici*, Grand Rapids, MI: Christian Classics.

Aragón Reyes, M. (2007). *Teoría del Neoconstitucionalismo, Ensayos escogidos, AAVV*. Madrid: Trotta.

Arato, A. (1995). 'Forms of constitution making and theories of democracy', *Cardozo Law Review*, 17: 191–233.

Ardant, P. (2007). *Institutions politiques et droit constitutionnel, libraire générale de droit et de jurisprudence*. Paris: E.J.A.

Arendt, H. (1963). *On Revolution*. London: Faber & Faber, pp. 125–6.

Aristotle (2010). *Politics: A Treatise on Government*. Seattle, WA: Create Space.

Atabaki, T. and Zürcher, E. J. (2004). *Men of Order, Authoritarian Modernization under Atatürk and Reza Shah*. London: I. B. Tauris.

Avril, P. (1997). *Les conventions de la constitution*. Paris: Presses universitaires de France.

Aydin-Düzgit, S. and Gürsoy, Y. (2008). 'International influences on the Turkish transition to democracy in 1993', Working paper, No. 87, Center on Democracy, Development, and the Rule of Law, Freeman Spogli Institute for International Studies, Stanford University.

Baker, L. A. and Dinkin, S. H. (1997). 'The Senate: an institution whose time has gone?', *Journal of Law and Politics*, 21: 24–9.

Balkin, J. M. (2007). 'Original meaning and constitutional redemption', *Constitutional Commentary*, 24(2):. 427–532.

Balkin, J. M. (2011). *Constitutional Redemption: Political Faith in an Unjust World*. Cambridge, MA: Harvard University Press.

Balkin, J. M. and Levinson, S. (2010), 'Constitutional dictatorship: its dangers and its design', *Minnesota Law Review*, 94: 1789–865.

Ballbé Mallol, M. (1983). *Orden público y militarismo en la España constitucional*. Madrid: Alianza Editorial.

Bartelson, J. (1995). *A Genealogy of Sovereignty*, Cambridge: Cambridge University Press.

Barthélemy, D (2005). *Critique textuelle de l'ancien testament*, 50/4, Fribourg: Academic Press Fribourg/Éditions Saint-Paul.

Barnett, R. (2006). 'Restoring the lost constitution, not the constitution in exile', *Fordham Law Review*, 75: 669–73.

Bates, D. (2005). 'Political unity and the spirit of law: juridical concept of the state in the late Third Republic', *French Historical Studies*, 28(1): 69–101.

Bates, D. (2007). 'Constitutional violence', *Journal of Law and Society*, 34(1): 14–30.

Baylac-Ferrer, A. (2009). *Catalunya Nord, Societat i Identitat, reflexions, vivències i panorama català*. Canet: Trabucaire.

Bell, D. (2005). 'Les origines de la guerre absolue, 1750–1815', in *La Révolution à l'ouvre perspectives actuelles dans l'histoire de la Révolution française*. Paris: J. C. Martin.

Bell, W. T. (2009). 'Graduated consent theory, explained and applied', available at: http://works.bepress.com/tom_bell/2.

Bello, A. (2004). *Etnicidad y ciudadanía en América Latina. La acción colectiva de los pueblos indígenas*. Santiago: Comisión Económica para América Latina y el Caribe (CEPAL).

Benhabib, S. (1996). *Democracy and Difference: Contesting the Boundaries of the Political*. Princeton, NJ: Princeton University Press.

Benjamin, W. (1977). *Zur Kritik der Gewalt*, Frankfurt am Main: Suhrkamp Verlag.

Biblioteca de la Academia Nacional de la Historia (1961). *El pensamiento constitucional hispanoamericano hasta 1830. Compilación de constituciones sancionadas y proyectos constitucionales (Colombia, Costa Rica, Cuba y Chile)*. Caracas: Biblioteca de la Academia Nacional de la Historia.

Biondi, A. C. (2007). 'Aristotle on the mixed constitution and its relevance for American political thought', *Social Philosophy & Policy Foundation*, 24: 176–98.

Bobbio, N. (1965). 'Law and force', *Monist*, 49(3): 321–8.

Bodin, J. (1992). *On Sovereignty*, Cambridge: Cambridge University Press.

Bohman, J. (1994). 'Complexity, pluralism, and the constitutional state: on Habermas's Faktizität und Geltung', *Law and Society Review*, 28(4): 897–930.

Brecht, A. (1976). *Politische Theorie. Die Grundlagen des politisches Denkens im 20. Jahrhundert*, Tübingen: Deutsche Ausgabe.

Briguglia, G. (2006). *Il corpo vivente dello Stato*. Milano: Mondadori.

Bulygin, E. (1967). 'Sentenza giudiziaria e creazione di diritto', *Revista Internazionale di Filosofia del Diritto*, 44: 165–202.

Bulygin, E. (1998). 'An antinomy in Kelsen's pure theory of law', in S. L. Paulson and B. Litschewski Paulson (eds), *Normativity and Norms: Critical Perspectives on Kelsenian Themes*. Oxford: Clarendon Press, pp. 297–317.

Cámara-Fuertes, L. R., Colón-Morera, J. J. and Martínez-Ramírez, H. M. (2006). 'The death penalty in Puerto Rico', *Centro Journal*, 18(11): 147–65.

Castells, M. (1996, 2nd edn 2000). *The Information Age: Economy, Society and Culture, vol. 1: The Rise of the Network Society*, Oxford: Blackwell.

Castells, M. (1997). *The Information Age: Economy, Society and Culture, vol. 2: The Power of Identity*. Oxford: Blackwell.

Castells, M. (1998). *The Information Age: Economy, Society and Culture, vol. 3: End of the Millennium*. Oxford: Blackwell.

Chemerinsky, E. (2006). *Constitutional Law: Principles and Policies*. Introduction to Law series, New York: Aspen.

Chopra, J. and Weiss, T. G. (1992). 'Sovereignty is no longer sacrosanct: codifying humanitarian intervention', *Ethics & International Affairs*, 6: pp. 95–117.

Cicero (1913–21). *The Orations of Marcus Tullius Cicero*. London: G. Bell.

Cicero (1961). *De Re Publica, De Legibus*, Cambridge, MA: Harvard University Press.

Clough, H. A. (1885), *Plutarch's Lives: The Translation Called Dryden's*. Boston, MA: Little, Brown.

Cohen, D. (1995). *Law, Violence and Community in Classical Athens*. Cambridge: Cambridge University Press.

Cohen, V. and Amar, A. R. (2006). *Constitutional Law*, 12th edn, St Paul, MN: Foundation Press.

Constable, M. (2001). 'The silence of law: justice in Cover's "field of pain and death"', in A. Sarat (ed.), *Law, Violence, and the Possibility of Justice*. Princeton, NJ: Princeton University Press.

Cover, R. (1983). 'Nomos and narrative', *Harvard Law Review*, 97: 4–68, esp. 4–10.

Cover, R. (1995). 'Violence and the world', *Yale Law Journal*, 95: 1601–29.

Dahl, R. (2003). *How Democratic is the American Constitution?* New Haven, CT: Yale University Press.

Derrida, J. (1990). 'Force of law: the mystical foundation of authority', *Cardozo Law Review*, 11: 925.

Derrida, J. (2005). *Rogues: Two Essays on Reason*, Stanford, CA: Stanford University Press.

Derrida, J. (2008). *Séminaire la bête et le souverain, I (2001–2002)*, Paris: Galilée.

Donahue, T. (2010). 'The scope of justice and global dark oppression', available at: http://papers.ssrn.com/sol3/papers.cfm?abstract_id=1483241.

Duverger, M. (1996). *Le système politique français*. Paris: Thémis Science Politique, Presses universitaires de France.

Farber, D. A., Eskridge, W. N. and Frickey, P. P. (2003). *Constitutional Law*. St Paul, MN: Thomson West.

Ferejohn, J., Rakove J. K. and Riley, J. (eds) (2001). *Constitutional Culture and Democratic Rule*. Cambridge: Cambridge University Press, p. 67.

Fishkin, J. S. (2004). *Deliberative Polling: Toward a Better-Informed Democracy*, available at: http://cdd.stanford.edu/polls/docs/summary.

Foster, J. C. and Leeson, S. M. (1998). *Constitutional Law*, Upper Saddle River, NJ: Prentice Hall.

Foucault, M. (1977). *Discipline and Punish: The Birth of the Prison*. London: Penguin.

Fromm, E. (1941). *Escape from Freedom*, New York: Henry Holt.

Frosini, T. E. (1997). *Sovranità popolare e costituzionalismo*. Milan: Giuffrè.

Frosini, V. (1991). 'Kelsen y las interpretaciones de la soberanía', *Revista Española de Derecho Constitucional*, 31: 61–74.

Galston, M. (1994). 'Contemporary critics of liberalism', *Ethics*, 104(3): 446–66.

Gardner, J. A. (2005). *Interpreting State Constitutions: A Jurisprudence of Function in a Federal System*. Chicago, IL: University of Chicago Press.

Garrido Falla, F. *et al.* (2001). *Comentarios a la Constitución*. Madrid: Civitas.

Gaus, G. F. (1996). *Justificatory Liberalism: An Essay on Epistemology and Political Theory*. Oxford: Oxford University Press.

Gerber, D. (1972). 'Levels of rules and Hart's concept of law', *Mind*, 81(321): 102–5.

Gordon, S. (1999). *Controlling the State: Constitutionalism from Ancient Athens to Today*. Cambridge, MA: Harvard University Press.

Green, L. (1996). 'The concept of law revisited', *Michigan Law Review*, 94: 1687, 1691–2.

Greenawalt, K. (1994). 'Dualism and its status', *Ethics*, 104(3): 480–99.

Greenidge, A. H. J. (1928). *A Handbook of Greek Constitutional History*. London: Macmillan, p. 76.

Habermas, J. (1969). *Theorie und Praxis*. Berlin: Hermann Luchterland Verlag GmbH.

Habermas, J. (1981). *Theorie des kommunikativen Handelns, Vol. 1: Handlungsrationalität und gessellschaftliche Rationaliserung*. Frankfurt am Main: Suhrkamp Verlag.

Habermas, J. (1985). *The Theory of Communicative Action, vol. 1: Reason and Rationalization of Society, vol. II: Lifeworld and System: A Critique of Functionalist Reason*. Boston, MA: Beacon Press.

Habermas, J. (1990a). *Die Nachholende Revolution*, Frankfurt am Main: Suhrkamp Verlag.

Habermas, J. (1990b). *Strukturwandel der Öffentlichkeit. Untersuchungen zu einer Kategorie der bürgerlichen Gesellschaft*. Frankfurt am Main: Suhrkamp Verlag.

Habermas, J. (1998). *Between Facts and Norms: Contributions to a Discourse Theory of Law and Democracy*. Boston, MA: MIT Press.

Habermas, J. (2000). *Theorie und Praxis, Socialphilosophische Studien*. Frankfurt am Main: Suhrkamp Verlag.

Habermas, J. (2001). 'Constitutional democracy: a paradoxical union of contradictory principles?', *Political Theory*, 29(6): 766–81.

Habermas, J. (2002). 'Three problems of social organisation: Institutional law and economics meets Habermasian law and democracy', *Cambridge Journal of Economics*, 26: 501–20.

Hale, W. H. (1994). *Turkish Politics and the Military*. London: Routledge.

Hamilton, A., Madison J. and Jay, J. (1787–1788). *The Federalist Papers*, available at: http:// Avalon.law.yale.edu/18th_century/fed02.asp.

Hansen, M. H. (1999). *The Athenian Democracy in the Age of Demosthenes: Structure, Principles and Ideology*. Norman, OK: University of Oklahoma Press.

Hardin, R. (1999). *Liberalism, Constitutionalism, and Democracy*. Oxford: Oxford University Press.

Hart, G. (2004). *The Restoration of the Republic: The Jeffersonian Idea in 21st Century America*. New York: Oxford University Press.

Hart, H. L. A. (1986). *The Concept of Law*. Oxford: Clarendon Press.

Havelock, E. (1990). 'Plato's politics and the American Constitution', *Harvard Studies in Classical Philology*, 93: 1–24.

Hegel, G. W. F. (1942). *Philosophy of Right*. Oxford: Clarendon Press.

Herzog, D. (1994). 'Democratic credentials', *Ethics*, 104(3): 467–79.

Hinsley, F. H. (1986). *Sovereignty*. Cambridge: Cambridge University Press.

Hobbes, T. (2009). *The Leviathan*. Oxford: Oxford University Press.

Holmes, D. L. (2006). *The Faiths of the Founding Fathers*. New York: Oxford University Press.

Honoré, T. (1998). 'The basic norm of a society', in S. L. Paulson and B. Litschewski Paulson (eds), *Normativity and Norms: Critical Perspectives on Kelsenian Themes*. Oxford: Clarendon Press, pp. 89–113.

Hume, D. (1985). *Essays, Moral, Political, and Literary (Of Civil Liberty)*. Indianapolis, IN: Liberty Found Books.

Hutton, C. (2009). *Language, Meaning and the Law*. Edinburgh: Edinburgh University Press.

Institut de Drets Humans de Catalunya (2008). *El pueblo mapuche*, Serie de conflictos olvidados.

Jacobsohn, G. J. (2010). *Constitutional Identity*. Cambridge, MA: Harvard University Press.

Jackson, B. S. (1995). *Making Sense in Law: Linguistic, Psychological and Semiotic Perspectives*. Liverpool: Deborah Charles.

Jackson, V. C. and Tushnet, M. (2006). *Comparative Constitutional Law*. New York: Foundation Press.

Jevakhoff, A. (1989). *Kemal Atatürk, les chemins de l'occident*. Paris: Tallandier.

Kaempfer, A. (2006a). 'Lastarria, Bello y Sarmiento en 1844: genocidio, historiografía y proyecto nacional', *Revista Crítica Literaria Latinoamericana*, 63–4: 9–24.

Kaempfer, A. (2006b). 'Alencar, Blest Gana y Galván: narrativas de exterminio y subalternidad', *Revista Chilena de literatura*, 69: 89–106.

Kahn, P. W. (1997). *The Reign of Law: Marbury v. Madison and the Construction of America*. New Haven, CT: Yale University Press.

Kahn, P. W. (2006). 'Political time: sovereignty and the transtemporal community', *Cardozo Law Review*, 28: 259–76.

Kahn, P. W. (2008). *Sacred Violence, Torture, Terror and Sovereignty*. Ann Arbor, MI: University of Michigan Press.

Kantorowicz, E. H. (1997). *The King's Two Bodies, Study in Mediaeval Political Theology*. Princeton, NJ: Princeton University Press.

Kay, R. S. (1998). 'American constitutionalism', in L. Alexander (ed.),

Constitutionalism: Philosophical Foundations. Cambridge: Cambridge University Press.

Keck, M. E. and Sikkink, K. (1998). *Activists beyond Borders*. Ithaca, NY: Cornell University Press.

Kelsen, H. (1961). *General Theory of Law and State*, New York: Russell & Russell.

Kelsen, H. (1979). *Das Problem des Parlamentarismus*. Wien: Wilhelm Braumüller, Universitäts-Verlagsbuchhandlung GmbH.

Kleinhaus, E. A. (2000). 'History as a precedent: the post original problem in constitutional law', *Yale Law Journal*, 110: 121–53.

Kraemer, J. L. (2005). 'Moises Maimonides: the intellectual portrait', in K. Seeskin (ed.), *The Cambridge Companion to Maimonides*. Cambridge: Cambridge University Press.

Kramer, L. (2004). *The People Themselves: Popular Constitutionalism and Judicial Review*. Oxford: Oxford University Press.

Kramer, L. (2006). '"The interest of the man": James Madison, popular constitutionalism, and the theory of deliberative democracy', *Valparaiso University Law Review*, 41(2): 697–754.

Kreseil, H. (2005). 'Maimonides political philosophy', in K. Seeskin (ed.), *The Cambridge Companion to Maimonides*. Cambridge: Cambridge University Press.

Kuo, M. S. (2009). 'Cutting the Gordian knot of legitimacy theory? An anatomy of Frank Michelman's presentist critique of constitutional authorship', *International Journal of Constitutional Law*, 7(4): 683–714.

Larry, A. and Solum, B. L. (2004). 'Popular? constitutionalism?', available at: http://papers.ssrn.com/sol3/papers.cfm?abstract_id=692224.

Lavroff, D. G. (1999). *Le droit constitutionnel de la V république*. Paris: Dalloz.

Lazare, D. (1996). *The Frozen Republic: How the Constitution is Paralyzing Democracy*. New York: Harcourt Brace.

Lemkin, R. (1944). *Axis Rule in Occupied Europe*. Washington, DC: Carnegie Endowment for International Peace.

Levinson, S. (1989). *Constitutional Faith*. Princeton, NJ: Princeton University Press, p. 11.

Levinson, S. (2008). *Our Undemocratic Constitution: Where the Constitution goes Wrong (and How We the People Can Correct it)*. Oxford: Oxford University Press.

Lieberman, J. K. (1999). *A Practical Companion to the Constitution: How the Supreme Court has Ruled on Issues from Abortion to Zoning*. Berkeley, CA: University of California Press.

Lindsay, A. D. (1943). *The Modern Democratic State*. Oxford: Oxford University Press.

Lintott, A. W. (1968). *Violence in Republican Rome*. Oxford: Oxford University Press.

Little, R. K. (1999). 'Federal death penalty: history and some thoughts about the Department of Justice's role', *Fordham Urban Law Journal*, 36: 347–57.

Loeffer, E. H. (1999). 'In re Hinnant: the relevance of competence in interstate extradition proceedings', *New England Journal on Crime & Civil Confinement*, 25: 469.

López Borja de Quiroga, P. (2004). *Imperio legítimo. El pensamiento político en tiempos de Cicerón*. Madrid: Machado Libros.

Luhmann, N. (1988). *Die Wirtschaft der Gesellschaft*. Frankfurt am Main: Suhrkamp Verlag.

Lutz, D. (1988). *The Origins of American Constitutionalism,* Baton Rouge, LA: Louisiana University Press.

Marmor, A. (2001). *Positive Law and Objective Values*. New York: Oxford University Press.

Mead Earle, E. (1925). 'The new constitution of Turkey', *Journal of Public and International Affairs*, 40(1): 73–100.

Mestre, A. and Guttinger, P. (1971). *Constitutionnalisme jacobin et constitutionnalisme soviétique*. Paris: Presses universitaires de France.

Michelman, F. I. (1998). 'Constitutional authorship', in L. Alexander (ed.), *Constitutionalism: Philosophical Foundations*. Cambridge: Cambridge University Press.

Michelman, F. I. (1999). *Brennan and Democracy*. Princeton, NJ: Princeton University Press.

Michelman, F. I. (2001). 'Suspicion, or the new prince', in C. Sunstein and R. A. Epstein (eds), *The Vote: Bush, Gore and the Supreme Court*. Chicago, IL: Chicago University Press.

Michelman, F. I. (2002). 'The problem of constitutional interpretative disagreement: can "discourses of application" help?', in M. Aboulafia, M. Bookman and C. Kemp, *Habermas and Pragmatism*. New York: Routledge.

Michelman, F. I. (2003). 'Is the Constitution a contract for legitimacy?', *Review of Constitutional Studies*, 8(2): 101–18.

Michelman, F. I. (2003–4). 'The integrity of law. Ida's way: constructing the respect-worthy governmental system', *Fordham Law Review*, 72: 345–62.

Morrow, G. R. (1993). *Plato's Cretan City*. Princeton, NJ: Princeton University Press.

Nedelsky, J. (1994). 'The puzzle of modern constitutionalism', *Ethics*, 104: 500–15.

North, D. W. (2001). 'The obstruction of the extradition derailment', *So. University Law Review* 28: 151–5.

Ohana, D. (2008). 'J. L. Talmon, Gershom Scholem and the Price of Messianism', *History of European Ideas*, 34(2): 169–88.

O'Higgins, B. (1997). 'Proclama a los Araucanos (1818)', in J. L. Romero (ed.), *Pensamiento político de la emancipación (1790–1825)*, vol. II. Caracas, Ayacucho.

Ostwald, M. (1986). *From Popular Sovereignty to the Sovereignty of Law: Law, Society, and Politics in Fifth-Century Athens*. Berkeley, CA: University of California Press.

Pattaro, E. (2009). *A Treatise of Legal Philosophy and General Jurisprudence*, vol. 9. Heidelberg: Springer Verlag.

Payne, G. S. (1987). *The Franco Regime 1936–1975*. Madison, WI: University of Wisconsin Press.

Plato (2006). *The Republic*. New York: Penguin.

Pocock, J. G. A. (2006). *El momento maquiavélico. El pensamiento político florentino y la tradición republicana atlántica*. Madrid: Tecnos.

Polybius (1962). *The Histories of Polybius*, vol. I. Bloomington, IN: Indiana University Press.

Popovic, D. (2009). 'Prevailing of judicial activism over self-restraint in the jurisprudence of the European Court of Human Rights', *Creighton Law Review*, 42(361): 396.

Popper, K. (1966). *The Open Society and its Enemies*. London: Routledge Kegan Paul.

Posner, R. A. (1992). 'Democracy and dualism', *Transition*, 56: 68–79.

Post, R. C. (1995). *Constitutional Domains: Democracy, Community, Management*. Cambridge, MA: Harvard University Press.

Proudhon, P. J. (1999). (Manuscrits – Documents Inedits), *De la critique et des idées dans la démocratie française, à propos d'un ouvrage sur la Guerre et la Paix (vers 1861)*. Paris: Éditions Tops/H. Trinquier.

Rawls, J. (2007). *Lectures on the History of Political Philosophy*. Cambridge, MA: Belknap Press of Harvard University Press.

Raz, J. (1979). *The Authority of Law: Essays on Law and Morality*. Oxford: Oxford University Press.

Risse, T., Ropp, S. C. and Sikkink, K. (1999). *The Power of Human Rights: International Norms and Domestic Change*. Cambridge: Cambridge University Press.

Roddey Holder, A. and Roddey Holder, T. J. (1997). *The Meaning of the Constitution*. Happauge, NY: Barron's Educational Series.

Rousseau, J.-J. (1954). *The Social Contract or Principles of Political Right*, ed. R. Maynard, Great Books of the Western World, 38, Montesquieu, Rousseau, Chicago IL: Encyclopaedia Britannica.

Rosenfeld, M. (1998). 'Constitution-making, identity building, and peaceful transition to democracy: theoretical reflections inspired by the Spanish example', *Cardozo Law Review*, 19: 1891.

Rosenfeld, M. and Arato, A. (1998). *Habermas on Law and Democracy: Critical Exchanges*. Berkeley, CA: University of California Press.

Rosenfeld, R. (2004). 'What democracy? The case for abolishing the United States Senate'. *Harper's Magazine*, pp. 35–44.

Rotunda, R. (2009). *Modern Constitutional Law*, 9th edn, St Paul, MN: Thomson West.

Sarat, A. (ed.) (2001). *Law, Violence, and the Possibility of Justice*. Princeton, NJ: Princeton University Press.

Sarat, A. and Kearns, T. R. (1991). 'A journey through forgetting: toward a jurisprudence of violence', in A. Sarat and T. R. Kearns (eds), *The Fate of Law*. Ann Arbor, MI: University Michigan Press.

Sarat, A. and Kearns, T. R. (1993). *Law's Violence*. Ann Arbor, MI: University Michigan Press.

Sarmiento, D. F. (1948–56). *Obras completas*. Buenos Aires: Luz del Día.

Saussure, F. de (2002). *Ecrits de linguistique générale*. Paris: Gallimard.

Schmitt, C. (1970). *Der Nomos der Erde im Völkerrecht des Jus Publicum Europeaum*. Berlin: Duncker und Humblot.

Schmitt, C. (1994). *Totaler Feind, totaler Krieg, totaler Staat*. Berlin: Duncker und Humblot.

Schmitt, C. (2008). *Constitutional Theory*. Durham, NC: Duke University Press.

Scholem, G. (1971). *The Messianic Idea in Judaism, and other Essays on Jewish Spirituality*. New York: Schocken Books.

Shapiro, S. J. (2008). 'What is the rule of recognition (and does it exist)?', *Yale Law School*, Public Law & legal Theory Research paper series, Research paper No. 181, available at: papers.ssrn.com/abstract#1304645.

Sikkink, K., Sanjeev, K. and James, R. (eds) (2002). *Restructuring World Politics: Transnational Social Movements, Networks, and Norms*. Minneapolis, MN: University of Minnesota Press.

Simma, B. (1999). 'NATO, the UN and the use of force: legal aspects', *European Journal of International Law*, 10: 1–22.

Simmons, B. A. (2009). *Mobilizing for Human Rights: International Law in Domestic Politics*. Cambridge: Cambridge University Press.

Skinner, Q. (2002). *Visions of Politics, vol. II: Renaissance Virtues*. Cambridge: Cambridge University Press.

Spooner, L. (1850). 'A defence for fugitive slaves against the Acts of the Congress, February 12, 1793 and September 18, 1850', Boston, Bela Marsh, 25 Cornhill, 'The illegality of the trial of John W. Webster', 1850, 'A plan for the abolition of slavery', 'Address of the free constitutionalist', 'Letter to Charles Summer', available at: http://lysanderspooner.org/node/4.

Stacy, H. M. (2009). *Human Rights for the 21st Century: Sovereignty, Civil Society, Culture*. Stanford, CA: Stanford University Press.

Stourzh, G. (1970). *Alexander Hamilton and the Idea of Republican Government*. Stanford, CA: Stanford University Press.

Strauss, L. (1963). *Introduction of Moses Maimonides, Guide of the Perplexed*. Chicago, IL: University of Chicago Press.

Sullivan K. M. and Gunther, G. (2004). *Constitutional Law*. St Paul, MN: Foundation Press.

Tamanaha, B. Z. (2006). *Law as a Means to an End: Threat to the Rule of Law*. New York: Cambridge University Press.

Taubes, J. (1982). 'The price of Messianism', *Journal of Jewish Studies*, 23: 1–2.

Taubes, J. (1983). *Religionstheorie und politische Theologie, vol. I: Der Fürst dieser Welt, Carl Schmitt und die Folgen, vol. II: Gnosis und Politik, vol. III: Theokratie*. Paderborn: Wilhelm Fink Verlag/Ferdinand Schöningh.

Taussig-Rubbo, M. (2009). 'Outsourcing sacrifice: the labor of private military contractors', *Yale Journal of Law & Humanities*, 21(1): 103–69.

Taylor, H. (1918). *Cicero: A Sketch of his Life and Works*. Chicago, IL: A. C. McClurg.

Tocqueville, A. de (2002). *Democracy in America*. Chicago, IL: Chicago University Press.

Tushnet, M. (2003). *The New Constitutional Order*. Princeton, NJ: Princeton University Press.

Tushnet, M. (ed.) (2008a). 'Introduction', *I Dissent: Great Opposing Opinions in Landmark Supreme Court Cases*. Boston, MA: Beacon Press.

Tushnet, M. (2008b). *Weak Courts, Strong Rights: Judicial Review and Social Welfare Rights in Comparative Constitutional Law*. Princeton, NJ: Princeton University Press.

Tushnet, M. (2010). *Why the Constitution Matters*. New Haven, CT: Yale University Press.

Tyler, T. R. (2006). *Why the People Obey the Law*. Princeton, NJ: Princeton University Press.

Vaky, V. P. and Muñoz, H. (1993). *The Future of the Organization of American States*. New York: Twentieth Century Fund Press.

Vergotinni, G. (1983). *Derecho Constitucional Comparado*. Barcelona: Espasa Calpe.

von Fritz, K. (1958). *The Theory of the Mixed Constitution in Antiquity: A Critical Analysis of Polybius Political Ideas*. New York: Columbia University Press.

Wachulow, W. J. (1994). *Inclusive Legal Positivism*. Oxford: Clarendon Press.

Wittgenstein, L. (1958). *Philosophishe Untersuchungen*, 3rd edn, New York: Macmillan.

Yankah, E. N. (2007–8). 'The force of law: the role of coercion in legal norms', *University of Richmond Law Review*, 1195–218.

Zagrebelsky, G. (2007). *Teoría del neoconstitucionalismo, Ensayos escogidos, AAVV*. Madrid: Trotta.

Zürcher, E. J. (2004). *Turkey: A Modern History*. London: I. B. Tauris.

Zurn, C. F. (2007). *Deliberative Democracy and the Institution of Judicial Review*. New York: Cambridge University Press.

Index